7ʔ

W9-CIH-642

From Gunboats to Diplomacy

From Gunboats to Diplomacy

New U.S. Policies for Latin America

Edited by
Richard Newfarmer

THE JOHNS HOPKINS UNIVERSITY PRESS
Baltimore and London

LIBRARY
COLBY-SAWYER COLLEGE
NEW LONDON, N.H. 03257

F
1418
.F9
1984

910

© 1984 by The Johns Hopkins University Press
All rights reserved
Printed in the United States of America

Originally published, 1984
Second printing, 1984

The Johns Hopkins University Press, Baltimore, Maryland 21218
The Johns Hopkins Press Ltd., London

Chapter 9, by William M. LeoGrande, originally appeared as "Cuba Policy Re-cycled," and is reprinted with permission from *Foreign Policy* 46 (Spring 1982). Copyright 1982 by the Carnegie Endowment for International Peace.
Chapter 10, by Albert Fishlow, originally appeared as "The United States and Brazil: The Case of the Missing Relationship," and is reprinted by permission of *Foreign Affairs* 60, no. 4 (Spring 1982). Copyright 1982 by the Council on Foreign Relations, Inc.

Library of Congress Cataloging in Publication Data
Main entry under title:

96430

From gunboats to diplomacy.

1. Latin America—Foreign relations—United States—Addresses, essays, lec-tures. 2. United States—Foreign relations—Latin America—Addresses, essays, lec-tures. 3. United States—Foreign relations—1981–   —Addresses, essays, lec-tures. I. Newfarmer, Richard S.
F1418.F9   1984   327.7308   83–16193
ISBN 0–8018–3025–7
ISBN 0–8018–3049–4 (pbk.)

Contents

v

Contents

III. U.S. Policies and Latin American Issues

Foreword

Relations between the United States and Latin America have entered a new and critical phase. In Central America, U.S. economic and military involvement is escalating with each new turn of events. The prospect for regional war has grown since 1981, increasing with it the possibility of U.S. troops intervening directly in that area of the world.

Recent events ranging from the strengthening of the extreme right in El Salvador to the retreat from badly needed reforms in that country, to the wholly unexpected war between Argentina and Britain, to the recent U.S. invasion of Grenada, raise new questions about the current course of U.S. policy in the region and the new challenges for U.S. diplomacy.

In Chile, the military regime that overthrew a democratically elected government in 1973 now teeters on the brink of collapse. On the positive side has been Argentina's return to democracy. The degree to which the United States demonstrates unequivocal support for Argentine democracy could have a measurable influence on whether or not this event is more than just another momentary aberration in the Southern Cone.

All too often, U.S. policy toward Latin America has been reactive and geared to short-term considerations. Unfortunately, in too many instances, long-term American interests have not been well served by this approach.

Therefore, this book is a timely and welcome contribution to the intensifying debate over American policy in the hemisphere. Richard Newfarmer put together a group of top-flight scholars with extensive experience in Latin America and policy circles to review past and current U.S.–Latin American policy. Their goal was to advance recommendations that together could form a consistent and effective hemispheric policy. Hopefully, this book will stimulate the broader and more informed debate on U.S.–Latin American policy which is required during this time of crisis.

While the policy recommendations in this book are solely those of the authors, the foreign policy of a nation such as ours can function effectively only in an atmosphere of free and open debate. Therefore, I hope you will find this study helpful in understanding the challenges facing the United States in this critical region of the world.

Robert C. Byrd
Senate Democratic Leader

Introduction: Issues in the Americas

Richard Newfarmer

Issues in the Americas

Henry Kissinger in June 1969 castigated Chile's foreign minister Gabriel
Valdès for having aggressively raised North-South issues at a White House
conference with President Nixon. "You come here speaking of Latin America, but this is not important. Nothing important can come from the
South. . . . The axis of history starts in Moscow, goes to Bonn, crosses over
to Washington, and then goes to Tokyo. What happens in the South is of no
importance."[1]

If Latin America was perceived to be remarkable for its unimportance to
U.S. strategic interests in the 1970s, quite the opposite is true today. Events in
Central America and the Caribbean, the conflictual politics of the Southern
Cone, and the "debt crisis" have kept the region on the front pages for the last
three years. Ironically, as the crisis in Central America increasingly assumed
the tar baby characteristics of Vietnam, President Reagan turned to the same
Henry Kissinger to head a national commission with the difficult task of
forging a policy of consensus.

The challenges facing today's policymakers are formidable. The American public is deeply divided over the course of U.S. policy in Central America.
Even though many are unable to identify which side the U.S. supports in the
region, a large majority express uneasiness with current policy. While a
majority feel that U.S. interests are at stake in Central America, an even larger
majority feel that whatever U.S. interests there may be, they are not so vital
that U.S. troops should be sent to support American allies.

The crumbling of military-dominated political orders established in the
seventies and the resulting emergence of democracy as a rallying cry present a
second set of issues affecting U.S. foreign policy in the region. In the early
1970s, Brazil moved tentatively toward reopening its political system. Peru
soon followed. The Carter administration welcomed both initiatives as part of
its human rights policies. Since the Reagan administration assumed office in
1981, voices clamoring for a return to democractic institutions rose in several

[1]Seymour Hersh, *The Price of Power* (New York: Summit Books, 1983), p. 263.

countries of the hemisphere, notably in Chile and Argentina. After a brief period of ignoring these voices, the Reagan administration has made democracy a key ideological pillar of its foreign policy toward the region, to be used selectively as part of its larger East-West perspective—even though the administration has shown remarkably little support for democratic forces in the Southern Cone.

A third pressing issue is the economic crisis of the region. After fifteen years of rapid growth during which the economies of the region never grew by less than 4 percent annually, 1981 ushered in the severest recession in the postwar period. Per capita income dropped by 1 percent in 1981, more than 3 percent in 1982, and continued to fall in 1983. The economic crisis dominated the politics of Mexico, Brazil, Argentina, Chile, and Costa Rica and played a central role in shaping U.S. relations with the Caribbean and Central American countries as well.

The papers that follow examine facets of these problems through the lenses of history, country studies, and issues. This essay draws upon the conclusion of these studies to discuss three major problems facing U.S. policy in the region: Central America, the transition to democracy, and the economic crisis.

Central America and the Caribbean Basin

By the fall of 1983, the situation in Central America was deteriorating rapidly. Economic stagnation gripped the region as all five Central American republics had lower per capita income than they did in 1977. Politics were marred by an increasing bellicosity throughout the region. The United States sent an armada of destroyers, aircraft carriers, and more than 35,000 troops into the region to carry out prolonged "military exercises" offshore and in Honduras that were to last well into 1984. The United States increased the CIA-funded operation based in Honduras and Costa Rica against the Sandinistas in Nicaragua, and the Nicaraguan government continued to build up its armed forces. In El Salvador, the military situation appeared temporarily stalemated, each side assessing the effectiveness of the other's tactics.

The main cause for optimism in this otherwise grim situation was the new peace efforts of countries in the Contadora group. The Contadora group—so named for the island off Panama on which ministers first convened—comprised Mexico, Venezuela, Panama, and Colombia. These countries began in earnest a series of peace moves designed to close the widening public gaps between the conflicting parties in the region. Their initial proposals dealt primarily with interstate conflict and did not cover the Salvadoran war, except to circumscribe the inflow of arms. The proposals included a reduction in arms flows and military advisers to countries in the region, the prohibition of new heavy armaments, an end to arms transfers to groups in other countries within the region, and bilateral and multilateral negotiations to establish nonaggression pacts. The Nicaraguans responded to these proposals—in what amounted to a concession—by reluctantly accepting the principle of a multilateral negotiation and by proposing to limit all military flows and remove foreign advisers. Cuba's policy, analyzed in depth by LeoGrande, was to abide by any agreement to limit arms and military advisers to the region.

The administration has approached negotiations with reluctance and suspicion, contending that neither the left in El Salvador nor the Sandinistas enjoy much popular legitimacy. The administration ignored the several Mexican and Venezuelan peace efforts of late 1981 and 1982. In early 1983, Spain's prime minister, Felipe Gonzales, offered his own peace proposals. Apparently without White House approval, Thomas Enders, the Assistant Secretary of State for Latin American Affairs, flew to Madrid to hold secret talks with Gonzales. This effort was immediately disavowed by the White House and Enders was later relieved of his position and reassigned to another post.

As public pressure to begin a dialogue began to build behind the Contadora proposals, the administration was pressed to offer reluctant gestures of support for the Contadora group, but the administration has not been willing to fully support the Contadora process. The U.S. reluctance seemed to stem from its unwillingness to participate in a peace process that American policymakers could not fully control. A National Security document made public in early 1983 revealed a deep mistrust of the Mexicans and their approach to the region, which implicitly accorded some legitimacy to the left in El Salvador and the Sandinistas in Nicaragua. Only when Congress made approval of the administration's aid requests in mid-1983 contingent upon an active diplomatic effort did the administration finally assent to establish a special envoy for the region.

To be sure, some within the administration, like Enders, had apparently argued for months for a two-track policy. The first track would maintain a diplomatic posture of openness to peace discussions and would capture the diplomatic initiative to preempt and perhaps coopt other peace proposals. The second track would pursue an essentially military strategy. With the firing of Enders, voices favoring two tracks fell silent.

More recent administration statements have indicated, if anything, a hardening of position against a diplomatic settlement. In September 1983, Under Secretary for Defense Policy Fred Ikle, in a major administration speech on its Central American policy, said: "the insurgents will never settle for a fair democratic process. We can no more negotiate an acceptable political solution with these people than the social democrats in revolutionary Russia could have talked Lenin into giving up totalitarian Bolshevism. . . . you have to defeat these 'rule or ruin' forces militarily. This is the purpose of our military assistance." Regarding Nicaragua, Ikle was equally straightforward: "we must prevent the consolidation of a Sandinista regime in Nicaragua." The alternative, he suggested, was the "partition of Central America" with the prospect of permanently stationing U.S. troops on Nicaraguan borders to prevent Soviet expansionism, "inexorably lead[ing] to a hostile confrontation of large military forces, a confrontation that could last for decades."

Thus, since the administration refused to recognize the legitimacy of the Democratic Revolutionary Front/Faribundo Marti National Liberation Front (FDR/FMLN) in El Salvador, the administration's negotiating position began with the premise that the left is not a legitimate political force and cannot, therefore, be consulted on the form and administration of future elections. This, by definition, ruled out serious negotiations. Similarly, the administration believes the Sandinistas enjoy no popular legitimacy and are dominated by the Cubans and Soviets, and so negotiations must include the make-up of the Nicaraguan government itself, something the Sandinistas, having just fought a revolution to obtain power, were not about to negotiate. Here, too, the U.S. position effectively ruled out serious negotiations. A political solution for the region's conflicts thus appears remote, at least before the presidential election in 1984.

But a military solution also appears remote. Without a major escalation of force, the government in El Salvador seems unlikely to achieve victory. Former ambassador to El Salvador Dean Hinton said in 1983 that the United States should be prepared for several more years of war. In the absence of a military victory, the conflict must eventually be settled politically. In the event that the position of the government in El Salvador does continue to deteriorate, the United States will be forced to provide ever larger amounts of economic and military aid, perhaps culminating in the sending of U.S. troops.

At the same time, in Nicaragua the offensive of the counterrevolutionaries (the *contras*) will probably not seriously threaten Sandinista rule in the forseeable future, certainly not within 1983 as reportedly forecast by some CIA spokesmen testifying before the House Intelligence Committee. As Schoultz points out in his chapter, the policy toward Nicaragua probably strengthened the hardline Sandinistas by providing them with an external threat around which to mobilize nationalism and anti-American sentiment. The policy also ran the high risk of provoking war between Honduras and Nicaragua. Increasing military aid to Honduras and carrying out massive military exercises there was seen as a signal to the more aggressive elements within the Honduran military that the United States would back them in a war with Nicaragua. If the Sandinistas should begin to chase the *contras* across the border, the Hondurans might well engage the Nicaraguans directly. A war between Honduras and Nicaragua would probably end in stalemate, neither dislodging the Sandinistas nor intimidating them into accepting stringent U.S. negotiating conditions—unless it served as a pretext for direct U.S. intervention. A regional war might also sow the seeds of protracted guerrilla war in Honduras and destabilize civilian rule.

By the fall of 1983 the prospects for peace in the region seemed as elusive as they had when the Reagan administration came into office. Neither $1 billion in American military and economic aid nor the presence of U.S. advisers, troops, and ships appeared to have created the conditions for a peaceful settlement, economic growth, or democracy.

The Transition to Democracy

The 1970s witnessed a strong resurgence of movements to establish constitutional democracies throughout the hemisphere. In some cases, the process grew out of the progressive strengthening of civil forces and institutions relative to the military, such as in Brazil. In other cases, the ineptness and repressiveness of military rulership coupled with economic deterioration have eroded civilian support for military regimes, such as in Peru and, more recently, in Argentina and Chile. In yet other cases, democratic pressures—to be sure, weaker than in the other countries but nonetheless perceptible—emerged with the consent of a tenuous alliance of elite and military groups and external actors, such as in Honduras and perhaps Guatemala.

The administration's rhetorical championing of democracy has been one of the most resonating chords of its policy. Some Latin Americans who two decades ago would have taken democratic rights either as an accepted right or as a bourgeois privilege to be easily sacrificed in the struggle against Communism or for more egalitarian societies now, after years of military dictatorships, take such rights more seriously. Actively identifying the United States with democratic causes held the promise of becoming one of the administration's greatest foreign policy successes in the region. Unfortunately, the rhetorical position of the administration has not been translated into sound policy actions, especially in the Southern Cone, where repressive rule has become closely identified with U.S. foreign policy. Therefore, the administration's initiative is viewed with cynicism by many Latin Americans.

The decisions to support democracy as a key tenet of policy appears to have arisen slowly from circumstances in the hemisphere rather than from initial design. In its first year, the administration disassociated itself from the Carter human rights program, claiming to opt for "quiet" advocacy through diplomatic channels. But the administration made a point of strengthening ties to the militaries in Argentina, Chile, and Brazil, as the chapters by Wynia, Valenzuela, and Fishlow make clear. The administration saw these regimes as natural allies of the United States in its East-West struggles with the Soviet Union. It associated military governance with political strength and, since these militaries were traditionally anti-Communist, these regimes were seen as stable allies.

By 1982, however, the administration saw the need for an ideological counterpoint to leftist movements. It began by engineering the March 1982 elections in El Salvador. Whatever the elections' real political meaning in El Salvador, the large turnout of the peace-hungry populace gave them a credibility *in the United States* and legitimized the Salvadoran government in the eyes of much of the U.S. public.

The administration increasingly couched its Central American policies in terms of promoting democracy. It accused Nicaragua of failing to provide for free expression and democratic elections. This, together with alleged human rights abuses in their treatment of the Miskito Indians and the Sandinista support of the guerrillas in El Salvador, constituted a reason to vilify the regime and mount a covert action to overthrow the Sandinistas. At the same time the administration could support a military build-up within Honduras as "a shield protecting Honduran democracy."

The administration also began to appreciate the deep roots of the Brazilian process, which clearly contained the seeds of an end to military rule. By the time of the Brazilian debt crisis in late 1982 and the subsequent trip of President Reagan through the region, the administration began rhetorically to make democracy a cornerstone of its entire Latin American policy. Stopping in Brazil, Colombia, and Costa Rica, the president proclaimed his support for democracies of the region.

The success of the policy, however, has been tarnished by its contradictory application and its naive articulation as part of the East-West struggle. The administration has used democracy as an ideological riposte to leftist insurgencies drawing their inspiration from Cuba. After the elections in El Salvador, it quickly proclaimed the country a democracy, despite the fact that the Salvadoran leftist insurgents in the FDR/FMLN chose not to participate and the fact that a dozen newly elected Christian Democratic mayors were assassinated by right-wing death squads shortly after their inauguration. Ironically, the elections of March 1982 have postponed the day of real democratic reconciliation of political differences through peaceful compromise rather than bringing it closer. As Blachman and Sharpe point out, the elections served to strengthen the forces of the repressive right within the Salvadoran government while doing nothing to incorporate the disaffected elements of the left.

It is legitimate to question the decision of the FDR/FMLN not to participate in the elections. Clearly the people of El Salvador are weary of war and the only just consensus must have democratic expression. On the other hand, the military has been implicated in the assassinations of opposition politicians, and civilian deaths from right-wing terrorist groups with ties to the security forces continue. The Office of Legal Aid in the Archdiocese of the Catholic Church of San Salvador, the authority most widely accepted as an objective observer of human rights abuse in the country, estimated that civilian deaths attributable to right-wing death squads had increased in the first half of

1983 to more than 400 per month, more than ten times the number attributable to the guerrillas. The left cannot be enticed into participating in the electoral process if their candidates will be shot or intimidated. A negotiated ceasefire, a restructuring of the security forces, the ouster of known human rights violators, and meaningful guarantees to protect civil rights are necessary preconditions to holding elections. Without such conditions, elections cannot be meaningfully termed democratic.

In the case of Honduras, the U.S. political strategy of supporting democracy is in conflict with the military strategy of strengthening the Honduran armed forces and using the country as a staging ground for the attacks against the Sandinistas. As Millett points out, to markedly expand the resources at the control of the military strengthens their position relative to civilian politicians. The military effectively controls many areas of political decisionmaking, most notably foreign policy. Civilian politicians cannot, therefore, object to foreign policy without directly challenging the military. As tensions with Nicaragua build, so does the temptation to stifle internal dissent on foreign policy issues. Feinberg notes that a similar, though more subtle, dynamic could well be unleashed in Costa Rica. An ironic casualty of creating a "shield for democracy" may be democracy itself.

But the policy has also suffered from inconsistent application. Administration spokesmen consistently chide Nicaragua for not holding elections and they justify the covert action of the United States against that country on the ground that it is not a democracy. At the same time, however, the administration has upgraded ties to the repressive military dictatorships of the Southern Cone and Guatemala and applied little public pressure to speed the transition to democracy. As Valenzuela shows in his study of Chile, if anything, administration policy throughout its first three years strengthened the forces of repression. Only by the summer of 1983, when the military government began to stagger under the pressure of economic collapse did the administration begin to put some distance between itself and the Pinochet regime. Similarly, in Argentina, only after the Falklands/Malvinas war and the subsequent deterioration of military rule did the United States indicate support for a return to constitutional democracy.

Thus, President Reagan has, to his credit, tapped a potential reservoir of moral power. But the inconsistent and ideological application of that power has rendered it less effective than it otherwise might be. By seeing authoritarian military regimes as strong allies to be enlisted in the containment of Soviet power the United States now finds itself allied with several unpopular, antidemocratic regimes whose political stability is in doubt.

The Economic Crisis

Another necessary step to attaining U.S. interests in regional stability is helping to create the conditions for broadly shared economic growth. As pointed out in my chapter on U.S. economic policy toward the region, the situation in Latin America is now worse than at any time since the Great Depression. Nearly all countries in the region are predicted to experience a decline in per capita income in 1983 and few have enjoyed sustained growth since 1979.

Most countries' difficulties were rooted in their incapacity to earn sufficient foreign exchange to pay the cost of their higher oil imports and debt service. Between 1981 and 1983, Mexico, Brazil, Costa Rica, Argentina, Chile, Peru, Venezuela, Honduras, El Salvador, Guatemala, Uruguay, Bolivia, and others faced severe liquidity crises and appealed to the International Monetary Fund to supply much needed short-term finance. Hit by an unfortunate sequence of international changes—the oil shocks, followed by high interest rates in the OECD countries, and then world recession and therefore falling commodity export prices and slow growth in exports—most of the region was plunged into economic decline. In retrospect, fault also can be found with the policies of the countries themselves in the 1970s: too many borrowed too much and delayed adjustment to the higher costs of imports too long. But a great many wise and not-so-wise bankers in the industrialized countries shared the optimism of planners in Latin America during the late 1970s and the voices of caution were not heard.

Once the dimensions of the debt crisis became obvious to the Reagan administration, it moved quickly to extend financial aid to particular countries. In late August of 1982, Mexico suddenly suspended payment on its international debt and sent a high-level team of economic policymakers to Washington to arrange a bailout. Fearing a wave of major bank failures, Paul Volker and the Federal Reserve led the push to arrange a multibillion-dollar rescue package, pending negotiations with the International Monetary Fund. Brazil then followed in Mexico's wake and the administration arranged a new financing package. Other countries in the region also made painful trips to the IMF.

Ironically, the administration had come into office urging a tightening of IMF lending conditions with the ostensible aim of curbing global liquidity. It also resisted expanding the role of all the international financial institutions. Weeks before the Mexican crisis in the summer of 1982, the administration had opposed European attempts to increase the financial base of the IMF. To its credit, the administration abandoned its initial position as it perceived the depth of the financial crisis. Unceremoniously, the administration reversed course and supported a large increase.

But the administration's support for the IMF increase remained tepid. The increase required congressional approval, which placed the administration in the difficult position of having to take on the Republican right wing. Some liberal Democrats also criticized the bill as a bailout for the large commercial banks. The Democratic leadership refused to take a position of firm support until the president made his position less ambivalent lest Republican opponents use the IMF increase as a campaign issue later. The Europeans and Saudis, disturbed by U.S. inaction, threatened to hold up their contributions, running the risk that the IMF would run out of available funds. In September 1983 the IMF was forced to cut off new negotiations for emergency loans for the first time in its history. By the fall of 1983 the fate of the IMF bill in Congress was not yet settled.

The administration also refused to change its position on increases in World Bank funding, despite the appeals of some allies. World Bank loans have become increasingly important to Latin America as new loans from private commercial banks have dried up after the Mexico-Brazil debt scare of late 1982. The administration vigorously opposed increases in World Bank capitalization. It proposed a sharp cutback on new U.S. contributions to the soft loan facility in the International Development Association (IDA).

Trade policy holds another key to the debt crisis. Countries must be able to export in order to pay debt service. The administration has fought a commendable battle with the forces of protectionism. Still, the administration has yielded some important turf: it acceded to the reinstatement of sugar quotas, which limit sales of the region's exports to the United States; it agreed to quotas in specialty steel products; it agreed to a tightening of the Multifibre Agreement, which limits textile imports; it has proposed tightening the Generalized System of Preferences, which affords developing countries free access to the U.S. market for a limited number of products; and it has not taken action on tariffs on processed raw materials that discourage manufacturing abroad of the region's primary product exports.

The administration's most innovative economic program was its Caribbean Basin Initiative (CBI). The CBI was designed as a package of aid, trade, and investment tax credits. The aid component amounted to $350 million in 1982, with most going to El Salvador and Jamaica. The trade component creates a one-way free trade zone in selected products by allowing businesses in the Central American and Caribbean countries to have tariff-free access to the U.S. market. The investment tax credit, which was eliminated by Congress in 1983, would have permitted all U.S. investors in the region to receive a 10 percent tax credit for new investment in the region. Estimates contained in the Feinberg-Newfarmer chapter indicate that the entire program could be expected to increase the region's foreign exchange earnings by 1 to 2 percent. As finally passed by Congress in 1983, the CBI offers slightly fewer benefits because of the elimination of several export products from the list of products eligible for the free-trade area.

The administration's most important foreign economic policy toward the region is its domestic macroeconomic policy with its effect on the U.S. growth rate. If the U.S. recovery is strong and enduring, it will pull up the economies of the South by creating a rapidly growing demand for the region's exports.

The first half of 1983 looked promising as recovery continued to be strong. Nonetheless, one ominous cloud remains on the economic horizon: high federal deficits may result in high interest rates and might cut short the recovery. A resurgence of high interest rates and slow growth would postpone recovery in the debt-laden countries indefinitely.

Thus, the administration's foreign economic policy considered as a whole works against its political objectives of stabilizing the region. On balance, its economic policies probably will not lead to sustained growth. To its credit, the administration has come up with an innovative program of regional aid to the Caribbean Basin; it has also managed to stave off the severest demand for protection against Latin American imports into the United States; and it has acted to bolster the International Monetary Fund. But these pluses have been overwhelmed by actions with negative effects: the domestic macroeconomic policies were not successful in creating new growth in the United States until halfway through the administration, and the prospect of high deficits threatens the international financial system with resurgent interest rates. Its proposals to limit access to IMF capital reduce available financing for developing countries and transmit the wrong signal to private capital markets whose capital is desperately needed to foster new growth and stave off future liquidity crises. Weakening the IMF's capacity to act as a lender of last resort in any given situation increases the risk to investors and will thus reduce the amount of private bank credit available to Latin America. Finally, the administration's cuts in multilateral aid undermined its other efforts to stabilize the international financial system. Ironically, the poorest countries of the Caribbean Basin probably will lose more in the long run from the U.S. reduction in funding to the World Bank than they will gain in aid contained in the Caribbean Basin Initiative. In limiting the international financial institutions, the administration seems to be sacrificing goals of global financial stability and long-term development—with their future security implications—to near-term concerns about domestic austerity and politics.

The Task for 1984 and Beyond

The situation confronting U.S. foreign policy in Central America is treacherous—full of slippery slopes that may plunge the region into war and may even draw U.S. troops into combat. If the Reagan course appears to be leading toward a military abyss, what policies might lead in a different direction and still achieve American interests?

An answer to that question must begin with a careful consideration of U.S. interests in the region. Kurth and McCall in their chapters formulate a vision of U.S. interests and power capabilities to achieve them. U.S. security interests, Kurth suggests, are threatened only when the Soviets are able to install military bases in the region, especially those with a missile capability of striking the United States. At its most basic level, then, U.S. policy must ensure that this does not occur.

The United States has the military power, as it showed in the Cuban missile crisis of 1962, to prevent the Soviets and client states from ever sustaining such a threat. Moreover, any new client state for the Soviet Union would be substantially redundant, offering few advantages that the Soviets do not already now have in Cuba. However regrettable a Soviet client state would be on other grounds, it need not represent a heightened security threat.

A second U.S. interest is economic. U.S. business has a legitimate interest in seeking access to regional resources and markets in a fair and equitable system of exchange. From time to time, nations disagree on what is "fair and equitable" and this requires negotiations. But no nation in Central America accounts for even a minuscule fraction of U.S. international assets or trade. If a nation nationalizes U.S. property, the United States should take appropriate diplomatic actions, but important national economic interests should not be seen as jeopardized.

Diplomatic activity is more likely to be effective in protecting American economic interests in the long run. Nearly all radical states eventually find it in their interest to seek access to U.S. resources and markets. Central America's trade and investment is predominantly with the United States, and the costs of disengaging are high. Even leftist regimes, therefore, might welcome U.S. investment and provide attractive terms to stimulate it. Realizing this, Cuba's Fidel Castro has exhorted the Nicaraguans to avoid breaking with the United States. The Soviets cannot compete with the United States in economic terms and the Nicaraguans have been generally disappointed with the amount of financing received from the Eastern bloc. This suggests that the fear of the administration of "the proliferation of Cuban model states" is, in economic terms, unrealistic. It is unlikely that the Soviets will support "another Cuba"—except in the case that Western hostility provides a noncompetitive opening for Soviet financial engagement.

One unfortunate consequence of the current policy for American economic interests is that the failure to negotiate a political settlement that would bring peace to the region as a whole is badly hurting American business interests there. U.S. investors have fled the region in droves because of the escalating military tensions. As Feinberg points out, even in peaceful, democractic Costa Rica, U.S. investors have felt their profits squeezed by political uncertainty. The Caribbean Basin plan, designed to stimulate investment and trade with the region, has been more than offset by the military and political conflicts.

Another unfortunate economic consequence of the military conflict is the huge emigration from the region to the United States and elsewhere. The President, recalling the "boat people" of Vietnam, raised the specter of thousands of "feet people" coming to the United States should governments there become communist. Fagen's paper shows that people are already fleeing—fleeing military conflicts, human rights abuses, and lack of economic opportunity. Once these situations have been reversed, she notes, emigrants tend to return to their countries.

The greatest threat to U.S. economic interests lies outside the Central American region: it is the threat posed by the enormous debt burden of Mexico, Brazil, Argentina, and Venezuela. Should these countries be unable to meet their international obligations and be unwilling to reach an accord with the banks involved, several leading U.S. banks would be in serious financial jeopardy. The international financial system could become unstable. The administration has coped adequately with the near-term crises, but real problems may still be in the future. Several steps that should be taken soon include expanding the IMF yet further and encouraging it to borrow on capital markets in the United States and Europe to maintain credit flows to cash-short, but otherwise sound, economies in the region; expanding the World Bank and IDA to provide additional long-term financing; opening new U.S. markets to Latin America's exports, expecially products now covered by quota arrangements, such as agricultural goods and textiles; and making a serious effort to reduce out-year deficits in the U.S. budget that portend high future interest rates and renewed economic stagnation in the United States. If U.S. growth were to falter and/or export markets be denied Latin America, the result could pose a serious threat to the international financial system.

The United States also has an interest in promoting human rights, including the right to economic participation in a broadly shared growth and political participation in democratic regimes. These principles must be advocated within a framework of inter-American relations that respects self-determination and nonintervention. Democracy, by its very nature, cannot be exported, even less so by coercion. The United States can, however, encourage those domestic forces that seek democracy and discourage those that make it impossible. It can promote democracy and human rights through example and incentives. The appropriate policy response to such regimes that abuse human rights in a gross and consistent pattern is to withdraw economic and political support and urge allies in the court of world opinion to do likewise. I am not suggesting conducting an economic boycott, but the relationship should be sufficiently arms-length so as to provide an incentive for political actors to make progress toward more open, humane societies.

To gain credibility among allies and a multilateral consensus, U.S. policy toward democracy and human rights must be administered with some degree of consistency. Unfortunately, *in*consistency has been the hallmark of the Reagan administration's policy. American spokesmen have attacked the Nicaraguans in nearly every public forum open to them while remaining virtually silent on Paraguay, Argentina, and Chile. U.S. human rights policies have focused almost exclusively on Cuba and Nicaragua while saying almost nothing about Chile, Argentina, Guatemala, and El Salvador (except where Congress has mandated direct attention).

Given these interests and general policy framework, what specifically should be done to address the conflicts in Central America? The papers suggest several policies that would contribute to a lasting peace consistent with U.S. interests and consistent with principles of self-determination and nonintervention that should be reaffirmed as cornerstones of inter-American relations.

As a beginning, U.S. policy has to recognize the imperative of seeking a political solution; a military solution, short of a massive American intervention, is highly improbable and runs the high risk of creating new, more severe problems for U.S. security, such as a regional war, protracted guerrilla conflict in more countries in the region, and a completely unstable political environment throughout the region. A massive American intervention would offer even a less secure outcome: not only would it not be acceptable to the U.S. public, it would not be acceptable to Latin Americans, who are as sensitive to U.S. hegemonic tendencies as they are to Soviet designs. Moreover, it would result in a quasi-permanent U.S. military establishment to ensure rulership, and that would feed rather than eliminate an interminable guerrilla struggle. Its tremendous cost would buy only less security and stability.

A diplomatic strategy, while containing no guarantees of success, holds far greater promise. As part of a new diplomatic initiative, the United States should vigorously support the proposals of Mexico, Venezuela, Panama, and Colombia and encourage the mediation of the Contadora group in the negotiations process. After all, no country has a greater interest in seeing a stable outcome to the region's conflicts than these regional actors. This process will certainly require recognition of—and compromise with—the left in El Salvador and with the Sandinistas in Nicaragua. The dialogue in El Salvador should concern the steps toward free, internationally supervised elections on the basis of security guarantees for all participants. This would necessitate a cease-fire, an end to violence against the civilian population, and the establishment of the conditions for an open political debate. The dialogue with Nicaragua should be directed at reducing hostilities between neighboring states, ending arms flows and training to rebel groups in other countries, placing limits on outside military armaments and troops, and not interfering in the internal affairs of other nations.

The United States does not need to compromise issues vital to U.S. national interests, such as the presence of Soviet bases, troops, or strategic weapons. To the contrary, U.S. policy should make clear to the Soviets and their allies that it will not tolerate military bases in the region nor the stationing of threatening offensive weapons systems—and that the United States will use its military force to prevent that occurrence. The United States could engage the Soviet Union in meaningful discussions to extend to the region as a whole the U.S.—Soviet understandings of 1962, 1970, and 1979 with respect to Cuba. As LeoGrande points out in his chapter, those agreements have consistently affirmed the U.S. right to expect that the Soviets would not establish strategic facilities or naval bases in Cuba in return for a U.S. pledge not to take aggressive action against Cuba. These agreements have for more than two decades protected the security interests of the United States. They now may form the precedent for a future agreement for the region as a whole.

The best long-term guarantee of U.S. security interests resides in the preponderant economic strength of the United States. Its abundant resources of capital and advanced technology as well as huge market for Central America's goods constitutes a powerful magnet that will keep even the most radical nation-state in the region in the U.S. orbit—provided that it is allowed to work. To work, economic relations require a stable and peaceful political environment as well as normal diplomatic relations. Military threats and economic blockades reverse the polarity of the economic magnet and propel nations to search for other economic ties.

Neither economic nor security interests now requires the U.S. to control the internal politics or make-up of a particular regime in Central America; in fact, the United States can tolerate radical nationalist states with a neutral indifference while waiting for the radical regime to come to terms with it.

Changing the direction of current policy will require some bold and innovative departures from past assumptions. No longer should the United States assume that every revolution will inexorably lead to Soviet domination and threaten U.S. security. No longer should the United States assume that its interests are served by trying to control the internal make-up of individual regimes in Central America. In the 1980s gunboats and troops are a sign that policy has failed. They do not augur military victories, but political failures.

As American diplomacy begins to reflect the new realities of the 1980s, it will have to be based upon the mutual interests of the United States and other states in the region. Common economic ties form the basis of enduring relationships in the hemisphere. Building on the natural strength of these ties, the United States can afford to relinquish unilateral hegemony in order to assert leadership in a new multilateral consensus. Democracy and human rights are integral to the new consensus as are rights of self-determination and non-interference. The challenge facing American diplomacy is to create diplomatic alternatives to what otherwise will be military misfortune.

I

Theory and Reality in U.S.–Latin American Relations: The Longer View

1. The New Realism in U.S.–Latin American Relations: Principles for a New U.S. Foreign Policy

James R. Kurth

The United States, Latin America, and the World: Four Conventional Assumptions of U.S. Foreign Policy

For many years, from the mid-1930s until the mid-1970s, U.S. policy toward Latin America was based on a set of four assumptions about the world and about the place of the United States within it: (1) the strategic assumption of bipolarity, which held that the world was essentially divided into two opposing alliance systems, that of the United States and that of the greatest European power of the time, first Nazi Germany and then the Soviet Union; (2) the economic assumption of American enterprise, which held that the principal motor of economic growth in the world was American investment and American markets; (3) the ideological assumption of bipolarity, which held that there were only two significant world views in world politics, liberal capitalism and totalitarianism (first fascism and then communism); and (4) the political assumption of military regimes, which held that authoritarian military governments were stable and loyal allies of the United States.

These assumptions together formed a set that was coherent, consistent, and comprehensive. And from the Roosevelt administration to the Johnson administration, these assumptions more or less corresponded to conditions in the real world. They are, however, dangerously unrealistic today. Yet these assumptions have been revived, indeed, exemplified, by the Reagan administration. As a basis for U.S. foreign policy in general, and for U.S. policy toward Latin America in particular, they will lead to failures and perhaps disasters. But out of these unrealities and failures, a future Democratic or Republican administration will have an opportunity to construct new realistic assumptions and new effective policies.

3

On *the strategic assumption of bipolarity,* or East-West competition, countries were either allies of the United States or allies of the Soviet Union (or, earlier, allies of Nazi Germany). This assumption was especially intense with regard to Latin America, "our own back yard," where it seemed obvious that "who is not with us, is against us" (as the case of Cuba seemed to prove).

On *the economic assumption of American enterprise,* or North-South division, countries were either developed or undeveloped, and they would be developed primarily by relying on American investment and American markets. This assumption was also especially intense with regard to Latin America, where American investment and markets had overshadowed other foreign investment and markets since World War II and where local state enterprises seemed overwhelmingly inept and corrupt.

Out of the combination of the strategic assumption of bipolarity and the economic assumption of American enterprise, there naturally grew *the ideological assumption of bipolarity* between capitalism and communism, the "Free World versus Communist bloc" image.

And out of the combination of strategic, economic, and ideological assumptions, there naturally grew *the political assumption of military regimes* as allies of the United States. Of course, the United States generally preferred stable liberal-democratic governments in other countries, but in Latin America liberal-democratic governments tended to be unstable, and stable governments tended to be military regimes. Whenever one of the central values of the first three assumptions (U.S. ally, American enterprise, capitalism) was threatened in a particular country, the U.S. government would give its support to a military regime (e.g., Guatemala in 1954, Brazil in 1964, Chile in 1973, and El Salvador in 1981).

This essay will argue that this set of four conventional assumptions of U.S. foreign policy should be replaced by a new set that will correspond to the new realities of the world: (1) a strategic assumption of multipolarity; (2) an economic assumption of multipolarity; (3) an ideological assumption of multipolarity; and (4) a political assumption about allies.

These new realities form the basis for new principles for U.S. policy toward Latin America. These new principles would provide a more effective and a far better defense of traditional and continuing U.S. national interests than does the current policy of the Reagan administration.

Innovations and Reversions in Latin American Policy: From the Roosevelt Administration to the Ford Administration

Four conventional assumptions, as we have noted, were commonly held by U.S. policymakers from the mid-1930s to the mid-1970s, and they are reflected today in the policies of the Reagan administration. But from time to time changes in the global balance of power and in the world economy caused a divergence in the world from the conventional framework. Each administration has, at some point and in some measure, recognized this divergence and has accommodated polices to the new realities. The administrations of Presidents Roosevelt, Kennedy, and Carter were most creative in effecting new policies to address new realities. But other administrations undertook such innovations also.

When Mexico nationalized American petroleum investments in 1938, President Roosevelt recognized that the real issue was not the protection of particular American enterprises, but the protection of American national security interests against expanding Nazi Germany. This required a friendly nation on America's southern border and the reestablishment of a natural commonality of interests between the United States and Mexico on a new and more solid basis. This meant U.S. acceptance of the Mexican nationalizations. Roosevelt understood that the United States had great strategic and economic strengths and that the Mexican leadership would recognize this. More importantly, he understood that if Mexico was politically autonomous within an American strategic and economic framework it would be a far more dependable friend than if it was a resentful and hostile country looking for a foreign protector, which at the time would have been Germany (as it nearly had been during World War I).

In 1949, with the implementation of the Point Four program of technical assistance, President Truman recognized that the United States had economic strengths to contribute to Latin American development that went beyond what American business alone could provide. The Truman administration's support of the Bolivian revolutionary government in 1952 demonstrated that, as in Mexico in 1938, there was unlikely to be a long-term conflict of interest between the United States and populist and nationalist regimes in Latin America. The Truman administration's policies toward economic assistance and the Bolivian revolution were accepted and expanded by the Eisenhower administration.

President Kennedy's 1961 Alliance for Progress program recognized that the economic growth of Latin America had given rise to new social groups and new social conflicts and that support for these new groups would be more productive for U.S. national interests than support for traditional landlords and traditional military regimes would be. During the Johnson administration leading Democrats in Congress came to understand the potential conflict between economic development and military expenditures. Consequently, Congress enacted prohibitions on the sale of U.S. advanced armaments to Latin American countries.

Some administrations, however, have resisted these wise and creative departures from, and have instead reverted to, the conventional policy as-

5

sumptions. Until the Reagan administration, the culmination of the old assumptions seemed to be in the Nixon and Ford (perhaps more accurately the Kissinger) administrations. Nixon and Kissinger gave unalloyed support to military regimes. And they subverted the most stable, institutionalized, and enduring democratic regime in Latin America, Chile.

Yet even Nixon, Ford, and Kissinger recognized that there had been a major change in the strategic assumption of bipolarity: this resulted in the opening to China and the policy of detente with the Soviet Union. It is often forgotten by neoconservatives, including several serving in the Reagan administration, that Republican administrations of the 1970s were the most enthusiastic salesmen for Soviet-American detente. (Indeed, it is apparently often forgotten by Nixon and Kissinger themselves.)

Conflict between the Old Assumptions and the New Realities: Response of the Carter Administration

Each of the four conventional assumptions had become increasingly remote from the world situation during the period of the mid-1960s to the mid-1970s. The strategic assumption of bipolarity and strong alliances confronted the strategic reality of multipolarity and shifting coalitions. The Sino-Soviet conflict (and the earlier Yugoslav-Soviet conflict) demonstrated that communist countries could be anti-Soviet and, indeed, that the Soviet Union could sometimes best be contained by another communist country. The defections of Indonesia, Egypt, and Somalia from the Soviet Union's camp to that of the United States had demonstrated that heavy Soviet influence in a country could be reversed with dramatic suddenness, so long as Soviet combat troops were not present to protect and preserve that influence. It was only in Latin America that there seemed to be no gap between assumption and reality, particularly since Cuba remained a loyal ally of the Soviets. On the other side of the bipolar assumption, France developed an independent foreign policy and Ethiopia's support shifted from the United States to the Soviet Union. The overall result was a multipolar balance of power with shifting coalitions of nations.

The assumption of the economic superiority of American enterprise confronted the economic reality of a multipolarity of major industrial countries. First, European and Japanese investment established major presences in Latin American economies. Then, European and Japanese enterprises began to compete fiercely with American enterprises in Latin American markets as well as in U.S. markets. And, recently, Latin American industrial products, especially from Mexico and Brazil, have begun competing effectively, even within the U.S. market. This reflects the development of a truly multipolar international economy in which American investment and American markets have been relegated to the role of "first among equals."

In many countries the ideological assumption of bipolarity between capitalism and communism began confronting the ideological reality of a third alternative. In Western Europe this alternative took the form of a renewed and vigorous Social Democratic party (i.e., West Germany) or a democratic Socialist party (i.e., France). In Latin America similar social-democratic movements received strong popular support in those few countries where free elections were permitted (e.g., Venezuela and Costa Rica).

In several other Latin American countries the new moral power was actually the oldest moral power of all—the church, particularly the Roman Catholic church. In their pilgrimage from Vatican II in 1962 through Medellin in 1968 to Puebla in 1979, important sectors of the Catholic church broke out of and transcended the old division between capitalism and communism. Guided by their ''theology of liberation'' and engaged in progressive political action, many Catholics condemned both capitalism and communism as inadequate and incomplete solutions. They insisted on the best of both, personal freedom and social justice (e.g., in Brazil, Chile, Nicaragua, and El Salvador). Protestant groups, too, have become increasingly important in some countries, such as Guatemala, and have advocated an end to repression and social injustice.

The last of the conventional assumptions to be challenged by the new realities was the idea that military regimes were inherently stable politically. In the mid-1970s several of those regimes in Central America, in particular in Nicaragua, El Salvador, and Guatemala, were demonstrating their growing incapacity to deal effectively with social change and the resulting social conflicts. Indeed, by their very efforts to maintain old systems of economic exploitation and political repression against the force of new social conditions and the rise of new social groups, these military regimes were actually promoting instability rather than preventing it.

The Carter administration recognized some of these historic shifts and attempted to construct a foreign policy based on new realities. The policy was not equally consistent in all regions of the world, but it was probably most consistent in Latin America.

Like Roosevelt with Mexico, the Carter administration recognized in the Panama Canal issue the value of a friendly and stable Panama within a wider American strategic and economic framework. Like Truman with the Bolivian revolution, the Carter administration recognized that the Nicaraguan revolution did not need to become a long-term threat to the United States, and it reached an accommodation with the Sandinistas in 1979. Like Kennedy with the Alliance for Progress, the Carter administration recognized the inherent instability of military regimes as a long-term threat to the interests and values of the United States, and it suspended military and economic aid to the most brutal and repressive Latin American regimes. And as an integrating principle for its new foreign policy, the Carter administration advanced the standards of human rights. With its human rights policy, the United States could speak to the growing professional middle classes in Latin America, a group whose members were so often the victims of the torture and the terror of military regimes such as those in Argentina, Chile, and Uruguay.

But, as in earlier administrations, so too in the Carter administration did global events overwhelm the microcosm of Latin American policy. The revolution against the Shah of Iran and the taking of the embassy hostages, the Soviet invasion of Afghanistan, and the related shocks to an already troubled American economy—these contributed to the electoral successes of the Republican conservatives. In turn these successes led directly to the restoration of all the old foreign policy assumptions in their purest form.

In fact, these world events should have confirmed that the old assumptions were unworkable. In particular, the overthrow of the Shah illustrated the falsity of the premise that military regimes are inherently stable, and the taking of the embassy hostages underlined the disasters that can ensue when the United States becomes identified with a state that engages in systematic torture.

Toward New Assumptions for Latin American Policy: The New Realism

It will be the task and the opportunity of the next administration to construct new assumptions to reflect global realities. I suggest that the new strategic, economic, ideological, and political assumptions might look something like the following.

Strategic multipolarity. Under this assumption the United States will continue to contain the military expansion of the Soviet Union but will do so as the ''majority leader'' of shifting coalitions of nations.

Most of these nations will be traditional allies of the United States, but some might be Marxist or even communist states, if they are willing to be pragmatic, realistic, and cooperative in their relations with the United States (following, for example, the models of Yugoslavia, China, Romania, Zimbabwe, and even Angola).

The history of the past twenty years shows that when Soviet influence in a country is based on military advisors, economic aid, ideological affinity, political clients, or even on all of these combined, it is still reversible and indeed has often been reversed (China, Indonesia, Egypt, Somalia). It is only when Soviet influence is based on military occupation (Eastern Europe, Afghanistan) or when it is based on military protection against the United States (Cuba, Vietnam) that it becomes entrenched, at least until that protection is no longer needed.

Consequently, the United States should continue to contain Soviet military expansion, including Soviet military bases and combat troops in other countries. But in executing this venerable policy of containment of Soviet military expansion, the United States may at times find that socialist, even Marxist, governments can be truly nonaligned and independent governments that are more effective and less costly allies for purposes of containment than are unstable "conservative" military regimes that cannot, in fact, conserve anything at all.

In Latin America this means that leftist movements that might come to power in the future would be enduring threats to U.S. strategic interests only if their fears of U.S. intervention led them to accept Soviet military bases and drove them into long-term alliances with the Soviet Union.

Economic multipolarity. Under this assumption the United States will continue its extensive trade and investment ties with Latin America, but it will do so as "first among equals" in a system comprised of many industrial and newly industrializing countries.

This multipolar system of industrial powers is, in fact, the fulfillment of the traditional foreign economic policy of the United States since Franklin Roosevelt and his secretary of state, Cordell Hull: the promotion of a fair and equitable system of international economic relations.

The multipolar industrial system will contribute enormously to our principal interest in containment of Soviet expansion. The old assumption of the central role of American business meant that there would be occasional economic conflicts between Latin American governments and American corporations, conflicts that would quickly escalate (for example, under the terms of the Hickenlooper amendment, which restricts U.S. aid to countries that seize American property) into conflicts between the Latin American government and the U.S. government. These conflicts would then drive Latin American governments to seek the protection of the other major power, the Soviet Union, as with Cuba in 1959 and 1960. In the new multipolar industrial system, however, such conflicts between Latin American governments and American corporations are likely to arise less often. At least, similar conflicts will arise with European or Japanese (or even Brazilian) corporations. In cases where such conflicts escalate to the intergovernmental level, the Latin American government may find it in its interest to seek aid not only from the Soviet Union but also from other Western industrial nations, as Nicaragua has done recently. For example, a revolutionary regime in El Salvador or Guatemala could readily turn for assistance to France, West Germany, or even Mexico.

The countries of Latin America now have production patterns and economic needs which make it most unlikely that they could decouple themselves temporarily from the Western industrial economic system with its essential markets, loans, and aid. A revolutionary Latin American country would at worst decouple itself temporarily from the United States while linking up with other Western countries to fill the gap. And then the structure

9

of international economic interdependence among the Western industrial nations would gradually draw the revolutionary Latin American country back, first indirectly and then directly, into new economic relations with the United States.

These new realities in the international economic system might be reflected in a more equitable distribution of authority within the major international economic institutions (such as the World Bank and the International Monetary Fund), with newly industrializing countries such as Brazil and Mexico being invited to play a larger role in developing the institutions' policies.

Ideological multipolarity. Under this assumption the United States will continue to press for the expansion of universal human rights in Latin America, cooperating with other institutions, such as the contemporary social democratic movement, the contemporary Catholic church, and other church groups.

In most Latin American countries, the Catholic church is perhaps the most relevant institution. Contemporary Catholicism is the unifying world view that is most likely to meet the moral needs of large numbers of Latin Americans while not being antithetical to the basic interests of the United States. Catholicism can speak to all classes and tries to integrate them into a social whole.

A political assumption about allies. In general the best allies of the United States in Latin America will be centrist-party regimes (in the more industrial countries) or national-populist regimes (in the less industrial countries) rather than conservative military governments.

The conservative military regimes in Latin America have provided an illusion of political stability, but in the end their political and economic abuses have brought about violent change. Supporting such regimes, the United States kept outdated institutions alive (e.g., the Somoza family system in Nicaragua, the coffee feudal system in El Salvador). Some current policymakers have revived the belief that the political stability of such institutions can be restored. This can only lead to greater political explosions (e.g., the restoration in Guatemala in 1954 which has led directly to unprecedented violence and repression in that country).

Conservative military regimes in Latin America have done their utmost to destroy the political forces of the Center and the Left. They seek to demonstrate that only Marxist revolutionaries remain on the Left and thus to force the United States to choose between two violent extremes, the Marxists and themselves. The United States should seek to prevent violent extremists from defining its options. One way to do this is to acknowledge and constructively deal with all democratic opposition groups in countries under military rule.

Conservative military regimes have proven to be opponents of U.S. national interests in other, more obvious, ways. The Soviet Union could hardly find a better supporter in Latin America than the military regime in Argentina. It sold wheat to the Soviets during the grain embargo imposed by the United States after the Soviet invasion of Afghanistan and continues to be a major trading partner, and it disrupted Britain's ability to participate in NATO defense efforts through its invasion of the Falkland/Malvinas Islands. It has demonstrated that conservative domestic policy is no guarantee of good relations with the United States.

At first glance the military governments in the Southern Cone of South America, which political scientists refer to as "bureaucratic-authoritarian" regimes, seem to have been very stable indeed—Brazil since 1964, Chile and Uruguay since 1973, and Argentina since 1976. A closer examination of these regimes, however, presents a rather different picture for the future.

First, just as the preauthoritarian regimes suffered economic dislocations so severe that they helped bring about the military coups, so have the current military regimes. This is especially true in Argentina and Chile. Even the conservative civilian groups that originally supported the military coups have become disillusioned and want major political reforms. Further, "stagflation" in the advanced industrial world in the 1970s has become a deepening economic recession in the early 1980s. The economic impact of this deteriorating situation is much more critical in the newly industrializing or underdeveloped states than it is in the advanced industrial countries.

In the Great Depression of the 1930s most Latin American regimes were thrown out, and their successors often adopted radically different policies. There is every reason to think that the unfolding world economic crisis, brought about in part by current U.S. economic policies, will bring down many of the military regimes in Latin America, those most loyal allies of the Reagan administration, sometime in the next few years. And if they are still identified with the United States (and the United States with them), their successors will, at least for a time, be deeply anti-American.

It would be far wiser for the United States to work for the establishment of centrist-party regimes in the more industrialized countries of Latin America, where the social conditions for such governments probably exist (Argentina, Chile, and Uruguay). And it would be wiser to work for the establishment of populist regimes in the less developed countries (much of Central America). These centrist-party or populist regimes, by supporting a more equitable distribution of power and goods, will be more stable in the long run than the present repressive and regressive military regimes.

One model for Latin America in the 1980s might well be Latin Europe in the 1970s, in particular Spain and Portugal. There, authoritarian regimes were succeeded by center-right democratic governments (in Spain directly, in Portugal after a few years). But the Franco and Salazar-Caetano regimes in their last decades or so were no longer torture and terror systems, like some of the Reagan administration's allies in Latin America. It is rare for an authoritarian regime to give up power peacefully, as happened in Spain, and to a degree, in Portugal. But it is impossible for a regime employing systematic torture to give up power without great violence and chaos, because the members of the regime know that they will be the first targets of revenge. Political transitions are inevitable, but extremely repressive systems make a smooth transition impossible. At minimum the United States would be wise once again to press the military regimes of Latin America to eliminate torture and terror, to move from being like Franco in 1950 to being like Franco in 1970.

Together, these four assumptions—strategic, economic, ideological, and political—recognize that today and in the years to come the United States will not be the only source of support for basic U.S. national interests. In fact, there are many such sources: other nations interested in containing Soviet military expansion, other industrial nations interested in participating in Latin American economic development, other moral forces that oppose totalitarianism, and other potential political leaders in Latin America who are capable of cooperation with the United States.

U.S. National Interests and New Principles for U.S. Latin American Policy

These four new assumptions about the new realities of Latin America in the world provide the basis for a more accurate and discerning definition of the continuing U.S. national interests in the region. These U.S. national interests, in turn, give rise to new principles as guides for U.S. Latin American policy.

Strategic principles. The United States continues to have a major national interest, as it has had for a century and a half, in protecting the physical security of the United States and Latin America from the military intrusion of new major powers from outside the region. This implies, as a clear strategic principle, that the United States should deter and prevent the Soviet Union from establishing military bases and combat troops in the region. Conversely, however, Latin American countries, even those as unfriendly as Cuba, need not in themselves pose a serious security threat to U.S. national interests. The United States should be willing to enter into diplomatic relations with all countries in the region, including Cuba.

Economic principles. The United States continues to have a major national interest, as it has for a century and a half, in maintaining fair access through international trade to the economic resources of Latin America. This implies, as an economic principle, that the United States should discourage revolutionary Latin American governments from closing their economies to trade relations with Western nations. However, any Latin American government, revolutionary or not, will normally find continued international trade with the West in general and with the United States in particular to be in its own interest. And, if trade relations with the United States are temporarily interrupted during periods of revolutionary enthusiasm, the United States should accept this in the knowledge that local and international economic needs and realities will soon bring about a restoration of trade with the United States, if the United States is willing.

Human rights principles. The United States continues to have a major national interest, growing out of the central values of the nation since its founding, in furthering the expansion of universal human rights in Latin America. As a principle, the United States should press conservative military regimes to eliminate their abuses of human rights and, in particular, to eliminate their use of torture and terror.

Political principles. These three major elements in our national interest—strategic, economic, and human rights—are in turn promoted by a fourth: genuine political stability in Latin America. This can only be achieved by governments that enjoy popular support and that are moving toward broadly shared political and economic development. This implies, as a political principle, that the United States should not oppose efforts by the peoples of Latin America to oppose their own political destiny and to be free from coercion and terror. This will entail, from time to time, some U.S. acceptance of short-term political instability in order to achieve a greater long-term stability.

In choosing policies to carry out this political principle, the United States can usefully differentiate between two kinds of governments. First are popularly supported governments that do not systematically violate human rights. Regardless of their ideological orientation, with these governments—as various as those in Mexico, Costa Rica, and Nicaragua—the United States should be willing to carry on a broad range of normal activities, unless these governments pose a military threat by providing military bases for the Soviet Union.

Second are governments that lack popular support and that systematically violate human rights. With these governments—such as those in Argentina, Chile, and El Salvador—the United States can usefully focus its attention on the true or domestic sources of unrest. Appropriate policies could be: (1) withholding military aid; (2) using economic aid as an incentive to reward movement by the government toward more humane and more popular policies or to help the conditions of the poorest and most suffering members of the society; (3) avoiding exclusive reliance on any one opposition group and maintaining contact with all significant political groups; and (4) encouraging negotiations, if possible, to bring about a nonviolent solution to problems and conflicts.

These policies contain much that might appear new in U.S. policy toward Latin America. But in their essence, in their support of a genuine and authentic political stability, they represent the continuation of earlier U.S. policies. And they also will provide the surest and soundest defense for the physical security of the Americas, for fair access through international trade to economic resources, and for the expansion of fundamental American values and human rights—those most traditional and most central of American national interests.

2. From Monroe to Reagan: An Overview of U.S.–Latin American Relations

Richard McCall

Contrasting Paths of Development: The United States and Latin America

The United States and Latin America share a common heritage of European colonialism. However, this is one of the few common experiences shared by the continents of the North and South during their colonial and postcolonial histories.

The United States was settled mainly by Anglo-Saxon immigrants fleeing religious and political oppression. The stepchildren of the Age of Enlightment, they brought with them a social ethic that recognized human and political equality (even when they did not always practice it) and the right of political resistance to autocratic rule.

The nations of Latin America, on the other hand, were settled not by pilgrims, but by conquistadores—the armed legions of Iberia's quest for gold and other riches—who subjugated the great Indian civilizations and imposed colonial rule on the societies they conquered. The conquistadores established a concentrated system of land ownership that enriched the few at the expense of the many. The subsequent exploitation of mineral wealth and plantation agriculture produced inequality as well as a provincial ruling class that was generally closed to the ideas and forces that were remaking northern Europe during the Age of Enlightenment.

In 1787, when the United States gained independence from Great Britain, the founding fathers used the arguments of the British political philosophers to justify their struggle for independence from the Crown. The young American republic began to develop a new society that deliberately sought to break from everything it found inimical in imperial Europe. Blessed by a large internal market and abundant fertile land, North Americans were able to build a new

15

society unencumbered by an agricultural sector that was stifled by highly concentrated land holdings or politics that were dominated by the power of a politically reactionary landed aristocracy. Family farms provided modest wealth for many and rewarded initiative. The large internal market created relatively unconcentrated economic power and opportunities for social mobility.

The emancipation of Latin America occurred between 1808 and 1926. Independence did not shatter the old order based on inequitable and rigid social structures. For the most part uninterested in democracy and hostile to any system that would weaken their privileges, the local elites now ruled through a succession of figureheads and caudillos.

Prospects for national economic development were set back by small markets and the social structures of the new states in Latin America. The impoverished rural populations could offer limited support for local industry. The old colonial division between a privileged minority, monopolizing land and office, and a barely subsisting mass of peasants and workers remained intact. The power base continued to be the great landed estates, mining, and plantation agriculture. The system soon became economically inefficient. It was carried ultimately on the back of cheap labor, seasonal or servile.

These differences in social structure and economic organization assumed new importance in the latter part of the nineteenth century as the effects of the industrial revolution were felt. From 1825 to 1910 the output of the U.S. economy grew at an average annual rate of 1.6 percent per capita. At the same time, the U.S. population doubled every twenty-seven years, and unencumbered trade across the states gave the country a large internal market. Developments in agriculture and railroad transportation, combined with abundant resources, a highly literate population, technological innovation, and large-scale capital investment, promoted the rapid industrialization of the United States during the nineteenth century. The greatest industrial growth occurred from 1877 to 1892, when American factories tripled their output. By 1890 the United States was the world's leading industrial power.

During the nineteenth century the United States imported capital. Much of North American economic growth was, in fact, a direct result of British and European investment. But in contrast to later waves of investment in Latin America, the incoming capital was mainly portfolio investments and debt capital without management control. It was only after 1918 that the United States became a net exporter of capital.

The situation was quite different in most of the new nations of Latin America. Most developed classic export economies in which cheap land and labor were exploited to produce raw materials for the world market. Their economies remained dependent on one or two crops or raw materials. These products accounted for the bulk of the foreign exchange earnings needed to feed their growing populations. However, these earnings soon proved insufficient to cover the cost of both essential imports and industrialization. The division between the privileged minority and the mass of impoverished peasants and workers grew even sharper.

This system gave a preponderant role to the military, while civilian political institutions were left to wither. Yet, while he was originally a war leader, the characteristic Latin American caudillo, or military dictator, also played other roles. He represented regional and, especially, economic power. He was a distributor of patronage, of office, and of land. The half-century following independence was the classic age of primitive caudillismo, when Santa Anna in Mexico, Rosas in Argentina, and Paez in Venezuela ruled whole nations as though they were haciendas.

External economic penetration of Latin America tended to buttress these social systems. Unprecedented investment in plantation agriculture and mines by the northern industrial powers, accompanied by a massive European immigration, drew Latin America further into the global economy. Argentina became a world supplier of grain and meat. Other countries—Brazil, Cuba, Mexico—modernized the production of food and raw materials and acquired docks and railways to speed their exports. However, such unbalanced development did not overcome dramatic extremes of wealth and poverty and did not foster the widening of domestic markets. In addition, the surplus of labor kept wages low, so that there was little trickle-down to the bulk of the population.

To be sure, the United States had its own problems with social, political, and economic inequities. Settlers pushing West persecuted fragmented Indian nations that were finally subdued by U.S. Army forces. In the South, large plantation agriculture shared many of the characteristics of the social structure found in Latin America. However, the ethos of "life, liberty, and the pursuit of happiness" and the relative decentralization of economic power eventually enabled the United States to undertake profound social change. These changes did not come easy. The United States endured a civil war and a constant struggle for basic civil and labor rights. Yet, over the course of two centuries of nationhood, the United States managed to move its diverse social structure very profoundly toward a more democratic and just society. Such changes, when they have occurred in Latin America, have tended to come later, more abruptly, and, at times, violently. But too frequently they have not occurred at all.

The Century of Expansionism

There is another element that explains the quite different paths of development taken by the United States and Latin America. After the War of 1812, the United States never had to contend with a dominant power that sought to impose its military and economic influence on its internal development. Such is not the case for Central and even South America. Latin America had to contend with the growth of the giant to the North. Ironically, in the period from the Monroe Doctrine to the inception of the Good Neighbor Policy, the commercial expansion of the United States, more often than not, reinforced Latin America's rigid social systems. In turn, U.S. foreign policy began to reflect support for local political elites who sometimes enjoyed limited domestic popularity.

MONROE AND MANIFEST DESTINY

In 1823 the young republic of the United States issued a declaration warning the so-called imperial powers of Europe to keep their hands off the Western Hemisphere. In exchange, this country promised to refrain from interfering in European affairs. Known as the Monroe Doctrine, the declaration meant little in the world of 1823, which was so thoroughly dominated by British sea power. The United States had neither the military capability to confront European expansionism beyond its own limited borders in the hemisphere nor the capacity to influence the course of events that so convulsed the European continent throughout the remainder of the century.

Even so, in the early 1800s ardent expansionist sentiment was already at work in the young republic. The expansionist program gave rise to the concept that later became known as "Manifest Destiny." Manifest Destiny was both an economic drive and an ideological attitude that grew out of the internal growth enjoyed by the people of the United States in the years from 1820 to 1850. By 1848 Americans had concluded that it was "their manifest destiny to overspread the continent allotted by Providence for the free development of our yearly multiplying millions." It was decreed by fate that the United States should be greater still. So its inhabitants thought as they pushed their country's frontiers southward and westward to the Gulf of Mexico and the Rio Grande, the Columbia River, and the Pacific Ocean. In the process they developed a philosophical justification for this "Manifest Destiny."

Yet this period of U.S. expansionism had been agrarian based and confined to contiguous territory. From 1850 on, the urge for an overseas expansion in which the businessman and the banker would figure more than the farmer took on new importance. The new expansionism sought commercial and economic advantage rather than agricultural opportunity. Farmers had wanted new land to settle and cultivate. The advocates of commercial expansion, planning no mass migration, were often satisfied with economic and political control.

The trade balance of the United States influenced this expansionism. For a century after independence this country had an unfavorable balance of trade, a natural situation for a young and growing agricultural nation. But in the

1870s the pattern changed. By the end of that decade the republic began selling more overseas than it purchased.

The character of the trade also changed. Previously the nation had imported manufactured goods and had exported raw materials, chiefly farm products like wheat and cotton. But following the Civil War and the rise of industry, export lists began to show more manufactured articles: textiles, farm implements, machines, railroad equipment. Imports included proportionately fewer finished goods, proportionately more raw materials like wool and sugar, copper and petroleum, coffee and rubber. Such items were demanded by the factories and by the growing urban population in the new industrial centers.

U.S. businesses with foreign operations were turning to the government for aid in locating and capturing markets overseas. Those who wanted raw materials from abroad had come to feel that the United States should be able to control the sources of supply. European competition had increased American demands for action, notably with reference to the tropics, the so-called backward areas of Latin America, Asia, and the Pacific. These were as yet unexploited sources of needed raw materials as well as great potential markets for manufactured goods.

American businessmen were already at work in Latin America. Unknown when he began building Costa Rican railroads in the 1870s, Minor Keith gained fame when he planted bananas to provide freight for his lines. Within a generation he had laid the foundations in Central America for the politico-economic empire of the United Fruit Company. Organized in 1899, this giant company did much to draw the northern part of Latin America into the U.S. sphere of influence.

While Keith developed United Fruit, the Guggenheims acquired copper and silver mines in Canada, Mexico, and South America. Other Americans developed sugar plantations in Spanish Cuba and the Phillippines. Americans put money into Mexican oil lands and Argentine meat-packing plants. They took over the foreign debt of the Dominican Republic and several Central American countries. Each step increased American diplomatic influence— and exposure—abroad.

The decade beginning in 1880 saw the establishment of the economic and intellectual foundation for a vigorous policy abroad. Agitation for naval rehabilitation was closely related to four general concepts that gained currency in naval circles during the period and served as basic premises for naval expansion. Broadly conceived, the concepts were commercial, ideological, geographical, and historical. These concepts not only provided a justification for the territorial expansion of the late 1890s, but also linked naval expansion to national expansion.

Thus the new version of Manifest Destiny had been set in place. This time, the argument asserted the moral right of this nation's superior civilization to establish order throughout the world.

When President William McKinley won the election of 1896, the war drums in the United States were already beating over Spain's attempts to deal with armed insurrection in Cuba. Until the mid-1890s the Monroe Doctrine had remained virtually dormant. The United States could not (because of the U.S. Civil War) invoke it when the French temporarily installed the Austrian Archduke Maximilian as Emperor of Mexico.

However, the turning point came in 1898, with the Spanish-American War. American ambitions were spurred on by the new spirit of Manifest Destiny and inspired by the doctrine that the United States must be supreme in the Caribbean. Spain's fate was soon sealed as the United States declared war against that country. The Spanish-American War plunged the United States into world politics. The rewards of victory were as plentiful as they were far reaching: Cuba was created as a U.S. protectorate in 1903; Puerto Rico became a U.S. possession; the Philippines and Guam were ceded to the United States by Spain in the peace treaty of 1898; and war launched the United States on a course of interventions in Latin America.

The United States' involvement in the Isthmus of Panama dates to the early 1850s and the advent of the steamship. In 1856 a treaty signed with Colombia had given the United States the right of transit through Panama, and in return this country agreed to help the Colombians maintain law and order in the isthmus. George Law, president of the United States Mail Steamship Company, and Willian H. Aspinwall undertook to build a railroad across the isthmus to facilitate the delivery of mail from the East Coast to the West Coast. The railroad was completed in 1855. This American-owned Panama Railroad inextricably linked the United States with the destiny of this region; as elsewhere, the economic beachhead, once established, grew into a permanent presence.

President Theodore Roosevelt's interest in a canal across the isthmus had predated the Spanish-American War. Early in his political career he became interested in a U.S. naval capability that would protect U.S. interests throughout the world. The time needed for the battleship *Oregon* to sail around the horn of South Africa on the eve of the Spanish-American War demonstrated to Roosevelt and many other Americans the need for an interoceanic canal, not only for its commercial value, but also because of its importance to American naval forces.

From the 1830s onward, Panamanians had tried periodically to secede from Colombia. In the fifty-seven years before Panama finally achieved its independence in 1903, the United States intervened thirteen times to restore order in Panama. Prior to the Senate debate on the Panama Canal Treaties, *U.S. News and World Report* noted:

> Tensions between Colombia and Panama came to a head in 1903 when
> the Colombian Senate, hoping to squeeze out a better deal, turned down

another canal treaty with the United States. Panamanians revolted in fear that the Canal they wanted would go to Nicaragua.

The U.S., suddenly reversing its earlier policies, refused to send troops to Colombia's aid. Instead, American warships prevented Colombian vessels from landing soldiers to regain control. The result: Panama attained independence on November 4, and on November 18 signed a treaty with the United States. Construction began the next year.[1]

U.S.–Latin American Relations in the Twentieth Century

THE ROOSEVELT COROLLARY

In December 1904 the total convergence of the Monroe Doctrine and Manifest Destiny as the basic political justification for U.S. foreign policy was finally accomplished. It was at this time that President Theodore Roosevelt announced his corollary to the Monroe Doctrine. The Roosevelt corollary declared to European governments that henceforth the United States would be responsible for the conduct of Latin American states. "We do not intend to permit . . . [the Monroe Doctrine] to be used by any of these republics as a shield to protect the republic from the consequences of its own misdeeds against foreign actions."

The Roosevelt corollary to the course of U.S. policy in the region was intended to legitimize the principle that Latin America fell solely within this nation's sphere of influence and that this nation would assume responsibility for the internal conduct of Latin governments, whether or not they had ties to any foreign powers.

Thereafter, strategic considerations became popular in the formulation of American foreign policy. But, in its precise meaning, *strategy* refers to long-term problems of military security. Using it to refer to the establishment of American economic and political predominance in other countries— something entirely different from trade or specific alliances—made every foreign policy issue a problem of military security. This use of the term *strategic*, which became more and more common, began in the course of America's economic expansion into Latin America between 1900 and 1914.

However, commercial considerations remained the overriding concern as the United States began looking to the south for new markets and sources of raw materials. The then secretary of war, William Howard Taft, focused on trade early in this century. On 20 November 1906 Secretary Taft made the following observation on commerce with Latin America:

Since the first election of President McKinley, the people of the United States have for the first time accumulated a surplus of capital beyond the

[1]"Panama a Doomed Treaty?," *U.S. News and World Report,* 19 September 1977, p. 24.

requirements of national development. . . . Our surplus energy is beginning to look beyond our own borders throughout the world, to find opportunity for the profitable use of our surplus capital, foreign markets for our manufacturers, foreign mines to be developed. . . .

Coincident with this change in the United States, the progress of political development has been carrying the neighboring continent of South America out of the stage of militarism into the stage of industrialism. . . .

Great opportunities for peaceful commercial and industrial expansion to the south are presented. Other investing nations are already in the field— England, France, Germany, Italy, Spain; but the field is so vast, the new demands are so great, the progress so rapid, that what other nations have done up to this time is but a slight advance in the race for the grand total.[2]

After World War I, U.S. industrialists launched major overseas expansion efforts. The search for markets for their goods continued unabated, but they added a new program of direct investments. This was the result of several developments. The prosperity brought on by World War I enabled the industrialists to recover control of their capital assets from investment bankers. This, in turn, made it possible for them to move to control the production and, sometimes, the processing of raw materials, particularly in Latin America.

GUNBOATS AND DOLLAR DIPLOMACY

William Howard Taft's vision of peaceful commercial and industrial expansion into Latin America proved to be illusory. Domestic clashes were common, especially in Central America, where social inequities of significant dimension remained. The United States responded to repeated political upheavals in Cuba with a series of American military interventions there (1906–9, 1911–12, and 1917–22). Similar interventions and occupations occurred in the Dominican Republic (in 1905, and from 1916 to 1924), Haiti (from 1915 to 1934), and Nicaragua (from 1909 to 1924). Friction with Mexico had led to two attempted, but unsuccessful, interventions in that country in 1914 and 1915. These incursions have permanently shaped Latin American perceptions of the United States.

Economic expansion became an integral part of U.S. foreign policy in the wake of the Russian Revolution. The rise of the Bolsheviks to power in the Soviet Union, facilitated by economic depression and war, significantly influenced the formulation of U.S. foreign policy. The prevention of revolutions, which challenged U.S. values and, in particular, American property rights abroad, became a major preoccupation of American policymakers during the decade of the 1920s. The era of dollar diplomacy was launched in earnest.

[2]William Howard Taft on "Commerce with Latin America," in *The Shaping of American Diplomacy*, ed. William Appleton Williams (Chicago: Rand McNally, 1963), 2:532.

Latin America became a primary focal point of this new policy, which President Calvin Coolidge's secretary of state, Charles Evans Hughes, outlined on 30 November 1923. Elements of the Hughes pronouncement included the following:

> A confiscatory policy strikes not only at the interests of particular individuals, but at the foundations of international intercourse, for it is only on the basis of the security of property validly possessed under the laws existing at the time of its acquisition that the conduct of activities in helpful cooperation are possible. . . .
>
> Fourth.—It is the policy of this Government to make available its friendly assistance to promote stability in those of our sister Republics which are especially afflicted with disturbed conditions involving their own peace and that of their neighbors. . . .
>
> We are seeking to establish a Pax Americana.[3]

During the 1920s overseas economic and political expansion was virtually unrestrained, particularly in Latin America. In addition to direct investments in raw materials on the part of U.S. industrialists, American bankers began making sizeable loans to Latin American governments (many of them unsound and leading to a refusal on the part of foreign creditors to pay their obligations), and American manufacturers began to build branch factories throughout the region in order to take advantage of cheaper labor and material. This massive flow of U.S. economic resources into international markets led President Calvin Coolidge to observe in a 1928 Memorial Day speech: "Our investments and trade relations are such that it is almost impossible to conceive of any conflict anywhere on earth which would not affect us injuriously."

Yet, in order to counter the potential spread of radicalism with this new policy, the United States was forced to maintain the status quo—a status quo in many countries in Latin America which was as inimical to American values as was Bolshevism. As a result, the new policy ran into difficulties. Critics of the policy warned that the establishment of American economic predominance in Latin America would lead to armed interventions to protect these interests and interference with the political processes of these nations, leading inevitably to the very revolutions the policy was designed to prevent.

Nicaragua is perhaps the most egregious example of how U.S. power entrenched the position of a privileged elite in return for its protection of American investments. After the American-supported insurrection culminated with the overthrow of Nicaraguan President Zelaya in 1910, the United States established a significant military presence in that country from 1912 until 1933. The United States controlled the macroeconomic policy of the country, even to the extent of inventing Nicaragua's local currency. During this period,

[3]Charles Evans Hughes, "The Foreign Policy of Secretary of State Hughes," *Shaping of American Diplomacy*, ed. Williams, 2:714.

the United States ruled the country on the basis of priorities set by American and European creditors. U.S. power in Nicaragua relied on its own military presence, the acquiescence of the privileged elite who benefited from the occupation, and eventually on the Nicaraguan national guard, which was created by and armed by the United States. After the United States had officially withdrawn from the country, American interests in Nicaragua were protected "by proxy" when the head of the national guard, General Somoza, assumed the presidency.

THE COMING OF THE GOOD NEIGHBOR POLICY

The 1929 crash of the stock market in the United States and the depression that followed it struck a shattering blow to Latin America, cutting off supplies of foreign capital and lowering the prices of primary products in world markets. This forced the area to look to its own resources and to undertake a program of industrialization. But the crash also fostered great social and political distress, particularly among those who lacked the power to protect themselves. Urban workers became disenchanted with the middle-class liberal or radical parties, which had been wooing them, and began to look for strongmen who promised immediate relief from their problems.

U.S. financial involvement in Latin America stemming from the policies of Secretary Hughes caused growing concern, particularly in congressional circles. This set of circumstances led Senator Hiram Johnson, a Republican from California, to observe on 15 March 1932: [The international bankers] were perfectly willing by their loans to maintain dictators in power and to be party to the suppression of every natural right of citizens of South American republics. Indeed, they contributed the money, in some instances, for the destruction of liberty itself. . . . Loans were made to Latin American countries sometimes to maintain dictators in power, dictators who laughed to scorn every fundamental principle of liberty and every cherished right of peoples. They were sometimes made to go hand in hand with concessions, out of which princely profits might be realized."[4]

With the advent of the administration of Franklin Roosevelt, U.S. policy toward Latin America shifted decidedly. Roosevelt strove to convince Latin America of this country's good intentions when his secretary of state, Cordell Hull, outlined the administration's "Good Neighbor Policy" in Montevideo, Uruguay, in December 1933. Numerous conferences were arranged, and a Pan American council was set up with headquarters in Washington. The emphasis in the hemisphere was shifted from unilateral action by the United States to collective action by all nations.

[4]Hiram Johnson, "Senator Hiram Johnson Discusses American Economic Expansion in Latin America," in *Shaping of American Diplomacy*, ed. Williams, 2:716.

To some extent this policy was born of making a "virtue out of necessity." The United States faced new constraints on the use of its military power abroad. Domestically, as the Great Depression ground onward, the United States had fewer resources and turned more and more insular.

The years leading up to the outbreak of World War II also saw the United States increasingly preoccupied with Europe and the Far East. Despite the fact that U.S. policy had promoted a commitment to neutrality on the part of Latin America in 1939, long-term economic ties with Great Britain, France, and their colonial spheres of influence were strengthened by the Roosevelt administration. Thus American economic interests, particularly access to raw materials, were placed in jeopardy by the increasing aggressiveness of the Axis powers of Germany, Italy, and Japan.

Darkening war clouds in Europe gave added impetus to the non-interventionist nature of the Good Neighbor Policy. In 1934 U.S. Marines were withdrawn from Haiti and America gave up financial control over the National Bank of that Caribbean nation. When U.S. petroleum interests in Bolivia and Mexico were expropriated in the late 1930s the Roosevelt administration reacted out of sympathy for the economic and social motivations underlying these actions. It was apparent that security considerations were now given precedence over commercial interests and the prior policy view that property rights were inviolable.

With the outbreak of war in Europe in 1939, it was imperative for U.S. policymakers to secure access to raw materials. The United States looked to the south. The Inter-American Financial and Advisory Committee was established, thereby launching a mutually beneficial economic relationship between the United States and Latin America during the war years. The United States required increasing quantities of strategic raw materials and became virtually the only market available to Latin America for the export of these materials.

Prior to the outbreak of World War II, some 25 percent of U.S. imports came from Latin America, while Latin America consumed 18 percent of U.S. exports. However, by 1945, the United States was importing 42 percent of its needs from Latin America, while Latin American markets accounted for only 14 percent of U.S. goods. This new trade relationship was somewhat illusory. U.S. demand for Latin American resources was fueled by the need to fulfill wartime requirements, yet access to U.S. manufactured goods was limited due to the necessity of devoting resources to the American war machines.

The problem of insufficient goods to satisfy demand within the Latin American economies led to the development of high-cost import-substitution industries in many countries to meet local demand. For the largest countries—Brazil, Argentina, Colombia, and, later, Mexico—import-substitution industrialization was undertaken on a major scale, precipitating significant migration to the major cities and the development of an urban industrial, labor, and

25

middle-class base. The small countries, such as Paraguay, languished in slow growth.

This aberration in U.S.–Latin American economic relations proved to be temporary in the aftermath of the war. New and cheaper sources of goods and materials competed with Latin American exports for the U.S. market. Meanwhile, U.S. exporters moved aggressively to reestablish their prewar commercial dominance of the Latin American markets. Latin American industries that had developed during the war now found themselves uncompetitive in the world market, giving rise to demands for tariff protection. Serious balance of payments difficulties arose, resulting in a new stimulus toward industrialization throughout Latin America.

THE CODIFICATION OF NONINTERVENTION AND MUTUAL SECURITY

In 1947 the United States and the nations of Latin America concluded the Rio Treaty, whereby the parties agreed that "an armed attack by any State against an American State shall be considered as an attack against all the American States, and, consequently, each one of the said contracting parties undertakes to assist in meeting the attack on the exercise of the inherent right of individual or collective self-defense recognized by article 51 of the Charter of the United Nations." The Rio Treaty was followed by the creation of the Organization of American States in Bogota, Colombia, in 1948. The OAS set out guidelines for hemispheric conduct which ruled out intervention by one state in the affairs of another.

The OAS Charter marked a new departure in Latin American relations with the United States. As Ronald Steel pointed out in his book *Pax Americana:*

> For the first time it seemed to free them (the Latins) from the fear of the big stick which had been applied against them so often in the past. For the United States, as well, it was a radical break with the past, a final and explicit repudiation of "gunboat diplomacy" and a recognition that the Monroe Doctrine could no longer be used as an excuse for unilateral interventions designed to punish or intimidate recalcitrant States.
>
> It was a noble declaration of intent, but it completely neglected to take into account the cold war with communism which was just coming up over the horizon.[5]

The Emergence of the Cold War in Latin America

The emergence of the cold war coincided with a new instability among the political regimes of Latin America. As the United States sought stable

[5]Ronald Steel, "Pan American Illusions," *Pax Americana* (New York: Penguin Books, 1977), pp. 198–199.

political regimes, cold war concerns forced American policy more and more into supporting rigid regimes that were striving to preserve the status quo. In some instances, supporting the status quo also benefited particular U.S. interest groups and played upon anticommunist fears on the domestic front.

With the creation of the OAS in 1948, Latin Americans had believed they could put to rest their fears of Yankee interventionism in the hemisphere. After all, national governments in Latin America emerged from the depression and war years with a new sense of strength and centralization of power, much as had the U.S. government. Moreover, the national economies, despite their small markets, were far more integrated than they had been at any time since the great Indian civilizations.

The Guatemalan revolution of 1944 inaugurated basic social change in that country. In fact, during the early 1950s, it appeared that Guatemala would join Costa Rica as the only Central American democracies determined to overcome the social, economic, and political inequities of the past. For ten years, until 1954, Guatemala had enjoyed a series of democratically elected governments. However, Jacob Arbenz, elected by a large vote in 1950, angered President Eisenhower and Secretary of State John Foster Dulles when he expropriated land owned by the Boston-based United Fruit Company under an agrarian reform act. The land expropriated was surplus to United Fruit's needs at the time and was not in production. The Guatemalan agrarian reform act provided compensation for owners who lost acreage, and ultimately one hundred thousand peasants were to have benefited from the program. However, Arbenz had appointed a small number of Communists to low-level cabinet positions within the government—though never in the army, cabinet, or the police forces. United Fruit executives successfully convinced the Eisenhower administration and large segments of the American public, through an extensive media campaign, that Arbenz was a Communist.

At Dulles's behest, funding was approved to begin covert action against Arbenz. In 1953, a few months after the Central Intelligence Agency overthrow of the Iranian government and return of the Shah to power, President Eisenhower gave a go-ahead for a coup in Guatemala. The CIA set up an exile army in Honduras and Nicaragua and persuaded a right-wing Guatemalan military renegade, ex-Colonel Castillo Armas, to head it. The agency also secreted a mini-air force in Nicaragua and the Panama Canal Zone to back up Armas's invasion and to bomb Guatemalan cities. As pilots for the planes, the agency hired U.S. Navy airmen to serve as mercenaries.

Arbenz fled Guatemala to Mexico on 27 June 1954. Armas took power and installed a right-wing military dictatorship. He immediately arrested, exiled, or executed thousands of Arbenz's supporters. He disbanded the country's labor union movement, returned all expropriated land to the United Fruit Company, and banned all political parties.

But, as Steel pointed out, this anticommunist, antirevolutionary policy created a new set of problems for the United States in the region:

Washington's insistence on linking anti-communism with Pan-Americanism had aroused the fear of Yankee intervention which they thought they had put to rest at Bogota in 1948. For Latin Americans the principle of nonintervention is one that overrides party and class, for it involves the very question of national independence, a cause Latin Americans care a good deal more about than they do about anti-communism. And in their eyes, the two are not identical.

This has posed a serious dilemma for American foreign policymakers. On the one hand, they would like the United States to be a "good neighbor" to the Latin Americans, encourage them to replace dictatorship with democracy, help raise their standard of living through such devices as the Alliance for Progress, and observe the rules of non-intervention in the charter of the OAS. They want, in short, to assure the Latin Americans that the days of "gunboat diplomacy" are gone forever, and that we are all members of one big inter-American family.

On the other hand, Washington officials fear that the nations of Latin America may fall into the hands of one of the various "international communist conspiracies" directed from Moscow, Peking, or Havana. Looking at Latin America, they see a continent ripe for revolution: a feudal landholding aristocracy which refuses to give up its ancient privileges, a politically impotent middle class without middle class values that normally support Western-style democracies, a tradition of violence and military dictatorship, an alienated industrial proletariat, and an impoverished peasantry beginning to be roused to political consciousness.

While Washington officials do not consider themselves to be hostile to revolutions per se, they are deeply antagonistic to any revolutions in which communists may play a role, or even which communists support. They assume—although more from fear than from experience—that communists, be they ever so few, will immediately seize control of any popular revolution. By such reasoning they come close to believing that any revolution is inherently dangerous for the United States because communists tend to support revolutions.[6]

THE CUBAN REVOLUTION

In 1959 another revolution—this in Cuba—was to mark a fundamental hardening in U.S.–Latin American policy, casting in concrete the link between support for the political status quo and anticommunism. While Cuba had attained high levels of per capita national income under Batista, the country suffered from high unemployment, repressive authoritarian rule, and large disparities in income distribution. For the majority of Cubans, any economic benefits from the country's association with the United States were largely irrelevant due to the problems of illiteracy, poverty, and joblessness.

When Fidel Castro, a self-proclaimed Marxist, succeeded in ousting the

[6]Ibid., pp. 201–2.

Batista regime, the United States hoped for accommodation. But Castro was guided by a naive egalitarianism and a surprising unawareness of the economics of development. Castro pushed change and social reform rapidly. The hostility of the United States to this political change interacted with Cuba's deep resentment over the U.S. role in the Cuban economy and soon polarized relations between the two countries. Each step taken by Castro, particularly the nationalization of U.S. business interests, produced a new cycle of U.S. antipathy and bellicosity. In turn, Cuba turned increasingly to foreign powers outside the hemisphere, and eventually to the Soviet Union, for assistance.

This turn in the Castro revolution sent shock waves through Washington, In 1961 the ill-fated Bay of Pigs invasion was launched against Cuba by the Kennedy administration. This was followed the next year by the Cuban missile crisis with the Soviet Union in which U.S. power was successful in preventing the establishment of a Soviet military presence in the hemisphere.

Confronted by this turn of events in the hemisphere, President Kennedy solemnly announced the Alliance for Progress program in recognition of the need for social change throughout Latin America. Some $20 billion was pledged for a regionwide crash program of development designed to ameliorate the social conditions that were providing fertile ground for communist-led insurrections.

That the alliance eventually faltered can be blamed on the dilemma faced by Washington policymakers. On the one hand, there was the drive to contain communism in the hemisphere. On the other hand, there emerged numerous right-wing military regimes whose alliances with narrowly based oligarchies resulted in national policies that were antireform in substance. However, American policy during the early years of the alliance did promote, for the first time, major social reforms in land tenure and tax policy. The alliance was heralded by important segments of Latin America as a new era of partnership and progressive change.

This short-lived era of good will was cut short by military intervention of the United States in the Caribbean. In 1965 President Lyndon Johnson sent the marines into the Dominican Republic on the assumption that the Dominican revolution was controlled by the Communists. The president proclaimed what soon became known as the Johnson Doctrine on 2 May 1965: "Revolution in any country is a matter for that country to deal with. It becomes a matter for hemispheric action only when the object is the establishment of a communist dictatorship."

The invasion prevented the return to power of Juan Bosch, who had been democratically elected in 1963. U.S. fears of communism had superseded our commitment to the principle of nonintervention and democracy. More importantly, it sent a signal throughout Latin America that the United States was more comfortable with military governments than with democratically elected reformist governments.

29

Latin America receded into the backwaters of U.S. policy during the latter part of the Johnson administration and the first Nixon administration as Vietnam consumed official Washington's attention. While the Nixon administration did not approve when the reformist government of Juan Valasco Alvarado in Peru nationalized a Standard Oil affiliate in 1969, it did not seek the invocation of the Hickenlooper amendment, although U.S. aid was reduced. Eventually a solution was negotiated. To a certain degree this was attributable to a more sophisticated perspective on the part of many U.S. businesses and U.S. policymakers. Many companies realized they could live with much-needed reforms undertaken by the military, while other companies facing expropriation were compensated and even encouraged to invest in other industries. Moreover, an assertive U.S. policy to destablize the regime did not have any logical allies, since the military was already in power and united in support of reform. Eventually the military government gave way to a new civilian regime in the late 1970s.

However, U.S. policy toward Chile took a different course. In 1970 Salvador Allende, representing a coalition of socialists and communists, was elected to the presidency. U.S. policy at the time was mutedly hostile. As U.S. companies, particularly those engaged in copper mining, were nationalized with disputed compensation, many American businessmen complained to the government in Washington. The United States brought heavy pressure to bear in the World Bank and the Inter-American Development Bank to diminish significantly the flow of economic resources to Chile. The Allende experiment was terminated by military force in September 1973 with support from the United States. The authoritarian dictatorship that followed is ranked among Latin America's most repressive, and elections have been postponed until 1989.

THE CARTER ADMINISTRATION AND TENTATIVE NEW POLICIES

The advent of the Carter administration brought a change in U.S. policy, including a strong advocacy of human rights. Although applied with some inconsistency, the advocacy regained for the United States some of the respect among centrist and democratic forces which had been lost in the wake of its Vietnam and Chile experiences. This, together with the successful conclusion of the Panama Canal Treaties, did much to improve U.S. relations with moderate forces through the continent. For all its inadequacies, the human rights policy promoted the development of a political Center while fostering much needed institutional change.

This policy emerged not so much out of so-called misguided idealism on the part of a handful of policymakers, but out of a recognition of hard realities. First, the only way the United States could reassert moral leadership in Latin America was to recognize the legitimate aspirations and rights of the poor majority. Second, the United States, because of its overwhelming economic

30

importance to the region, could tolerate reformist change without jeopardizing fundamental security interests. After all, the ability of reformist regimes to survive was of necessity tied to the Western economic system, so these regimes would eventually have to reach an accommodation with the United States.

The greatest test of the Carter policy was the Nicaraguan revolution of 1979. The U.S.-supported dictator, Anastacio Somoza, whose family had been brought to power by U.S. Marines in the 1930s, faced a general uprising from nearly all sectors. In the final days of the regime even the most conservative business interests abandoned support for the government and at the very least gave tacit support to the guerrillas. U.S. policy, which recognized that change was inevitable, threw its support to moderate elements in Nicaragua in an effort to accommodate this turn of events. After the revolution, President Carter attempted to build bridges to the Sandinistas, but the election of Ronald Reagan short-circuited the policy.

The Reagan Era

When President Reagan took office in January of 1981, he brought with him a deeply ingrained Cold War perspective of inter-American relations. The victory of the Sandinistas in Nicaragua was seen not as a massive internal insurrection throwing off a corrupt and brutal (albeit friendly to the United States) dictatorship but as a Cuban-inspired revolution that would soon lead to the establishment of a totalitarian dictatorship.

Policymakers in the Reagan administration view the insurgency in El Salvador as being "directed and controlled by Havana and Moscow." Some recognition is given to the fact that the insurgency represents the final decay of an old, narrowly based landed system. However, in the absence of such an insurgency, one wonders how much stress would be given to agrarian reform in El Salvador as a condition for receiving U.S. assistance.

In the administration's view, Guatemala is next in the line of dominoes in Central America. Therefore, U.S. military support should be given the Guatemalan government if the internal situation is to be stabilized, even if this means supplying arms to a repressive regime. Little attention has been given to the fact that Indians, who represent more than one-half of the Guatemalan population, have been systematically brutalized in the twenty-eight years since Arbenz's overthrow.

Costa Rica, which has enjoyed impressive stability as a dynamic democracy largely because the military had been disbanded in the late 1940s, is now seen as being vulnerable because it does not have a military. Little attention is given to the fact that Costa Rica's problems stem from escalating petroleum costs and the deep plunge in prices it receives for its primary commodities in the marketplace.

31

Two countries of the Southern Cone, Argentina and Chile, were perfect allies, in the eyes of the administration's policymakers, to assist the United States in containing communism in the hemisphere. The "bad policies" of the Carter administration would be replaced by this administration's policy of good will and realpolitik, moving the United States closer to both authoritarian regimes. Little attention was paid to the history of both countries—a history that contains ample evidence of their "marching to their own drummers." The war over the Falkland/Malvinas Islands is a graphic demonstration of Argentina's commitment to historic claims to the islands at any cost.

Taken together, the Reagan policies ignore changes in the international system which have markedly diminished the ability of the United States to control events. Power to control, or even to dictate, internal political processes within Latin American nations has been weakened irreversibly by the natural historical processes of growth, the integration of nation-states on the continent, and the release of pent-up political, social, and economic aspirations of the vast majority of the populations in many of these countries. The time has long passed when the United States could cavalierly send troops to install regimes of its own liking.

At the same time, the post–World War II international economic system has become stronger, more diverse, and yet more interdependent. While the United States no longer completely dominates the economic system, it remains by far the most important market and source of capital and technology. Moreover, the spread of foreign investment, greater access to the banking system of industrialized countries, and the development of an international system of multilateral finance have promoted the interdependence and trade that tie the Western nations together. Any nation wishing to opt out of the Western economic system could only do so at great cost. The Soviet Union operates at a distinct disadvantage in this system because it has far fewer trade, capital, and technology resources to offer and none of the management and other skills of Western enterprise. Basic control of the international economic system remains in the hands of the United States and the other industrialized countries. This has become the most important tool in the West's diplomatic arsenal.

In spite of this reality, three historical lessons continue to be ignored by the administration—with potentially catastrophic consequences. First, historical inequities traceable in large measure to colonialism can usually be overcome only through reform and social change. Social structures founded on landed elites and narrowly based oligarchies who resist broad-based participation in economic development are likely to be swept aside by aggressive social movements. Nicaragua is a prime example. The Somoza family had cornered a large part of the entire nation's wealth and had virtually ignored the problems of the vast majority of Nicaraguan society—illiteracy, the virtual absence of health care in rural areas, and the virtual denial of opportunity to

32

participate in the Nicaraguan economy. In El Salvador, fourteen families and a handful of wealthy entrepreneurs controlled most of the productive land of that country.

Second, movements to change antiquated, inequitable social structures like those in Central America do not draw their primary inspiration from Soviet communism. To be sure, factions within such movements may receive support from Cuba or even the Soviet Union. However, these movements tend to be highly variegated, often comprising frustrated democratic elements worthy of U.S. support. American support for repressive governments that seek to preserve undemocratic societies can lead to results directly opposite to those being sought. Providing assistance to these regimes because the United States has done so in the past or, worse yet, simply because the Soviet Union supports the other side, plays into the hands of the anti-U.S. elements in these political movements. The United States proves for them that it stands for the status quo and against equity and representative societies. They use this argument against the United States all over Latin America and will continue to do so as long as America provides them the proof of its true intentions by following these misguided policies.

Finally, the United States must recognize that it can no longer exercise its power freely and unilaterally within the hemisphere. The nations of the world are no longer exclusively dependent on the United States for economic and political support. They can now also turn to Europe and Japan. Ironically, this is true for the Soviet Union's traditional satellites and allies as well.[7]

Multilateralism has grown in intensity and strength during the post–World War II era, largely through the increased interdependence of the Western economic system. With multilateralism has come the acceptance of the concept of both economic and political burden sharing. Unfortunately, while the Reagan administration's policymakers have demanded more economic support from U.S. allies, they are irritated by their growing political independence. The strength of multilateralism depends on consensus among the major countries and can be successful only when predicated on shared principles such as self-determination, the basic rights of the individual,

[7]In the past four decades the major powers of the world have seen their spheres of influence, and even their colonial empires, altered by grass-roots movements that linked revolutionary elites with major segments of the mass populace. The Soviet Union has had its Polands, Czechoslovakias, and Hungarys. Rumania has pursued an independent foreign policy. Yugoslavia moved into the nonaligned camp early on, much of the move due to American help. And as if to demonstrate that communism can also be nationalistic rather than only monolithic, the People's Republic of China has emerged as a major ally of the United States in countering Soviet expansionism. In the third world, the Soviets lost Egypt and Indonesia. Angola looks to the West for assistance in addressing its development needs. Mozambique still has denied base rights to the Soviet Union, and Zimbabwean relations with Russia remain cool at best. Somalia is now an ally of the United States, having formerly been solidly entrenched in the so-called Soviet Camp. Russian troops have been unsuccessful in subduing Afghanistan nationalism. All of this hardly constitutes a record of unswerving loyalty and obedience to the world's premier totalitarian power.

33

96436

LIBRARY
COLBY-SAWYER COLLEGE
NEW LONDON, N.H. 03257

nonintervention, and the promulgation of democratic values. This strength is the most formidable weapon in the U.S. arsenal. It is crucial to American long-term interests. The United States must have the support of the other democracies. The old adage that there is strength in numbers is particularly relevant to this day and age. And this is the challenge for American diplomacy in the decade of the 1980s and beyond—a challenge that can be met only if American policies abroad remain true to the underlying principles on which this country's freedoms and institutions are built.

II

U.S. Policies toward Latin American Countries

3. Mexico: The Continuing Quest for a Policy

Peter H. Smith

A little bit of knowledge can go a long way—toward misunderstanding. In late 1982 the U.S. media suddenly discovered "the Mexican crisis." News reports and editorial columns expressed dismay over Mexico's 80- to 85-billion-dollar foreign debt, usually hinting that it resulted from inefficiency, irresponsibility, and corruption (or some combination thereof). An hour-long television documentary intimated that the country's socioeconomic inequities might lead to political breakdown. In December *Time* magazine devoted a full-length cover story to the Mexican presidential inauguration; the reportage itself was thorough and responsible, while the lead quotation next to a picture of the new chief executive was meant to catch the eye: "We are in an emergency."

The overall media message was mixed, but it could produce at least two plausible interpretations of Mexico's contemporary crisis—with corresponding U.S. policy prescriptions. First, Mexico is in the throes of an enormous debt; if the United States helps its neighbor through this period of difficulty, then petroleum reserves and other blessings will make everything well. Second, and alternatively, Mexico is heading for a Central American–style revolution; the United States can either stand by helplessly or intervene decisively, but the time for decision will probably arrive during the 1980s.

Neither one of these views is correct. Mexico's main problem is neither its debt nor the prospect of peasant revolution. It is a long-term socioeconomic crisis that threatens to challenge and transform the political order. The United States' main problem is that it does not have a coherent policy toward Mexico that responds to this reality.

Peter H. Smith

Overview

What is the Mexican political regime? It is a wondrously complex, intricate system that has maintained itself in power for the last half-century by controlling the terms of political debate, absorbing potential challenges with modest reforms, and repressing uncooperative opposition movements. As the institutional heirs to the Mexican Revolution of 1910, the current government and its semiofficial Partido Revolucionario Institucional (PRI) have exerted a virtual monopoly on political power. Presidents rule for nonrenewable six-year terms, during which time they command supreme authority: they possess the final word on all major policy questions, they control vast amounts of patronage, and, despite the limitation on incumbency, they can have enduring influence on the path of national development. There is a constitution, of course, and there are regular elections. There have been political prisoners, a fact the government has often denied, and there have been moments of violent repression. In October 1968 army troops killed approximately three hundred participants in a large-scale demonstration in Mexico City, an outpouring that had swelled from a student protest against university policies to a critique of police brutality and, finally, as Mexico's Olympic Games approached, to a broad denunciation of social and political inequities. In 1971 scores of students were again shot down by paramilitary thugs as police stood casually by, and peasant leaders and labor agitators have mysteriously disappeared from time to time.

Opposition parties exist, but at the moment they are fragmented and relatively powerless. Until the late 1970s a handful of political parties—principally the Partido de Acción Nacional (PAN), the Partido Popular Socialista (PPS), and the Partido Auténtico de la Revolución Mexicana (PARM)—provided the regime with loyal, parliamentary dissent: with low to minuscule electoral support, their leaders accepted seats in the congress, criticized occasional decisions (but never the system itself), made frequent deals with the PRI, and, by their mere existence, strengthened the government's claim to popular support and legitimate authority.

In recent years a more radical, less collaborationist party movement has appeared. Led by the Partido Socialista Unificado de Mexico (PSUM), a variety of leftist organizations has stressed the unfulfilled hopes of the masses, the long-lost dreams of the Mexican Revolution, and the persistence of injustices. Partly because of its internal divisions the Left has yet to capture a large electoral following, winning about 10 percent of the vote in the presidential election of 1982. Consolidation of these competing factions into a single party of the Left could create a formidable political force in the future.

Outside the party structure there have been terrorist movements, both urban and rural, but their importance has diminished since the mid-1970s.

Crackdowns and antiguerrilla campaigns by army and police units appear to have subdued terrorist groups.

One of the most pervasive popular feelings, however, is apathy. Voter turnout in presidential elections ranges from 43 to 76 percent (though the ballot is obligatory), and as a whole the Mexican people tend to perceive their government as distant, elitist, and self-serving. A sizeable share of the populace, perhaps one-quarter to one-third, is underfed, underschooled, underclothed—and so marginal to the political process that it represents, in the phrase of one Mexican sociologist, an "internal colony." Apathy and marginalization do not necessarily constitute a clear and *present* danger to the regime (indeed, they often permit the regime to do what it does), but they offer ominous warnings about the potential for *future* discord and strife.

But if the Mexican political system exhibits authoritarian features, it possesses flexibility too. Top-heavy as it is, the PRI is organized around three distinct sectors: one for peasants, one for workers, and one, quixotically called the popular sector, for almost everyone else. This structure provides at least token representation for broad strata of Mexican society and helps explain the passive acceptance, if not enthusiastic endorsement, that the regime enjoys among the masses. A steady rotation of political personnel means that new people, some with new ideas, are able to gain access to high office. When signs of discontent have appeared, Mexico's rulers have frequently co-opted mass leaders by providing them with public positions, further broadening the base of support for the system. And every decade or so, most recently under president José López Portillo (1976–82), the system undergoes a period of self-examination that often leads to some kind of reform (in the latest instance, expanding opposition representation in the national Chamber of Deputies to one-quarter of the total seats). The results are less than dramatic but they affirm the system's basic code, which one close observer has succinctly summarized this way: two carrots, even three or four, and then a stick if necessary. Thus Mexico has created its unique political system—a highly institutionalized dominant-party regime under the control of civilian officeholders.

Such methods demonstrated extraordinary effectiveness in resolving the governmental crises that beset Mexico from the 1910s through the 1960s. The political challenges now looming before the country reflect tremendous social and economic forces, however, and they cannot be met through electoral adjustment and administrative tinkering.

World War II helped inaugurate the pattern of economic growth that has since become known as "the Mexican miracle." Loans poured into the country, investment flowed, petroleum exports multiplied, and with both the supervision and participation of the state, the gross domestic product (GDP) increased at annual rates of 6 to 8 percent. But not all Mexicans shared in this expansion. By 1969 the wealthiest tenth of families received 51 percent of the national income, while the bottom half had only 15 percent—and it seems likely that the disproportion worsened in the 1970s. (In the United States, by contrast, the wealthiest tenth in 1970 took in about 17.5 percent of the national income and the bottom half received 26 percent.) About 40 percent of Mexico's labor force is underemployed, according to best estimates, causing a degree of social hardship usually associated with an unemployment rate of 20 percent or so—over and above the open unemployment rate of 6 percent in the urban industrial sectors. Laborers struggle for work, peasants clamor for land, one-fifth of the population cannot read or write, and poverty continues to spread in both the cities and the countryside. An especially poignant indicator of social deprivation is the persistence of infant mortality: despite great progress in Mexican medical and public health services, about fifty-five of every one thousand children still die before their first birthday, compared to fifteen per thousand in the United States.

Especially worrisome for the future is the fact that, due to one of the highest rates of demographic growth in the world, nearly one-half of Mexico's seventy-two million people are under the age of 15. To be sure, the annual rate of population growth appears to have slackened in recent years, dropping from 3.5 or 3.6 percent to 2.9 percent or so, and this pattern may continue for some time. No matter what kind of birth control programs start now, however, the age structure of the Mexican population presents a fundamental, unchangeable reality: the pressure for new jobs from now to the end of the century will be immense.

This is a critical problem. Recent estimates project that 700 to 800 thousand Mexicans will enter the job market every year between now and the end of the century. There is no convincing sign that Mexican industry, with its tendency to rely on technology instead of labor, will be able to supply sufficient jobs. Indeed, some analysts believe Mexico will be fortunate to meet *half* the imminent demand.

The contradiction between economic growth and popular welfare intensified in the late 1970s. Then came the crisis of 1982.

1982: YEAR OF THE SHOCKS

The political dimensions of an impending crisis began to appear in September 1981, when López Portillo revealed his selection of Miguel de la Madrid as president-designate for 1982–88. The choice seemed understandable on its merits and consistent with tradition. A personal friend (and one-time student) of López Portillo's, De la Madrid had played a prominent role in the formulation of economic policy. Handsome and well educated (with a master's degree in public administration from Harvard), he showed every sign of the intellectual and bureaucratic capacity required by the presidency. De la Madrid had only one drawback: a technocrat par excellence, he had

40

never held elective office and he had weak connections with the PRI. This made it all the more significant when the president of the PRI expressed his unhappiness over the De la Madrid nomination—and lost his job in the bargain.

Economic difficulties became apparent in February 1982, when the López Portillo administration decided to let the peso "float" on the international market—and it promptly plummeted from twenty-six per dollar to around forty-five per dollar. In March the finance minister resigned. In August the government decreed another devaluation. The peso fell to between seventy-five and eighty per dollar and Mexico announced that, given its shortage of foreign exchange, it might not be able to meet its debt obligations. While the international banking community scrambled to provide some short-term relief López Portillo decried the existence of speculation against the peso, denounced the "vultures" seeking ill-gotten gains, and stunned onlookers by declaring state expropriation of privately owned banks in his annual message on September 1 (foreign-owned banks were exempted). Hand in hand with this decree was the imposition of government control on the foreign exchange rate, set promptly at seventy per dollar for commercial purposes and fifty per dollar for preferential transactions. Inflation was by this time running at a yearly rate of close to 100 percent.

The Left applauded the nationalization and López Portillo claimed his place in history. Though he won the 4 July election with nearly 75 percent of the vote, De la Madrid kept his silence, as custom demanded, until his own inauguration on 1 December. When his opportunity finally came he roundly criticized "financial populism" (without naming names, of course) and called for the "moral renovation" of society and government. The bank expropriation itself was "irreversible," he conceded, but his administration would take the true road to recovery. "The first months of the government will be arduous and difficult. The situation requires it. The austerity is obligatory."

The new president moved with remarkable speed. De la Madrid appointed a cabinet full of proficient technocrats like himself, holding over Jesús Silva Herzog as minister of finance and reinstating Miguel Mancera (who had opposed exchange controls) as head of the central bank. He accepted the International Monetary Fund's (IMF) conditions for renegotiation of the debt, including a provision that the budget deficit be gradually reduced from 16.5 percent of GDP in 1982 to 3.5 percent in 1985. He lifted price controls on twenty-five hundred consumer items and provided pricing flexibility on two thousand more. Through Mancera he floated the peso once again, and its free-market value fell to around one-hundred-fifty per dollar. And he sent a bill to congress that would authorize the sale of 34 percent of the ownership in the newly nationalized banks to private investors.

De la Madrid was struggling with three related problems. One was to restore Mexico's credibility in the international financial community, and on

41

this front he was taking swift action. A second problem was either to restore or to redefine the structure of the country's ruling elite, and here he was facing several key choices: whether to uphold and reintegrate the national private sector (as the bank-shares bill suggested), how to handle the old-line PRI *políticos* (who were almost completely excluded from his cabinet), and whether to make special accommodations for the role of the military (about which he released no early signs). His third major problem came from the Left and from the masses, who would bear most of the burden of the International Monetary Fund–approved recovery plan. Somewhat predictably, the PSUM expressed its "outright rejection" of De la Madrid's austerity program. Less predictably, and more significantly, labor leaders vowed their opposition to measures that "affect the working class."

U.S.-Mexican Relationships: Perspectives

These conditions have serious implications for U.S.-Mexican relations, for in dealing with Mexico, this country is dealing with a government simultaneously beset by two kinds of challenges: first, an almost overwhelming set of socioeconomic problems that will be exacerbated (but were not created) by the IMF conditions for debt rescheduling; and second, the long-term need to broaden its own political support. At times these two goals may seem mutually inconsistent, if not downright contradictory. It is frequently argued that dictatorship, either reactionary or revolutionary, constitutes a necessary prerequisite for economic growth or income redistribution, as the examples of Chile and Cuba allegedly attest. To avoid such stark outcomes Mexican leaders must strike a delicate balance. In order to maintain the peace, to meet the needs of their people, and to improve representation within their political system, they may well have to adopt far-reaching, radical-appearing policies. They will continue to feel a patriotic need to protect their country's resources, assert their nation's autonomy, and insist on pursuit of their own interests—especially against pressure from their giant neighbor to the north. And yet, in the process, they will not want to frighten off the U.S. capital and technology they still want for national development. If the Mexicans cannot attain these goals, the choice will be a most unpleasant one: either a major upheaval from below, from restless urban masses and laborers, or, more probably, an increase in repression and perhaps conspicuous encroachment by the military into politics.

Political stability in Mexico is therefore a major concern for the United States. For all its imperfections, the Mexican government represents the kind of regime the United States should encourage and support in Latin America. It responds to popular needs, it attempts (at least in its fashion) to articulate programs for the masses, it speaks for the national will: in short, it has the support, active or passive, of most segments of the population. The Mexicans will not always follow the U.S. lead, but this country must accept that likelihood. We Americans must comprehend the difficulty of the choices that the Mexicans will have to make. And Americans must recognize that stability, if it is to persist, will mean accommodation to change.

Throughout the transitions of the 1980s, however, basic characteristics of the U.S.-Mexican relationship are certain to endure. Four features come to mind.

Asymmetry. The United States is bigger, stronger, and richer than Mexico, and has been ever since the early nineteenth century (though not before). There is no bargaining between equals. Overall, the United States will continue to have the upper hand—and this will continue to engender suspicion and resentment. "Poor Mexico," one well-known slogan goes, "so far from God and so close to the United States."

Conflict. Despite some common outlooks and goals, there will be disagreement on specific issues. What is good for Mexico is not always good for the United States, and vice versa (or, in more refined terms, what is good for certain interests in Mexico might not be good for certain interests in the United States).

Diplomatic limitations. Government-to-government negotiations do not and will not have the capacity to resolve some key bilateral issues in a definitive manner. This is partly due to the nature of the issues—such as migration, which responds to socioeconomic stimuli and stoutly resists official regulation. It also reflects diversity and contradictions in policy making, particularly in the United States (where multitudinous government agencies, each with its own perspective and constituency—including almost all departments of the executive branch plus both houses of Congress—take part in the policy process). Inconsistency is more apparent in U.S. decision making toward Mexico than toward Cuba, for instance, or even toward Nicaragua, where the bilateral agendas are more clearly defined. This situation contrasts sharply with the centralized apparatus in Mexico, where presidential will prevails.

Cultural differences. Underlying all these factors are divergent value systems and senses of history. North Americans look to the future while Mexicans, like most other civilized people of the earth, remain aware of the past. As the philosopher-poet Octavio Paz once said, "North Americans consider the world to be something that can be perfected, while we [Mexicans] consider it to be something that can be redeemed."

This concern with history has instilled Mexicans with deep-seated suspicion of the United States. They recall with bitterness the disputes over Texas and the "war of the North American invasion" that led to the loss of half the nation's territory. They remember U.S. intervention in the Mexican Revolution of 1910, including U.S. acquiescence in the assassination of Francisco

Madero (since revered as the "apostle" of the revolution) and the U.S. Navy's occupation of the port of Veracruz. Pridefully noting the prestige of Pemex, the government-owned petroleum company, they are reminded of U.S. strident opposition to the nationalization of oil in 1938. Such recollections directly affect the style and tone of bilateral negotiations. As López Portillo declared on one occasion after the discovery of the new energy reserves, Mexico "suddenly found itself the center of American attention—attention that is a surprising mixture of interest, disdain and fear, much like the recurring vague fears you [the United States] inspire in certain areas of our national subconscious."

Current U.S. Policy: Explanation and Critique

Mexico occupies an important place in the Reagan administration's strategy toward Latin America as a whole. Because of its political stability, it appears to offer a viable alternative to communist (or even Marxist) solutions. And because of its relative strength and prestige, Mexico seems to have the capacity to play the role of diplomatic broker between the United States and other parts of Latin America. Viewed within an East-West framework, Mexico can thus contribute to the containment of communism. It is also the ultimate domino. As one Reagan administration official has declared, "Mexico is the decisive battleground. If we make no headway in El Salvador or in Guatemala in forestalling Marxist-Leninist takeovers, I do not know what the U.S. or anyone could do to prevent Mexico from falling to a similar regime."

Given this outlook, the Reagan administration has tried hard to create a positive atmosphere for U.S.-Mexican relations. Unlike Jimmy Carter, Ronald Reagan established excellent personal rapport with López Portillo and may do so with De la Madrid. The elimination of the "consultative mechanism" and of the Office of Special Coordinator for Mexican Affairs, both closely identified with the Carter approach, have underscored this administration's determination to improve matters. Despite initial ridicule over his appointment, U.S. Ambassador John Gavin has earned respect in some quarters for his modest manner (and fluent Spanish). Visits to Mexico by topmost officials—including the president, the vice-president, and the secretary of state—have gratified Mexican sensibilities. Within the State Department, too, Mexican affairs are managed by people with some experience in Mexico.

Mexico thus constitutes a high priority. Indeed, as one seasoned observer has noted, the Reagan administration's approach to Latin America appears to consist of three parts: no more Nicaraguas, good relations with the Southern Cone, and good relations with Mexico.

There is no question that the tenor of this country's relationship with Mexico has improved markedly within the past two years. But this is not really a *policy*; it is a *posture*. "It's all very nice," another insider has said, "but so far there's nothing of substance. It's just atmospherics."

The Bilateral Agenda

At present, and for the foreseeable future, the agenda for Mexico and the United States will consist of two sets of issues: bilateral and regional. Bilateral questions focus mainly on socioeconomic matters. There are no military or territorial disputes. The principal concerns relate to trade, energy, the debt, and migration.

Trade. Points of conflict stem from U.S. opposition to Mexico's quest for national self-sufficiency, the promotion of export-led growth, and occasional protectionist policies—in other words, to Mexico's resistance to complete integration in the international economic system. The Carter administration expressed acute disappointment over López Portillo's 1980 decision to refrain from joining the General Agreement on Tariffs and Trade (GATT); Mexico's inclusion eventually would have lowered duties on North American goods. The Reagan administration has imposed countervailing duties on Mexican leather products and has been pressured to take similar action on auto parts, pharmaceuticals, and winter vegetables. In such dealings asymmetry is harshly apparent: the United States takes up about 60 percent of Mexico's trade, while Mexico accounts for only 4 percent of all of this country's international transactions.

Energy. Mexico has oil and gas the United States would like to buy. Proven hydrocarbon reserves now amount to 72 billion barrels, and potential deposits are estimated at 250 billion barrels, second only to Saudi Arabia. Here the interests of producer and consumer cannot coincide. The United States wants to purchase large amounts at modest prices, while Mexico wants (1) to conserve as much oil as possible for its own industrial development, setting a ceiling on exports of 1.5 million barrels per day; (2) to obtain a good price for its exports, usually staying around OPEC levels; and (3) to diversify its customers (Mexico recently announced its intent to sell no more than 50 percent of its exports to any single buyer, i.e., the United States, which was at one time purchasing 70 percent). Through the 1980s Mexico can supply about 5 percent of total U.S. energy needs.

The Reagan administration appears to have accepted Mexico's petroleum policies; it has at least refrained from applying unnecessary pressure. The current oil glut has no doubt facilitated this stance and helps explain Mexico's surprising mid-1981 decision to provide supplies for the U.S. strategic reserve. Conditions are apt to change if the oil glut disappears, and it remains to be seen how the United States will respond.

Debt. The prospect of large-scale earnings from oil and gas tempted the López Portillo administration to embark on an overambitious development

45

program. To obtain capital, Mexico borrowed heavily on the international market, running up a total debt of between 80 and 85 billion dollars by mid-1982 (about two-thirds of which belonged to the public sector). For a variety of reasons—the oil glut, rising interest rates, declining prices for agricultural exports, capital flight, corruption, and mismanagement—Mexico ran out of money for its payments.

After some initial hesitation the Reagan administration decided to furnish help. By late 1982 the United States joined the international banking community in providing Mexico with a multipartite package consisting mainly of:

a 5-billion-dollar loan from European and U.S. creditor banks;

a 3.8-billion-dollar authorization from the IMF;

rescheduling of the $19.5 billion in public debt due before the end of 1984;

a staggered grace period on principal payments; and

an advance payment of $1 billion on U.S. purchases for the strategic oil reserve, plus

credit guarantees for the purchase of agricultural commodities from the U.S., while

Mexico undertakes the austerity program set forth by De la Madrid.

Even as the ink was drying on these agreements, observers began to wonder if Mexico could keep its end of the bargain. Others noted that it was the "overexposed" U.S. banks, not Mexico, that had the most to lose. (Almost incredibly, the nine largest U.S. banks had tied up 44 percent of their capital in Mexico!) Both points became clear through speculation in early 1983 that a collapse of OPEC could lead to a $10 drop in the international price of oil per barrel, which could cost Mexico $7 billion in export earnings. And if Mexico were to announce that it could not pay the interest on just 20 percent of its loans, Chase Manhattan, Citibank, and Bank of America would each stand to lose $60 million in 1983. "That would be very dangerous," said a senior official with a New York bank. "Not every bank can afford to lose $60 million."

Migration. This is probably the most difficult, volatile, and emotional issue on the bilateral agenda. It calls for understanding, compassion, and a rational assessment of the facts. Despite alarmist assertions that eight to twelve million "illegal aliens" from Mexico are participating in a "silent invasion" of American society, in truth it appears that there are between 2.5 and 3 million undocumented migrants in the United States at any given time (and the number may be substantially lower). One or 2 million hold jobs of one sort or another. The size of the annual flow of migrants from Mexico is between .5 and 1.5 million; most migrants come to this country for limited periods of time and then go back home.

Many U.S. employers approve of this migration, since it provides them with a cheap and dependable source of labor. North American unions staunchly oppose it, arguing that it keeps wages low and unemployment high. For Mexico, where unemployment is rampant and worsening, where under-employment may be as high as 40 percent, it represents a safety valve. "To the United States," sociologist Jorge Bustamante has observed, migration "has been a problem, but to Mexico it has been a solution." López Portillo firmly expressed his own view on the subject: "It is not a crime to look for work," he declared more than once, "and I refuse to consider it as such."

In this area the Reagan administration has taken an explicit stand, proposing in July 1981 an immigration program with these key components:

> creating a temporary guestworker program, permitting up to fifty thousand Mexican nationals per year to enter the United States for periods of nine to twelve months (they would not be allowed to bring spouses or children, and they would not be eligible for welfare assistance);
> granting "amnesty" to illegal aliens who can prove continuous residence in the United States since 1 January 1980 or before;
> imposing fines of $500 to $1,000 on U.S. employers who knowingly hire illegal aliens; and
> strengthening the U.S. border patrol.

The program might seem sensible at first glance, but it is inadequate and unworkable. The plan for fifty thousand guestworkers does not begin to address the fact that one million or more Mexicans cross the border every year. The amnesty proposal is complicated in detail and will prove cumbersome in practice: many "undocumented" workers will find it hard to furnish documentary proof of residence. The sanctions against offending employers are too weak to be effective, and a 40-million-dollar increase in the border patrol's budget will hardly stem the flow of migrants. "The effect," says Wayne Cornelius, "is simply to speed up the revolving door, generate ever-more-impressive apprehension statistics, and bid up the fees charged by the 'coyotes' who smuggle undocumented aliens across the border." As it stands, the administration's plan is likely to bring us the worst of all worlds: its implementation will neither reduce nor regularize the inflow of Mexican migrants, while its enforcement may cause enormous difficulties for relations with the Mexican government.

During 1982 congressional attention focused on a general immigration bill sponsored by Senator Alan Simpson (R-Wyo.) and Representative Romano Mazzoli (D-Ky.). The bill passed the Senate by an eighty to nineteen vote, attracted bilateral support, and received President Reagan's approval. Simpson-Mazzoli is a sprawling piece of legislation incorporating the main provisions of the administration's program with at least three aspects of special relevance to Mexico:

47

inclusion of immediate family members in the formal yearly quota of twenty
thousand visas;
rollback of the permanent amnesty date from 1980 to 1977; and
increase of the penalty for U.S. employers who hire undocumented workers.

The overall point of the bill is to reduce illegal migration, and its principal
strategy is to eliminate hiring incentives for employers through the threat of
severe sanctions. This, too, seems logical enough. The problem is that it will
not work, since employers can find numerous ways to skirt the penalties (as
they have in California, where a decade-old employer-sanctions law has not
resulted in a single conviction). If passed it may also lead to bias against
Chicanos and legal migrants, adding yet another complication to
U.S.-Mexican affairs.

The Regional Agenda: Central America

Different responses to conflagrations in Central America have led to
sharp disagreement between Mexico and the United States, and the reconciliation or exacerbation of these differences will have a crucial effect on relations
between the two countries. The Reagan administration has chosen to interpret
insurrectionary movements in El Salvador and elsewhere as the result of
external subversion, mainly originating in Cuba. This view places Central
America's upheavals directly within an East-West cold war framework and
stresses the need to halt the perceived spread of communism in the hemisphere. Nicaragua's Sandinista regime is cited as both a source and a demonstration of the danger.

For their part, most Mexicans tend to see the conflicts in Central America
as logical and perhaps inevitable responses to historic conditions of repression
and inequity. Partly because of their own revolution and its heritage, they do
not assume that social upheaval necessarily leads to catastrophic consequences. Their hope is to encourage negotiated political settlements, in
anticipation that emergent left-of-center governments will stabilize the region.
Hence López Portillos's outspoken support for the Sandinista movement in
Nicaragua and Mexico's joint call with France in August 1981 for recognition
of the Salvadoran Democratic Revolutionary Front (FDR) as a "legitimate"
political force.

Despite their differences in approach and premises, it should be noted that
the two countries have overall goals that are not entirely incompatible. As
Cathryn Thorup has written, Mexico's strategy in Central America is not to
"indulge" revolution, but rather to contain it. "Mexican aid to these
countries—diplomatic and/or commercial—may be seen as a way to promote
stability, interdependence, and economic growth, thus avoiding a rad-

48

icalization of tensions. In this sense, the ultimate goals of U.S. and Mexican policies toward Central America are not so dissimilar after all."[1]

For a time the Mexicans and the Reagan administration took care not to emphasize divergences. In February 1982 López Portillo publicly offered Mexico's help to unravel what he called "three knots that tie up the search for peace" in the region: the internal conflict in El Salvador, distrust between the United States and Nicaragua, and hostility between the United States and Cuba. He reiterated the call for a negotiated settlement in El Salvador, proposed a nonaggression treaty between the United States and Nicaragua, and urged futher dialogue between the American government and the Castro regime. Then Foreign Secretary Jorge Castañeda said in explanation that such settlements are essential for the tranquility of the region and even for President Reagan's own Caribbean Basin Initiative:

> Programs for economic development of the Caribbean Basin, no matter how ambitious or generous, cannot succeed in the midst of political confrontation and military threats. Gracious gestures of political accommodation must go hand-in-hand with the altruism of economic aid.
>
> Mexico is prepared to serve as a bridge, as a communicator, between its friends and neighbors. Together, we must find a solution that seves the interests and enhances the security of all the Caribbean Basin Countries.[2]

The U.S. response to the Mexican attempt has turned out to be lukewarm. In his proclamation of the Caribbean Basin program, President Reagan failed to mention the Mexican proposal. Some discussions took place and then withered away. Apparently the Reagan administration has little interest in pursuing the possibility of enlisting Mexico's aid. More's the pity, since the arrival of the De la Madrid administration—with its extremely able foreign secretary, Bernardo Sepúlveda—provides us with a fresh opportunity for resolving the conflicts in Central America.

Regional issues such as these can seriously jeopardize the United States's relationship with Mexico. They are not intrinsic parts of the bilateral agenda, but they are likely to persist in the future. So long as they can be contained and remain isolated they might not cause excessive damage to U.S.-Mexican affairs, but there are limits to the plausible range of toleration.

If the United States were to resort to flagrant military intervention in Central America (as Nicaragua has warned before the United Nations), Mexico would have no choice but to disrupt its dialogue with Washington. López Portillo committed himself to moral support of the Sandinistas and to a negotiated settlement in El Salvador—and there seems little doubt that, given the clarity of these positions, De la Madrid will follow this same line. Outright U.S. intervention in either country would make it impossible for the Mexicans

---

[1]*Washington Post,* 6 February 1981.
[2]*New York Times,* 10 March 1982.

to maintain their current conciliatory stance. It is hard to know what they would do, but options might include: a declaration of solidarity with the Sandinistas, the pursuit of negotiations with El Salvador without U.S. participation, and a firm diplomatic alignment with Western Europe, Venezuela, and Cuba on regional matters. Depending on the character of the American intervention, Mexico might conceivably suspend diplomatic relations with this country.

These unpleasant prospects reveal fundamental conceptual weaknesses behind the Reagan administration's pursuit of a "special relationship" with Mexico. The underlying idea, it appears, is to recognize a special role for Mexico in maintaining regional security. Mexico thus assumes importance in a geopolitical sense, as a friendly middle-range power that can serve as an effective diplomatic broker between the United States and the rest of Latin America. Mexico is not so crucial itself; what matters is the part it plays in the promotion of U.S. designs and strategies.[3] This perspective not only overlooks Mexico's intrinsic value to the United States, it also rests on the dubious premise that Mexico can be consistently persuaded to run diplomatic errands on behalf of the United States—or even to play a large role in the implementation of President Reagan's Caribbean Development plan.

An Alternative Approach: The Need for a Coherent Policy

In contrast to the Reagan administration's emphasis on East-West conflict and regional security, I believe the United States should construe its paramount national interest in Mexico as the maintenance of political stability. The United States does not want Mexico to become El Salvador—or Guatemala, either. Nor does Mexico's leadership. Indeed, the costs of major social upheaval in Mexico would be enormous for both countries. As one *político* declared to an American observer,

> For a long time, the United States never thought about us. Now you're worried about oil. You would do a little better to worry about the whole country or one day you could have a surprise.
>
> It may not happen for ten or twenty years. But the day Mexico catches fire because people do not have enough food, part of the United States will burn. This will be your final Vietnam.

The question is how to collaborate on bilateral issues in ways that will contribute to the achievement of genuine political stability in Mexico. To gain more support from its people, the Mexican government will eventually need to stimulate economic growth, distribute benefits to broad segments of society,

[3]As Cathryn Thorup points out, there is an underlying administrative inconsistency in the current approach to Mexico: the United States appears to want a "special" bilateral relationship but relies on informal ad hoc mechanisms.

alleviate the plight of the poor, and, at times, assert national pride and independence of the United States. This much the United States will have to accept and understand.

The Reagan administration has justifiably placed a high priority on establishing "good relations" with Mexico. It has created a positive atmosphere and taken fairly reasonable stands (thus far) on trade, energy, and the debt. It does not yet have a coherent and substantive policy toward Mexico, however, and the most problematic areas are the most important ones: the regional question of Central America and the bilateral question of migration.

SHORT-TERM POLICIES (1983)

The United States should drastically revise its policy on Central America as soon as possible. Mexico's participation in the "Contadora" group (with Colombia, Panama, and Venezuela) provides a chance for peace by mediation, and the U.S. should accept the offer. Mexico is in a unique position to help achieve a settlement—since it has simultaneous good relations with Cuba, Nicaragua, the United States, and the Salvadoran insurgents—and this country should take advantage of the opportunity. One beneficial side-effect would be to remove a potential source of conflict from the U.S.-Mexican agenda. The primary reason for changing America's policy on Central America, however, is to bolster this country's position in the region as a whole.

On the bilateral front, the United States should refrain from any major initiatives for a time so De la Madrid can settle in as president. This merely reflects some of the chronological realities of political life in Mexico. It also has the advantage of giving the United States an opportunity to devise reasonable and practical policies on matters of substance. In the meantime, this country should be prepared to offer a sympathetic hand if Mexico runs into trouble meeting its IMF obligations on the debt. Whatever else occurs, this is *not* the time to tighten diplomatic screws on Mexico if financial problems arise.

LONG-TERM POLICIES (1983–88)

The United States should shape a coherent policy toward Mexico that helps promote development and stability within that country. This would have to be a flexible and dynamic policy, one that can respond to economic and political changes within the two countries and to far-reaching changes in the international arena.

It can be safely assumed that De la Madrid will pursue the foreign policies established by López Portillo. If anything, in fact, the new president may eventually try further to assert and enhance Mexico's role as an independent power in third world areas and especially in Central America and the Caribbean. In this regard the United States should give Mexico a fairly free hand

and should try to encourage cooperative approaches. At the very least, the United States should refrain from public criticism of Mexican foreign policy.

Trends in domestic policy are harder to predict. De la Madrid has initially placed more emphasis on growth than on equity, stressing infrastructural development rather than redistribution, though he might eventually be pressured into pursuing more far-reaching goals. He may at least feel the need to use more radical (that is, liberal) rhetoric in an appeal to the Left. In any event, his administration will be straining to confront a difficult situation. There is every reason to believe that many Mexicans will eventually blame the United States—as the IMF's most influential donor—for socioeconomic hardships deriving from (or in any associated with) the IMF stabilization program. As William Cline has observed, "The potential for recrimination is vast, as is the challenge to statesmanship on both sides to pursue jointly beneficial economic goals."[4]

Within this context, the United States should explore ways of collaborating with Mexican authorities on questions of trade, energy, investment, and finance. Close and careful consultation will be absolutely necessary.

The United States should develop a position on the possibility of Mexican membership on OPEC. The United States might not want to encourage it; the question is whether and how to discourage it. Mexico obviously has the right to join OPEC if that turns out to be the preference of Mexico. How much difference would it make to the United States? At any rate, we cannot afford a knee-jerk reaction on an issue of such symbolic and substantive importance to the Mexicans.

But the overriding issue, the one with deepest significance, is Mexican migration to the United States. There are no easy solutions. Migration to this country is going to continue. There is little point in hapless attempts to bring it to a halt. Militarization of the border would be inappropriate, unacceptable, and counterproductive. What is to be done? The United States has three principal choices:

Ignore the problem. Under present circumstances migration might be illegal, according to this view, but it is effective in an economic sense. Mexican workers earn money and U.S. employers obtain cheap labor. The Mexican government shows no great interest in a major policy initiative here, so why bother?

Explore the feasibility of a large-scale guestworker program. The purpose would be to *regulate* and *legalize* the flow of migrant workers from Mexico, thus reducing if not eliminating the abuses of the present system (if it can be called a system).

Declare the border to be open, with no formal limits on crossing from Mexico. This would provide legal recognition of present de facto realities. It

---

[4]William Cline, "Mexico's Crisis, The World's Peril," *Foreign Policy* 49 (Winter 1982–83):118.

would also remove the need to create an apparatus for enforcement, which a guestworker program would require.

Assessment of these alternatives would necessitate thorough consultation with several key constituencies: the Mexican government, U.S. employers, and perhaps most importantly, U.S. labor unions. In the course of these deliberations it would be necessary to determine (1) whether Mexican workers in fact take jobs from U.S. citizens—an argument that does not stand up to recent research, which has revealed sharp segmentation in the American labor market, and (2) what practical effect the presence of Mexican workers exerts on prevailing wage rates.

Finally, and in general, the United States should develop a substantive policy toward Mexico that explicitly acknowledges this country's stake in Mexico's well-being and stability. Like it or not (and Mexicans often like it less than Americans), the two countries have had a unique, inescapable relationship. This demands a unique set of policies. The United States should recognize a special preference for Mexico and devise a bureaucratic means of pursuing this orientation.

4. Guatemala: The Long-Term Costs of Short-Term Stability

Robert H. Trudeau

Overview

To understand the politics of Guatemala today, we must consider the country's economy. Neither dimension can be fully appreciated if not studied in conjunction with the other. This chapter focuses on the totality of the political economy, the combined set of structures and processes by which any society produces its goods and services and makes decisions about their distribution. Several elements of the political economy of Guatemala are discussed. The first of these is the basic organization of economic processes and some of their social consequences.

Guatemala has never been truly "feudal"; since colonization, its economy has been oriented toward the exportation of agricultural products. After the Great Liberal Reform of the 1870s and 1880s, the economy was increasingly divided into an export sector and a subsistence sector. To be sure, there were overlaps: many members of the subsistence sector, especially in recent years, have been involved in the export sector as seasonal laborers. And there is a growing middle class and services sector. Nevertheless, in terms of ownership, control, orientation, and benefits, the economy is structured around two principal groups: the export sector and the subsistence sector.

Compared to the subsistence sector, the export sector has shown greater dynamism over the years, becoming increasingly "modernized." A higher proportion of the nation's resources has been directed to the export sector, including foreign exchange reserves used to purchase technological inputs, the lion's share of available credit and technical assistance, and access to the state's coercive apparatus. Over the past two or three decades, the amount of land used for the production of domestic foodstuffs has decreased while the land used for export agriculture has increased.

No one denies that this modernization process has had great direct benefits for the individuals and corporations who own and control the resources in question. But to what extent does this economic process benefit other groups in society, specifically the subsistence sector mentioned earlier? Have benefits trickled down?

In fact, the impact on the subsistence sector has been devastating. Social statistics reflect the impact of changes in resource allocation. The number of families with no access to land is increasing dramatically because land is more valuable when it is used for export production. When the export sector is in a decline, as it has been since 1980, times are hard for the subsistence sector. But they are equally hard, if not worse, in times of export booms, for during these periods resources are allocated to the export sector elite at the expense of the subsistence sector. In effect, the subsistence sector is no longer able to exist as such, and the individuals involved must compete with each other for scarce employment in the export sector.

As these dynamics continue, the results are interesting. From an economic perspective, the majority of the Guatemalan people are irrelevant except as seasonal workers. The production of goods, especially in agriculture, is not organized with domestic consumption in mind. Workers earn too little to purchase what they produce. Moreover, export markets are much more lucrative, even for those products that might be consumed in Guatemala.

The increased use of the nation's resources for agricultural export production and the consequent decline in the subsistence sector generates deeper poverty and inequality—a basic socioeconomic cause of the political unrest currently dominating Guatemalan life. Policies that ignore this cannot address the root causes of political instability.

How serious is the extent of inequality and poverty in Guatemala today? What are the trends? No thoughtful visitor to Guatemala can escape being stunned by the scale of social and economic inequality and the abject poverty in which the vast majority of the country's citizens live. Almost any commonly accepted socioeconomic indicator documents these conditions. The most brutal statistic reveals that 81 percent of Guatemala's children under the age of 5 suffer from measurable malnutrition. The daily cost of a basic beans and tortilla diet for a family of six people (the average family size) costs about twice the legal minimum daily wage, a wage that is rarely paid in rural areas. Even people lucky enough to find work often cannot feed themselves and their families. In the past twenty years, the situation has been deteriorating for the majority of Guatemala's citizens. The reality in Guatemala today is one of grinding malnutrition, widespread unemployment, and very little hope for at least two-thirds of the population.

The decline in the standard of living among the subsistance sector is a symptom of the recent collapse in the more modernized export sector of the economy. Commodity prices in the international markets have dropped;

55

revenues from tourism have been cut by half since 1979; and investment is increasingly difficult to locate, given the political climate. Capital flight has become a serious problem, in spite of efforts to stem the tide. Foreign exchange reserves have declined to essentially nothing.

A second important element affecting Guatemala's political economy is the role of the military. Since the early 1960s the Guatemalan officer corps has become direct owners of much of the export-oriented resources of the nation. The current economic downturn, together with the military's direct role in the economy, has led the army to use the governmental apparatus to retain and improve its economic position. These economic dynamics explain much of the electoral fraud and human rights abuse that have become characteristic of Guatemalan politics. In the 1982 election, for example, assassination was used to eliminate progressive candidates and fraud was used to "defeat" important sectors of the economic elite—business groups perceived by the military as short-term competitors for pieces of a dwindling economic pie.

Under these conditions elections cannot be interpreted as evidence of democracy. In Guatemala, persistent electoral fraud has caused elections generally to be regarded as farcical. Turnout is low. Elections have offered no chance for the people to control the military or the government, which is the basic meaning of democracy. Furthermore, there has been no possibility of constructive change on behalf of the dispossessed masses. In fact, progressive individuals who have participated as candidates have been thereby identified and then assassinated, so that elections under conditions of persistent violence and fraud have served to reduce the extent of democracy in Guatemala.[1]

Fraud in elections and assassinations of political leaders have usually been sufficient to keep the electoral process from becoming a serious threat to military/elite dominance. But generalized repression against the masses is also a characteristic phenomenon. Why? After the CIA-sponsored coup in 1954, foreign missionaries were invited to Guatemala to help eliminate "communist" attitudes among the peasantry. Much organizing on a local level took place, marked by the creation of improvement committees, cooperatives, catechist groups, etc. Attitudes of hopelessness and fatalism began to fade as participation in local groups created a new sense of dignity. Other forces, such as mobility, increased communication, and the presence of agencies such as the Peace Corps fostered this new level of awareness.

After the earthquake of 1976 many local groups sought international assistance directly when it became evident that the military would not or could not organize effective relief programs. The military perceived these successful local organizations as threats to its unquestioned domination of society.

[1]For a more detailed discussion of the relationship betwen elections and "democracy" in Guatemala, see, in addition to many published sources, Robert H. Trudeau, "The Guatemalan Electoral Process and Democracy: Implications for Public Opinion in the United States" (revised version of a Paper originally presented at the National Conference on Guatemala, Washington, D.C., 14 November 1981).

Systematic military repression directed against local organizers began only weeks after the earthquake and has increased in rate and ferocity since. After 1978, and especially since mid-1981, massacres of entire village populations have taken place regularly, especially among the indigenous Indian populations; some ten to fifteen thousand victims of police and military violence have been documented since 1978.

As electoral fraud and violence precluded efforts at change through that avenue, people wishing to implement reforms turned to organizing on a local level. In the past five years, as this avenue has also been closed by the military, those seeking to improve—or at least prevent further decline in—the quality of life of the majority have had no choice but to turn to clandestine activity.

Clandestine activity is now widespread. This is the third major element in the overall politicoeconomic situation. The guerrillas in Guatemala are not tiny, isolated groups; much of the population, particularly the indigenous Indians, has become involved in some way in an organized effort to change Guatemala's political and economic systems. This involvement of the indigenous communities has been called the single most important event in Guatemala's history since the Spanish conquest. The result of widespread government terrorism has been to increase mass participation, not to eliminate it.[2]

Increased resistance is one result of state terrorism. Another is the ruin of the political system as a avenue for social change. A fourth element of the political economy is the ideological spectrum of the political process. Very little remains of the political Center. Moderate politicians have been killed or driven into exile. Today the formal political system reflects only one ideological tendency, that of the extreme Right. Any dissent is repressed or has to express itself clandestinely. In 1980 even the vice-president of Guatemala, Dr. Francisco Villagrán K., thought it prudent to flee after he had disagreed with some of the positions taken by the military.

To summarize and focus on the trends, the following observations can be made. Overall, the situation is quickly becoming worse. Poverty and malnutrition are increasing, as is inequality. The population is increasingly aware of and outraged by these conditions, and Guatemala is fast becoming a severely polarized society. The military presence, in both economic and political life, continues to grow. The economic decline is accelerating as the political climate deteriorates. Dozens of progressive political candidates have been assassinated since the 1978 election of General Lucas to the presidency, making the 1982 election even more fraudulant and unrepresentative than the past two national elections were.

The coup of 23 March 1983, while changing some aspects of the situation

---

[2]For a more detailed discussion of these dynamics, see Robert H. Trudeau, "Politics and Terror: The Case of Guatemala" (Paper presented at the Annual Meeting of the New England Political Science Association, Hartford, Conn., 2 April 1982).

in Guatemala, has done nothing to solve the basic problems of the political economy. In fact, the increased level of direct military involvement in Guatemalan life since the coup may have exacerbated the situation in the long run. Government repression of the civilian population has reached unprecedented heights since late 1981, as the targets of violence have shifted from individual leaders and organizers to entire villages.

Finally, there is the yawning gap between the aspirations of the Guatemalan masses and those of the elite, an elite that has resorted to extreme violence in order to retain its position in society. One cannot exaggerate the importance of this "aspiration gap" in understanding Guatemala today. The masses, faced with a hopeless and worsening situation, increasingly see the need for basic change in society. The past and the present reveal a basic political truth about Guatemala: change will not occur within the existing political structure.

Where has the United States stood?

U.S. Policy: Description and Analysis

Ethical and moral issues are important factors in any analysis of U.S. policy in Guatemala. In the world of international politics these issues may inspire concern, but policy analysis must be based on more pragmatic considerations. The following analysis is based on a consideration of U.S. national interests.

The long-range national interests of the United States lie first of all in the protection of physical and military security. A second element is economic and commercial: it is in this country's interests to maintain access to needed resources and to commercial opportunities. Finally, political relations should be open and characterized by mutual respect for the legitimate activities of citizens within borders. In other words, it is the long-range goal of the United States to avoid, especially in nations it considers to be within its "sphere of influence," political and economic situations that threaten this nation's physical security and impair its ability to conduct normal economic and business activities necessary to its national economic security.

What are the sources of potential threats to these interests? In Guatemala, U.S. citizens have enjoyed relative freedom to travel as tourists and to engage in business activities, including investment and other long-term arrangements. Guatemala is likely to continue to conduct business with the United States. Given the nature of Guatemala's geography and economic development patterns, its economy is interdependent with, if not dependent on, that of the United States. Guatemala's economy needs to be involved in international commerce. Historically, the United States has been Guatemala's main trading partner. It is impossible to imagine a scenario in which Guatemala will not be at least moderately dependent on international trade, though it *is* possible to imagine that the United States might not be involved in this trade.

But there are factors beyond the economic. If ideological hostility were severe enough to make it impossible for leaders of either nation to allow "business as usual," and if another outside power were to become involved in Guatemala, there could be a potential security threat to the United States. In other words, while it is "natural"—and it certainly is the historical pattern—for Guatemala and the United States to be interrelated strategically and economically, this relationship might to interrupted if Guatemala's internal politics were to shift in such a way that the United States no longer had either influence or leverage, short of the use of military force, with the Guatemalan government. The issue is how likely such an eventually is and what sorts of U.S. policies might best avert it.

The overview to this chapter examined the conditions causing unrest in Guatemala. It is also necessary to examine how U.S. involvement over the past few decades has affected Guatemalan society.

The Guatemalan revolution of 1944, led by urban, democratic, progressive groups, marked the beginning of a moderate transformation of Guatemalan society. The sources of this revolution were disparate domestic social and economic conditions plus the lack of sufficient opportunities for change within the political system dominated by the dictator Jorge Ubico.

It was unfortunate that this process began during the opening rounds of the cold war, when the perceptions of the U.S. government were filtered through a global lens. The Guatemalan revolution was misperceived in East-West terms, resulting in hostility that could have been avoided. By 1953 John Foster Dulles had decided that Guatemalan social reform programs were nothing less than communism on the march in the Western Hemisphere. In 1954 the CIA financed, trained forces for, and participated in an invasion of Guatemala from Honduras. This led to the overthrow of the democratically elected government of Jacobo Arbenz, who had succeeded Juan José Arévalo in the presidency in 1951.[3]

The 1954 invasion had two major consequences. The first was the end of the social and economic reforms of the 1944–54 period. Land that had been redistributed under the agrarian reform program was returned to the previous

---

[3]Under terms of the Freedom of Information Act, many documents relating to the role of the United States in the 1954 counterrevolutionary invasion in Guatemala have become public. Based largely on these documents, two full-length works on this period have been published. See Richard H. Immerman, *The CIA in Guatemala: The Foreign Policy of Intervention* (Austin: University of Texas Press, 1982), and Stephen Kinzer and Stephen C. Schlesinger, *Bitter Fruit: The Untold Story of the American Coup in Guatemala* (Garden City: Doubleday, 1982). A third work, by Blanche Wiesen Cook, *The Declassified Eisenhower: A Divided Legacy* (Garden City: Doubleday, 1981), considers the Guatemala episode as part of an overall study of the Eisenhower-Dulles period and its policies. The three works analyze what happens when bilateral relations between the United States and Guatemala become "understood" in the context solely of the cold war or East-West confrontations.

owners—the United Fruit Company of Boston was a major beneficiary of this policy. All existing peasant and labor federations were disbanded, and thousands of organizers and leaders of these groups were assassinated. The 1954 counterrevolution marks the beginning of the Guatemalan government's systematic repression of its own citizens, a process that has continued unabated.

The second major consequence was that the end of the Arbenz reform period increased the level of radicalization and polarization in society. This was not the result intended by U.S. policymakers when they decided to support the counterrevolution. Cole Blasier, in his study of U.S. responses to revolutionary situations in Latin America, writes:

> Suppressive policies toward Guatemala and Cuba tended to polarize these societies and radicalize opposition groups. United States pressures on Guatemalan President Arbenz made him increasingly dependent on anti-American forces, including the Communists. After Arbenz fell, many of the former Guatemalan moderates, such as [former President] Juan José Arévalo, become bitterly anti-American.[4]

By undermining a moderate reformist movement, and by supporting a group that has systematically used repression to prevent any reforms since 1954, U.S. policy in Guatemala has not alleviated the pressures on the Guatemalan system. Today we are seeing the legacy of this policy: a worsening socioeconomic situation, repression, and mass resistance. Within the State Department, the legacy is a reduced set of policy options, as one comment from an official suggests: "If only we had an Arbenz now. . . . We are going to have to invent one, but all the candidates are dead."[5]

In the years since 1954, U.S. aid as well as U.S. military assistance have had the effect of exacerbating the situation. The U.S. government is clearly not responsible for the existence of poverty and misery in Guatemala. And there is no doubt that the quality of life for many Guatemalans has been improved over the years, in part because of U.S. assistance, especially in response to natural disasters. But by providing the major portion of its assistance to the modernizing sector in a nation so heavily oriented toward production for export, the United States has done little to alleviate the basic economic inequalities. Although foreign assistance may have been beneficial to international trade balances and to the industrial sector, the net effect has been to drain resources from the subsistence sector, creating more inequality and hardship for the majority of the citizenry.

[4]Cole Blasier, *The Hovering Giant: U.S. Responses to Revolutionary Change in Latin America* (Pittsburgh: University of Pittsburgh Press, 1976), p. 233.

[5]Marlise Simons, "Guatemala: The Coming Danger," in *El Salvador: Central America in the New Cold War,* ed. Marvin E. Gettleman et al. (New York: Grove Press, 1981), pp. 318–27.

It is no surprise that citizens will organize to defend themselves against these economic hardships. The Guatemalan government, since 1954, has responded to dissent with co-option or physical coercion. Unfortunately, U.S. assistance has been supportive of this unsavory (as measured by our American ideals of justice and fair play) side of the dynamic, has undermined Guatemala's democratic structures, and has contributed to repression in Guatemala. From 1950 to 1977, 3,334 Guatemalan military officers received training at U.S. military facilities.[6] From 1950 to 1979, the United States provided Guatemala with over $60 million in military assistance. In terms of actual deliveries, none of the three main avenues of military assistance— Foreign Military Sales, the Military Assistance Program, and the International Military Education and Training program—was cut off after the 1977 ban on military assistance imposed by President Carter.[7]

In May 1981, shortly after Reagan became president, his administration announced that it "would like to establish a more constructive relationship with the Guatemalan government. . . . We hope changes in the situation will soon permit a closer cooperative relationship."[8] This statement was followed by visits to Guatemala by officials of the State Department and a renewal of military assistance—albeit renamed in order to avoid legislative restrictions— consisting of jeeps, trucks, and pilot training. Efforts to send helicopter parts were headed off in Congress.

At a public forum in November 1981, a State Department representative argued that while the Reagan administration was severely critical of the Lucas García regime, U.S. military assistance to Guatemala was needed to gain leverage in order to reduce the violence of the Guatemalan government. It is important to note that the level of violence directed at the civilian population of rural Guatemala increased dramatically in the period following the election of Ronald Reagan and the visits of his administration's pre- and postelection emissaries to Guatemala. These massacres continued to occur after the June 1981 delivery of military vehicles, and they involved the use of military trucks and helicopters—exactly the type of aid the Reagan administration sent. Assuming the purpose of U.S. policy is to *reduce* the incidence of such massacres, the attempt to "gain leverage" by sending military assistance has failed. Plans to permit Guatemala to legally import U.S. technology so that it

[6]Gabriel Aguilera Peralta, "El proceso de militarización en el Estado guatemalteco," *Polémica* (San José, Costa Rica), no. 1 (September–October 1981), p. 32. By way of perspective, the regular military in Guatemala as of 1978 consisted of about fifteen thousand people, with an officer corps of about fourteen hundred.

[7]Ibid., pp. 36–37. Also see testimony and data from Lars Schoultz, "Hearing before the Subcommittees on Human Rights and International Organizations and on Inter-American Affairs of the Committee on Foreign Affairs of the House of Representatives," 97th Cong., 1st Sess. (Washington, D.C.: U.S. Government Printing Office, 30 July 1981).

[8]Cited in Schoultz, "Hearing before the Subcommittee on Human Rights," p. 26.

may become self-sufficient in the production of small arms and ammunition bode ill for the future.[9]

In sum, the net effect of U.S. policy in Guatemala has been to support an oppressive and increasingly repressive regime. While this may not be the intended goal of U.S. policy, and although the State Department may genuinely believe that there is no current "policy" toward Guatemala, the facts show that this support has indeed been the result. As conditions worsen in Guatemala and the consequences of U.S. support become more apparent and serious, a critical question must be asked: Is this continuing support of the Guatemalan system in the best long-term interests of the United States?

The vast majority of the Guatemalan population do not have an economic stake in the current system; their only goal is day-to-day survival. The government of Guatemala has succeeded in organizing society so that the nation's wealth is held by a tiny percentage of the population and has organized its coercive power so that only clandestine dissent is possible. Within Guatemala there seems to be virtually no active political Center. Efforts by the Christian Democrats (DCG) to rebuild the Center in the aftermath of the Ríos Montt coup in 1982 may be too little too late, given the indefinite postponement of elections by Ríos (until "at least 1985") and the increased polarization produced by the military's ongoing rural violence. The majority of the population who favor change are increasingly mobilized by clandestine groups who in some cases, albeit reluctantly, feel that change can only come through violence. In such an atmosphere, radical leadership of the mass of the population is much more likely to emerge.

General Ríos announced with great bravado in October 1982 that the guerrillas had been soundly defeated.[10] However, observers believe that the Guatemalan army could not last long against the organized population of the nation in the absence of significant superiority in military technology. Foreign sources supply military hardware, communications and transportation capabilities, and training in the use of advanced weapons and computers. If the Guatemalan regime is to survive the current economic decline and the problem of capital flight, it must attract military assistance from abroad to fuel its coercive apparatus.

Revolutionary rhetoric aside, it also seems clear that the Guatemalan government cannot win a military victory against its own people. The very *most* that can be expected is a compromise solution that will provide a major role for the present insurgent elements within Guatemalan society. Short of a

---

[9]Council on Hemispheric Affairs, 14 September 1981.

[10]According to a report published in *La Nación Internacional* (San José, Costa Rica) 1, no. 46 (21–27 October 1982), General Ríos Montt declared that the guerrilla forces in his country had been completely defeated in the military sense, but that the ideological defeat had not yet occurred. He went on to say the ideas behind the guerrilla movement had to be eradicated before there would be an end to the violence.

successful policy of genocide, the most likely outcome is a defeat for the Guatemalan army.

What, then, are the policy options for the United States?

Policy Options: A Look to the Future

Increasingly large numbers of Guatemalans of all social classes feel the injustice of the Guatemalan system and the lack of opportunity for change within the existing political process. Given the extent of popular involvement in this process, and given the repression and economic injustice the Guatemalan government and military establishments support, it is a foregone conclusion that the current system can survive only if it makes major concessions to the needs of the masses. The nature of the existing system makes this unlikely. Guatemala is facing a revolutionary situation. Safeguarding the long-range interests of the United States requires acknowledging this fact. Policymakers must recognize that this revolutionary situation can be resolved (other than by genocidal means) only under the leadership of willing, progressive Guatemalans dedicated to basic changes in the structure of Guatemalan society—changes that many North Americans might find less than completely palatable, especially in the short run. If the United States does not recognize this, it will make policy judgments that will undermine its long-range goals.

Finally, realistic policy analysis must accurately assess the limits of this country's ability to change the current situation. It is arguable whether or not the United States has ever been able to exercise completely its will in the Caribbean and Central American regions—its "sphere of influence." But at present, few believe that U.S. power is boundless. Most thoughtful observers, both within and without the U.S. government, agree that Guatemala is such a "mess" that there are serious limits on what the United States can realistically expect to achieve.

Precisely because the situation is revolutionary and must be resolved in Guatemala by Guatemalans, U.S. policy should focus on the long-range considerations that are more important than those aspects of the policy picture that can change abruptly. Specifically, short-term policy options that endanger this country's ability to retain long-term influence with a revolutionary government should be considered carefully before adoption.

As a nation, the United States needs to reassess its definition of *friends*. It needs to redefine the specific nature of its goals, even while it retains its ideals. And it needs to bring in new approaches to help in these reassessments of policy. It is in this context that the following policy alternatives need to be studied.

Military assistance. The record of U.S. military assistance to past Guatemalan regimes is the single best example of the dynamics discussed in this paper. U.S. military and police assistance has led to increased levels of governmental repression against individuals and groups perceived as dissenters. Regardless of the short-term rationale in the past, such assistance at the present time is not in this country's long-term interests, for it will inevitably lead to increased social hostility toward the United States among an increasingly aware and mobilized populace.

It would have been in the best interests of the United States to identify and support a moderate, centrist, progressive element in Guatemala with whom it could have worked. But the U.S. past policy of military and police assistance contributed significantly to the disappearance of this very sector of the political spectrum and thereby lessened the likelihood that the long-term interests of the United States would be achieved.

Many policymakers in the United States, including members of Congress who have opposed military aid to El Salvador, hoped that the new regime of General Ríos Montt would make sufficient human rights progress to justify a renewal of military assistance to Guatemala. And, in fact, the early months after the 23 March coup did show some improvement, as evidenced by the sharp decline in assassination in urban areas. Although some officials in the State Department still cling to this as evidence of substantial progress, it is increasingly apparent that the hoped-for changes have been illusory.

Initially, the coup of 23 March took place with at least some active participation by the civilian National Liberation Movement (MLN). In the days that followed, the Christian Democratic party indicated, if not support, then certainly not outright rejection of the sort that has characterized DCG statements about previous military governments. This is not surprising when we recall that General Ríos was the DCG candidate for president in 1974. But much more than old loyalties were involved. Statements by General Ríos promised an early, swift, and just end to corruption and political violence. These positions long have been supported by the Christian Democrats, a group that has been severely victimized by government violence and electoral fraud.

Within weeks of the coup, however, General Ríos eliminated all civilian participation from the Guatemalan policymaking process. He removed from office his two fellow junta members. He postponed elections indefinitely. He named himself president as well as chief legislator, disbanding the Guatemalan congress. He declared that the constitution of 1965 was no longer the de jure law of the land. He prohibited activities of all political parties. He did not bring to trial any of the high military officers of the previous regime; in fact, he named the former minister of defense, Benedicto Lucas García (brother of the deposed president) to the position of counterinsurgency director for the Petén area of northern Guatemala.

In the area of human rights violations, equally noteworthy events occurred. General Ríos declared an amnesty, which was to last for the month of June 1982, during which all individuals who had committed violations of humans rights would be pardoned for the crimes. Few guerrillas took advantage of this general amnesty. However, there are reports that many individuals in the government and paramilitary units did avail themselves of it. The amnesty seems to have absolved any guilt from government violators of human rights. At the end of the amnesty period, the president declared a State of Seige, during which all constitutional rights were abrogated: individuals suspected of acting against the interests of the government can legally be summarily tried and executed. This provision was extended to include making any mention of military activities in the press, unless the information was obtained from the military's own press operations.

For the rural areas, General Ríos's statements in effect amount to a declaration of war. The fictions that the guerrillas are a small, isolated group of individuals and that the civilian population is caught in the middle of an armed struggle between them and the army are clearly not believed by the Guatemalan government. Several government statements have been made intimating that the entire indigenous community seems to be supporting the armed resistance, that it is, in effect, combatant and so following a "scorched-earth" policy is appropriate. This is what the government is now doing in rural Guatemala.[11]

The illegal and horrible violations of human rights under the Lucas García regime continue to exist under the Ríos Montt regime. The main difference is that such violations have been declared legal by the new government. Some U.S. policymakers have pointed to this as an improvement, one that justifies a renewal of military assistance. Yet the main source of tension, the overwhelming presence of the military in both the economy and the political system, remains more imposing. Proposals to renew military assistance must be measured against the long-term trends, not against superficial changes.

In other words, from a variety of perspectives, granting military assistance to any Guatemalan military regime seems to be harmful to the long-term interests of the United States. It may be in the short-term interests of some Americans who seek to gain continuing U.S. support for the Guatamalan regime. This is the approach of the American Chamber of Commerce of Guatemala, some of whose members have even supported the use of government death squads to eliminate labor unrest. But this group's easy access to the executive branch of the U.S. government contributes to policies that do not

[11]The events recounted in these paragraphs are reported in a variety of newspapers and newsletters that are not readily available in the daily press in the United States but that are available to individuals who wish to consult newsletters published by various organizations following events in Guatemala. For an extensive list, see Robert H. Trudeau, "Guatemalan Human Rights: The Current Situation," *LASA Newsletter* 13, no. 3 (Fall 1982): 13–16, or consult with the Network in Solidarity with Guatemala (NISGUA) in Washington, D.C.

serve this nation's national interests in Guatemala. The group continues to encourage U.S. policymakers to believe that a permanent military victory over the insurgents in Guatemala is not only possible, but also is desirable for the country's long-range interests.[12]

In spite of their ideological rhetoric, this group and others with similar interests recognize certain facts very clearly. First, the Guatemalan military is primarily an economic institution: its role in society is to defend the economic status quo and only secondarily to "defend the nation." Second, the Guatemalan people will not tolerate indefinite continuation of the present system. The economy no longer allows even the subsistence sector to subsist, and no amount of government terror can overcome the basic need and desire of the people to improve their conditions.[13] The draining of Guatemala's foreign exchange reserves is an indication that the Guatemalan elite, including North Americans doing business in Guatemala, recognizes that situation. The elite is hitching its star to capital flight and abandoning the sinking ship of state. To keep that ship afloat, however, the elite, especially through the American Chamber of Commerce and the Amigos del País, has pressured the U.S. government for assistance even while it has removed its own resources. Although external assistance is vital to the short-term interests of this tiny group, the long-range interests of the United States require a better understanding of the situation. Otherwise, this country will witness a continuation of policies that will lead inexorably, as in a Greek tragedy, to the very outcome these groups claim to be opposing.

Economic assistance. The granting of economic assistance to Guatemala has depended in the past five years on evidence of fewer human rights violations and more satisfaction of humanitarian needs, and rightfully so. But economic assistance can only be effective if the government of Guatemala is willing to permit programs to achieve these goals. "Effectiveness" depends on the degree to which developmental assistance actually reaches the intended

[12]From a presentation by Mr. Allen Nairn at the National Conference on Guatemala, Washington, D.C., 14 November 1981. Mr. Nairn has conducted extensive interviews with this group and has published work on the role of the Bank of America in supporting the Guatemalan regime. See Allen Nairn, "Controversial Reagan Campaign Links with Guatemalan Government and Private Sector Leaders" (Washington, D.C.: Council on Hemispheric Affairs, October 1980), and idem, "Bank of America Asked to Explain Its Support for the Guatemalan Death Squads," *Multinational Monitor* 3, no. 3 (March 1982): 14–15. For a direct representation of the point of view of the American business community in Guatemala, see statement of Fred Sherwood on CBS News' Special Report, "Central America in Revolt," 20 March 1982.

[13]Support for this contention on the limits of government terror can be found in Jorge E. Torres Ocampo, *Reflexión, Análisis, Crítica, y Autocritica de la Situación Política de Guatemala* (Guatemala City, 1980). Until his assassination shortly after the cited work was published, Torres was one of the top leaders of the National Liberation Movement party in Guatemala, the party of the extreme right wing. Torres' thesis is that the people of Guatemala would only support a government that could satisfy basic human needs. His analysis of Guatemalan history and of the present situation leads him to conclude that terror, i.e., government violence, only serves to weaken the ability to the government to rule.

population. The United States has shown a willingness to accept a high degree of corruption, however unpalatable, on the grounds that the net effect of the economic assistance has been positive for its long-range interests.

This is no longer the case in Guatemala. Providing funds for huge infrastructure projects allows national resources to be diverted to military endeavors so that economic assistance becomes, in effect, indirect military assistance.

Even humanitarian programs, such as those set up after the 1976 earthquake, which are aimed at improving the quality of life for deprived groups are no longer effective. Any Guatemalan who is willing to participate in such projects runs the risk of assassination.[14] In other words, because of the attitudes of the government and its supporters, providing even humanitarian assistance to Guatemala can lead to an increase in violence against the populace. This only contributes, albeit indirectly, to public hostility toward the United States for providing the assistance. The long-range threats to American interests are clear.

American policymakers must evaluate economic assistance programs, including humanitarian programs, on the basis of impact as well as on the basis of intentions. It is difficult for genuinely concerned Americans to question the value of humanitarian assistance, but such an attitude is required because of the current Guatemalan situation.

Political relations. The long-range interests of the United States are most severely threatened by a policy of reliance on, and support for, the current Guatemalan political and economic system. Yet support for the existing elite has often been justified by citing the threat from the Left and the absence of a reasonable alternative in the Center.

The Left may indeed be a threat in the sense that it proposes to organize societies differently from the U.S. system. But the Left is not necessarily a threat to U.S. physical or economic security, if this country can avoid ideological hostility and maintain reasonable economic and political relations. It would be helpful if the United States were to eliminate assistance to the current military regime, but these objectives can also be achieved through more positive political action.

Specifically, the United States should recognize that progressive groups

---

[14]The extent to which such violence occurs in Guatemala and the impact of this on development programs, especially in rural areas, is best discussed in Shelton H. Davis and Julie Hodson, *Witnesses to Political Violence in Guatemala: The Suppression of a Rural Development Movement* (Boston: OXFAM-America, 1982). The findings here are based on lengthy questionnaires from over one hundred respondents who had worked in development programs in Guatemala for an average of five years each. These respondents had extensive firsthand knowledge of rural development efforts and the responses of the Guatemalan elite to such programs. Davis and Hodson chronicle the destruction of rural development programs, and their respondents attribute this to government violence. This destruction is an intended outcome. Policymakers—and others who wish to understand Guatemala—would be well advised to consult this short booklet.

in Guatemalan politics exist and should maintain channels of communication with them. Although it is difficult to do this within Guatemala given the repressive practices of the government, it is certainly possible to develop these relationships outside of Guatemala. Many democratic, progressive leaders have organized in exile, creating groups representing various ideals and professions: the Church, the business community, the University, and several political parties of recognized popular appeal. An umbrella organization, the Democratic Front Against Repression (FDCR) has representatives in the United States. The organization of CGUP, the Guatemalan Committee of Patriotic Unity, is a major development, for it provides a unified group with which the U.S. government can legitimately establish working relations. The United States has maintained such a relationship throughout the past few years with the Guatemalan Christian Democrats. The United States should sustain this relationship but should not depend solely on this group for its future influence and access to Guatemalan policy. Unfortunately, the Christian Democratic party has lost much of its legitimacy with the Guatemalan population. The need for clandestine organization, the tremendous increase in rural violence, the early appearance of possible collusion with the Ríos government—all these led the Guatemalan people to bypass the DCG, formerly a major political force. The United States must keep abreast of changes such as these.

In addition to the opportunity to work with the opposition groups mentioned, other avenues exist for the United States to make a long-range investment. For example, there should be an accurate travel advisory for U.S. citizens traveling to Guatemala. The tourist industry, one of the principal earners of foreign exchange in Guatemala, obviously suffers under the current generalized armed conflict. A strong travel advisory would acknowledge that changes are coming in Guatemala and that the United States may wish to disassociate itself from the intransigent groups seeking to prevent those changes.

The role of the Peace Corps and other exchange programs should be re-evaluated. The United States ought to question whether or not it is appropriate to send U.S. exchange professors to Guatemala while Guatemalan professors are being murdered or driven into exile. The United States needs to assess the long-term impact of sending Peace Corps volunteers to work in social action projects; any Guatemalan working in such projects risks assassination. Regardless of the intentions of our current policies—intentions that on the whole are realized in more or less "normal" situations—the impact of such policies in Guatemala, because of the particular nature of the situation at this time, is very threatening in the long term.

In looking for policy alternatives, two aspects of the situation need to be examined. The first are the ongoing massacres in indigenous areas of the Guatemalan countryside. Well documented by many international and domestic groups in spite of attempts by the Ríos Montt government to disguise the origins of the violence, these massacres are a blot on the history of the Western Hemisphere. The second problem, namely, the growing number of dislocated refugees, many in Mexico and in other nations, results from the first. The Maya-based culture of Guatemala's majority is being destroyed—a grievous loss to the entire hemisphere.

Faced with these aspects of political/military life in Guatemala, the U.S. government has been relatively quiet. Conversations with, for example, U.S. embassy personnel in Guatemala (during 1980) suggest that the reason for the quiet is to pursue U.S. influence behind the scenes. Yet this strategy has not produced the desired leverage. This is acknowledged when the subject is the Lucas García regime of the 1978–82 period. Yet, since the military coup of March 1982, the U.S. government apparently seeks to follow the same strategy, even in the face of growing evidence of increased levels of violence directed against the civilian population. The treatment of the refugees can only be contrasted with the administration's indignation about the Sandinistas' relatively placid treatment of the Miskito groups in Nicaragua.

Although opportunities for building long-term policy in Guatemala have been available, the U.S. government has not taken advantage of them. In spite of widespread feelings of horror among the American people about the massacres and widespread humanitarian concerns about refugees and human rights and civil liberties, the U.S. government has remained essentially silent or, worse, has sought to support the misinformation programs of the Guatemalan government that attribute rural violence to guerrilla groups.

Long-range pragmatic considerations require that our policy not be dragged along in the cockboat of short-term goals. Without a reexamination of current policy, the United States will soon find itself facing the agonizing question of whether or not to support a genocidal regime as the only way possible to retain any influence in Guatemala. The only way out of that dilemma seems to be to develop the long-term perspective, for the current course, as followed by recent administrations of both major political parties, has only served to limit U.S. options.

Domestic reassessment. The key to American policy is the concept that the United States can peacefully coexist with nations whose governments are not of U.S. choosing or even of the type of democratic structure preferred by the United States. The United States is able to maintain relationships with brutal dictatorships of the Right and the Left in many countries, arguing that it is in the national interest to do so. President Nixon was able to establish relationships with the People's Republic of China. Unless the United States recognizes that it can live with revolutionary regimes in Guatemala and throughout Central America, it will help create serious long-range threats to its military security and economic interests.

This is difficult for U.S. policymakers to accept because of the paramount role of the executive branch of our government. Congress must appreciate the limits of bipartisanship in foreign policy; that is, Congress must accept the partisan nature of information conveyed by policy proposals developed by the executive branch. This does not imply that partisanship is evil; in many ways it is the foundation of the U.S. system. But it does mean that Congress should actively seek alternative sources of information and policy recommendations, including making visits to areas such as Central America and having consultations with the many professional and religious groups that combine much personal experience with deep understanding of the present situation in Central America in general and Guatemala in particular.[15]

Conclusion: The Central Question

In the past four decades many major powers have seen their spheres of influence, and their colonial empires, reduced by grass-roots movements that brought "revolutionary" elites together with major segments of the mass populace. Rarely have these processes been stopped. Often, however, far-sighted leadership has been able to affect the course of events, if not determine them.

Rarely has there been a case study that fits this pattern as clearly as Guatemala. The domestic causes of popular movements—injustice, inequality, and violent repression of any moderate attempt to improve conditions—have been present in relatively large doses for several decades. Furthermore, in reviewing the case of Guatemala, we should learn from the "lessons of history." We need not rely solely on other nations' experiences. We need only to look at the attempt in 1954 to determine the course of Guatemalan history and compare the intentions of U.S. policymakers then with the legacies of their policies now.

The long-term interests of the United States in Guatemala depend on a politically stable situation. At some moments in history this stability—or, rather, its illusion—may have been achievable through brute authoritarianism. Modern weaponry, modern communication, and modern levels of public awareness preclude that possibility. Today, in most of the world, stability depends on the satisfaction of the people's basic economic and social needs. Governments unwilling or unable to provide this will suffer levels of instability that will render them ineffective, regardless of the level of authoritarian control. Sooner or later they will fall. The national interests of the United States are not advanced—when this occurs in its "sphere of in-

---

[15]Again, the reader is referred to Davis and Hodson, *Witnesses to Political Violence in Guatemala*. For a deeper understanding of the situation from the indigenous perspective, the reader should consult Rarihokwats, ed., *Guatemala! The Horror and the Hope* (York, Pa.: Four Arrows, 1982).

fluence''—if the United States supports such governments. For when they fall, U.S. "influence" evaporates.

The central question is whether U.S. policymakers and opinion leaders will recognize this basic change in modern politicoeconomic dynamics. Will policy options be considered from this perspective rather than from the basis of wishful thinking that would turn the clock of history back to a period that no longer exists?

5. El Salvador: The Policy That Failed

Morris J. Blachman and Kenneth Sharpe

Overview

The roots of El Salvador's present crisis lie in the fertile soil of her complex yet comprehensible history. The dominant economic and political structure was established in the last two decades of the nineteenth century, when changes in land tenure patterns led to a coffee-growing oligarchy commonly referred to as "los catorce," or "the fourteen families." By virtue of a court ruling in 1882 the families were able to gain control over vast amounts of the most fertile land. They parlayed their economic clout into political control and ruled the country, even alternating the presidency between two families for nearly twenty years, until 1931, when President Araujo was overthrown by General Maximiliano Hernández Martínez. Martínez ruled with an iron fist until 1944. He had presided over the most ruthless repression in Salvadoran history when, in response to a rebellion in the rural area led in part by local Communists, he unleashed the military on the peasantry, slaughtering between ten and twenty thousand people in what became known as "la matanza," or "the butchering."

Peasant uprisings were not unknown in El Salvador. Four times in the last thirty years of the nineteenth century peasants had revolted. When the rebellion began in 1931, Martínez and his supporters were determined to see that it would not happen again. The use of violence both to squelch opposition and as a means to express opposition was firmly established. The military, in concert with the oligarchy, has remained in control ever since, and has often resorted to the legacy of violence to control and destroy opposition.

The source of opposition attempts at reform can be found in the highly skewed distribution of land, income, goods, and services. Virtually all of the

72

best land, nearly 80 percent of the farm land, was owned by only 10 percent of the landholders. Fewer than one hundred families owned 60 percent of all farm land. Roughly 60 percent of the population lived in rural areas, and by 1975 over 40 percent of those living in rural areas were landless, a condition that had worsened considerably since 1950, when that figure was just under 12 percent. The resultant pressures had been heightened by the sense of change sweeping Latin America in the early 1960s as embodied in the Cuban Revolution, which explicitly called for structural reform in land tenure.

Organized public opposition began to emerge in the early 1960s and centered around the Christian Democrats, led by José Napoleón Duarte, and the Social Democrats, under Guillermo Ungo. As the opposition grew it gained an increasingly broad base among the Salvadoran population, but the reaction of the oligarchy and the military forced it to change its character and its strategy: in a series of four crucial struggles with the military and the oligarchy the opposition was systematically closed off from expressing itself through the arena of democratic electoral politics until its only options were to accept the repressive character of the regime or move into open insurgency. Failure of the Reagan administration to take into account adequately these historical struggles led it to undertake misguided policies that actually have stimulated continued insurgency: it supported a government unable or unwilling to control those who have systematically prevented any meaningful alternatives from emerging.

The first struggle was a purely electoral one. The opposition parties that emerged in the 1960s and successfully competed for local offices joined forces in the 1972 presidential elections and challenged forty years of military rule. Duarte and Ungo teamed up as presidential and vice-presidential candidates. This broad center-left coalition challenged Colonel Arturo Molina of the military-controlled Party of National Reconciliation. Despite the activities of ORDEN (a right-wing, paramilitary group organized in 1968) and other such groups, the 1972 elections were the first honest ones since the early 1930s. By all accounts Duarte and Ungo won, but the army and the oligarchy voided the elections; a colonel was declared president. A short-lived rebellion broke out in response to the fraud and was put down harshly. Duarte was among those imprisoned, tortured, and then exiled. The 1972 election was important because it taught many in the opposition that the electoral route to change was blocked.

Following the electoral fraud, a second struggle began. As moderate opposition leaders became targets of government repression, some, like Duarte, were driven into exile. Many who remained funneled their energies into a nonelectoral yet peaceful alternative, the "popular organizations." These community groups drew their membership from peasants, workers, student organizations, and professional groups and enjoyed Catholic church support. They pressed for immediate social improvements, relying on petitions, letters, demonstrations, civil disobedience, and strikes. The response from the security forces and oligarchy was often severe. Security forces opened fire on demonstrators. ORDEN and other paramilitary "death squads," often linked to the security forces, assassinated popular leaders, priests, and politicians and attacked meetings of the popular organizations. As reforms were blocked and repression continued, some members of the opposition began to see open insurgency as their only alternative and became willing to support or join the slowly emerging guerrilla movement. Most groups, however, continued to look for nonviolent alternatives despite the fact that their peaceful protests were often confronted with government-condoned violence.

The "election" of General Carlos Humberto Romero in 1977 was even more blatantly controlled than the 1972 election. Romero rationalized repression with the Draconian "law to defend and guarantee public order." Conditions deteriorated rapidly as kidnappings and shootings became increasingly widespread. In March 1978 only the government's Party of National Reconciliation participated in the local elections. By 1979 the Inter-American Commission on Human Rights had released a report recommending that ORDEN be disbanded and accusing the government of murdering opponents and engaging in torture. As the repression worsened, the Carter administration unsuccessfully sought "openings to the Center." Washington was relieved when apparently moderate military officers staged the October 1979 coup and set up a junta that promised reform.

There was some limited optimism as the opposition groups in El Salvador entered this third struggle. The first junta had excluded official representation of the popular organizations but had sought their active support, promising democracy, an end to corruption and repression, and economic reform. Its two military members included Colonel Majano, a reform-minded officer and leading figure behind the coup. Its three civilian members included Ungo and Román Mayorga, rector of the Central American University. The popular organizations and even some of the guerrilla groups agreed to a "wait and see" period to give the junta a chance to implement its promises. But violence, largely from the security forces and death squads, led to the first major defection of moderates from the junta in January 1980. Unable to oust Defense Minister José Guillermo García, who would not or could not control the violence of the security forces and death squads, Ungo, Mayorga, and the entire cabinet (except Garcia) resigned in protest, blaming the Right's intransigence for government impotence. A second junta formed with Christian Democratic support, but that party split. Conservative members were willing to gain rightist support for reforms even at the price of their growing isolation and of the continuing uncontrolled repression of the increasingly broad-based opposition—killings were occurring at a rate of about one thousand each month and were overwhelmingly attributable to the security forces and the paramilitary Right. In March 1980 the more moderate wing of the Christian Democratic party defected from the junta and the cabinet, echoing resigning junta member Hector Dada's words: "We have not been able to stop the repression and those committing acts of repression . . . go unpunished: the promised dialogue with the popular organizations fails to materialize; the chances for producing reforms with the support of the people are receding beyond reach."

Duarte joined a third junta, which was supported by more conservative Christian Democrats. The junta announced a sweeping agrarian reform program. But it became increasingly apparent that hard-line military officers were really in control and that they had no intention of ending repression and beginning serious reform. Despite some important successes, the hastily conceived and inadequately supported land reform program faced formidable barriers. The security and paramilitary forces on some occasions assassinated peasant leaders who had come forward to run the new cooperatives and on other occasions forcefully evicted former sharecroppers and tenants from their farms. The legitimacy of the junta was also undermined by the growing repression of moderate opposition leaders and civilians: the assassinations of Archbishop Romero, the four North American Catholic churchwomen, and two labor advisors were only the most publicized examples of the frequent killings.

In April 1980 moderate leaders who had been forced out of the government joined forces with the major popular organizations and opposition groups in the country and formed a broad-based center-left coalition, the Democratic Revolutionary Front. It united most of the important political opposition groups that had emerged in El Salvador during the preceding twenty years, the major exception being the small group of Christian Democrats remaining in the government. The FDR chose as its president Enrique Alvarez, the former minister of agriculture in the first junta, and it established close relations with the Faribundo Marti National Liberation Front (FMLN), a coalition of the major guerrilla groups. It also received encouragement and support from major elements of the Catholic church. The FDR operated relatively openly until November 1980, when Alvarez and five other FDR leaders were assassinated after uniformed soldiers surrounded the Jesuit High School where they were meeting and heavily armed men in civilian clothes took them away. Ungo replaced the murdered Alvarez as FDR president, and the leadership took sanctuary underground and in Mexico City. That the junta, in effect, stood squarely behind the growing repression, i.e., that repression was not merely attributable to a few right-wing extremists, was further clarified in December 1980, when Colonel Majano was forced to resign. He charged the government with complicity in the activities of the rightist death squads. Majano's replacement was Colonel García, the same minister of defense whose actions, or lack thereof, had contributed heavily to the civilian resignations in January. Although Duarte was named president of the junta to give it greater legitimacy, his actual power was severely restricted from the beginning.

The election of Ronald Reagan in November 1980 had sent a sharp signal to El Salvador. That message had reduced the incentive for restraint as elements of the security forces and the oligarchy came to believe that they could now engage in repression with relative impunity. This same message was also heard by the members of the FDR as well as of the FMLN, comprised of predominantly nationalistic leftists and Marxists. With public, nonviolent alternatives effectively closed off in El Salvador and a U.S. administration that was perceived to be unlikely to restrain the military, the opposition saw little choice but to work underground and turn increasingly to violent insurgency. This fourth and latest phase of the struggle had been taking form as government-supported repression increased throughout 1980, but it broke into the open when the insurgents launched an offensive against the junta in early January 1981 in the hopes of toppling the junta before Reagan assumed office.

The FMLN's offensive failed, and the resulting military situation for most of 1981 and into 1982 was aptly described by then Secretary of State Haig as a "stalemate." But the "stalemate" continued to take a toll. In 1981 Salvadorans were being killed at the rate of about one thousand per month. Insurgent forces continued their attacks on utilities, bridges, and military outposts and bases. Peasants fleeing from their homeland in increasing numbers have sought refuge from the fighting in neighboring Honduras. On occasion they were threatened even there by Salvadoran troops crossing the border, at times with the participation of the Honduran military. The repression of civilians by security and paramilitary forces seems to be creating more and more opposition and a substantial pool of recruits for the insurgents.

In an effort to reach a political solution, the FDR had repeatedly offered to negotiate with the junta, but its offers were rejected by the military and the United States. The FDR asked that two broad issues be put on the agenda. The first was the development of a new economic and political order. The FDR sought a mixed economy, a foreign policy of nonalignment, and a political program involving pluralistic representation of different social and political groups and a respect for human rights. The second issue was the restructuring of the armed forces. The FDR argued that two opposing armies cannot exist if there is to be a lasting political settlement and that elements of both the insurgent army and the government forces would have to be integrated into a single military force. The FDR also insisted that such talks take place without preconditions (a cease-fire itself would be a matter for discussion), that they include the FMLN as well as the FDR, that witnesses from other governments be present at the talks, that the Salvadoran people be fully informed about the talks, and that the talks be comprehensive, addressing the fundamental problems of the current situation.

The Salvadoran junta, partly in response to pressures from the United States, had organized the March 1982 election of the Constituent Assembly, which would appoint an interim government and begin writing a constitution. Meanwhile the U.S. administration had accused the FDR of being against democracy because it ''chose'' to oppose those elections rather than participate. From the point of view of the FDR, however, opposition to those elections was quite sensible. Freedom of the press, speech, and association were severely restricted by dint of security or paramilitary reprisals. Since 1980 assassinations by security and paramilitary forces had made public political activity too dangerous for the opposition.

Christian Democrats, who had broken with Duarte, along with Social Democrats and other moderate opposition groups initially joined the FDR and later went underground; some joined the armed insurgency. The atmosphere of terror and repression had worsened, making it life-threatening for these groups to participate openly in the elections. Asking their supporters to sign nominating petitions or make public statements would have been tantamount to asking them to put their names on death lists. Having seen so many of their associates assassinated, it would have been irrational for such candidates to risk their lives. Indeed, none of the candidates dared campaign on a platform criticizing the military and calling for increased control; none could have done so and lived.

The U.S. State Department has pointed to the large voter turnout as evidence of a popular rejection of the FDR/FMLN since those organizations urged voters to boycott the elections. But in assessing the meaning of the turnout, one must consider the full context of the process prior to the balloting. The FMLN did state that it would seek to disrupt the elections and did call on the population to refuse to participate. As the time drew near, several of the FMLN factions stopped short of the use of violence to disrupt the process. While the Reagan administration went to some length to point out these threats from the FMLN, it rarely, if ever, made public the fact that the far Right and the military also conducted a large public relations campaign that said that not voting was equivalent to supporting the insurgents. There is ample evidence that segments of the population feared that if, subsequent to the elections, they were stopped by the security forces at a checkpoint or for other reasons and they could not show proof of having voted, they might well end up dead, they might disappear, or they might land in jail as a suspected ''sympathizer'' with the insurgents. Because the majority of the killings have been attributed to the security and paramilitary forces, the rational person, facing a threat from both sides, might well have chosen to vote to avoid facing the greatest threat— the security and paramilitary forces.

Many believed that not having proof of voting would cause them to lose all governmental benefits, including their jobs if they were employed. Even in rural areas, people feared that not voting or null ballots might lead to reprisals against their village. These factors help to explain not only the size of the turnout, but the direction of the vote as well. Finally, careful study of the figures given by the El Salvadoran government leads one to conclude that the numbers are probably somewhat inflated. None of the above is stated to indicate that the turnout was unimportant. Rather, it is to make the point that the interpretation generally put forth in the United States is far too simplistic and either ignores or glosses over many of the factors (such as the threats from the Right) which must be taken into account. What is impressive about the turnout is that it signifies the high degree of politicized mobilization that exists in El Salvador and suggests that, given the appropriate mechanisms, this human resource potential could be channeled in fruitful rather than destructive directions.

While the large election turnout surprised many observers, the results strengthened the position of the Right, not the Christian Democrats as the Reagan administration had hoped. The Christian Democratic party received 35.3 percent of the vote, or twenty-four of the sixty seats in the assembly. The National Republican Alliance, an ultra-rightist party headed by Robert D'Aubuisson, received 25.7 percent of the vote, or nineteen assembly seats. D'Aubuisson, a cashiered army officer associated with coup attempts, was reportedly the founder of the White Warrier Union, a death squad involved in paramilitary terror campaigns. Alleged by former U.S. Ambassador Robert White to be the ''pathological killer'' responsible for ordering the assassination of Archbishop Romero, he had referred to the Christian Democrats as ''Communists'' during the election campaign and had vowed to remove human rights restrictions on the military and ''exterminate'' the guerrillas in three months. The National Conciliation Party, also an ultra-conservative foe of the Christian Democrats, received 16.7 percent of the vote and fourteen assembly seats. As the official government party from 1961 to 1979, this group fronted for a series of military presidents and was responsible, along with the army, for voiding the 1972 presidential election won by Duarte and Ungo. Two other right-wing parties won the remaining three seats in the assembly.

Efforts by the United States to pressure the military and the Right to give the Christian Democrats an important postelection role were largely unsuccessful. Roberto D'Aubuisson was chosen to head the Constituent Assembly, and Christian Democrats were excluded from all important assembly positions. Napoleon Duarte, the U.S.-favored candidate, was dropped from the government. A stalemate over the presidency was broken when the military high command, fearing restrictions on aid by the U.S. Congress, convinced the National Conciliation Party to compromise with the Christian Democrats and to support an independent, Alvaro Mágana, as interim president. Magaña, former head of the Salvadoran Mortgage Bank, is reputed to have close ties with the military. The weak position of the Christian Democrats was further reflected in the distribution of cabinet positions. They were given only the ministries of foreign relations, labor, and education, while the right-wing parties controlled the important ministries of the presidency, agriculture, economy, justice, and public works.

In the year since the March elections progress on land reform has come in limited fits and starts. The new minister of agriculture, a member of D'Abuisson's right-wing ARENA party, has been an outspoken opponent of the reform. Assistance to land recipients has been cut back, peasant leaders have often been intimidated and forced to pay protection money and, in some instances, have even been murdered by the security and paramilitary forces. Some segments of the Left have also resorted to tactics of intimidation to disrupt the reform.

Phase II, involving the lands of the powerful coffee oligarchy, has effectively been cancelled. Decrees 3 and 6 issued by the new Constituent Assembly have undermined the legal basis for further land expropriation and suspended the Phase III "Land to the Tiller" program. Furthermore, well over thirty thousand peasant families who were beneficiaries under the program were illegally evicted following the March elections. As of January 1983 only about half had returned, and the prospects for substantially more were dim at best.

The elections produced little progress on prosecuting those responsible for murdering the four American Churchwomen and the two American land reform advisors. Although five national guardsmen had been scheduled to go on trial for the murder of the women, the El Salvadoran government refused to investigate or indict the officers who gave the orders. This decision followed an October 1982 ruling by two Salvadoran judges that there was "insufficient evidence" (despite FBI and U.S. State Department reports to the contrary) to try two politically well connected officers and a businessman identified as having given the orders for assassinating the two U.S. advisors. U.S. Ambassador Deane R. Hinton was so taken aback by the blatant disregard for justice (and U.S. pressure) that he publically criticized the rightest "Mafia" in El Salvador and called on the government to end human rights "abuses" by the security forces and to bring to justice "the murderers of our citizens including those who ordered the murders."

Perhaps most seriously, the March elections did not move those in power any closer to bringing democracy to El Salvador, let alone finding a political solution to the crisis. Those in power have created new forces and factions: there are power conflicts within the military, some associated with a growing chism between supporters of D'Aubuisson and those of García. Indeed, García's attempts to shift his opponents out of key military positions in late 1982 and early 1983 led to a short-lived but somewhat successful mutiny by Colonel Ochoa, which reflected generalized opposition to García within the military. In early 1983 this opposition forced García's resignation. He was replaced by General Vides Casanova, former head of the national guard. But such factionalism is not as important as what is shared by many of the officers in the various security forces and by rightest political leaders such as D'Aubuisson. They are vehemently against real democratic participation by the opposition; they have condoned and even assisted the death squads in their campaigns of terror; and some have actively engaged in systematic repression, torture, and massacre. Repression continues to leave the opposition believing that they have no choice other than to continue armed insurgency. Dramatic evidence of this occurred again in October 1982, when the government of El Salvador refused to enter discussions with politicians representing the most moderate elements of the FDR regarding future electoral participation. Instead, security forces and death squads abducted five of the very politicians who were to be involved, making credible the claim of the FDR that they could not and cannot participate in elections organized by a regime that threatens the lives of opposition candidates.

Offering the opposition the option of laying down their arms and participating in elections is no option at all under these conditions. The opposition believes it must respond to the military repression with military resistence. The real strategy of the military in El Salvador, which is supported by the United States, remains what it has been: a military solution. The electoral strategy pushed by the United States, however well intentioned, merely masks what is in fact reliance upon a military strategy dependent primarily on military actions to solve the crisis. Illustrative of this are the efforts of the U.S. government to discourage the El Salvadoran government from pursuing FDR/FMLN offers for unconditional dialogue, such as the initiatives taken in October 1982. Indeed, there has even been considerable international support for the alternate strategy of a negotiated settlement. European and Venezuelan Social Democratic parties and the governments of Mexico, France, and Holland have recognized the FDR as a legitimate party to a political solution and have urged negotiations. In February 1982 Mexico's former President José López Portillo proposed a comprehensive package aimed at concluding a negotiated settlement of the El Salvadoran civil war as well as diffusing the tensions between the United States and Nicaragua and the United States and Cuba. The López Portillo peace initiative met with considerable congressional interest and was received favorably by the Cuban and Nicaraguan governments and by the FDR. The Reagan administration initially reacted with mixed signals and then effectively ignored and smothered it, as it has other similar proposals.

Despite the much-heralded elections, the situation in El Salvador remains bleak:

Violence and repression continue at an alarming, albeit reduced, rate.
The agricultural foundation of the economy has been crippled.
The economy continues to register overall negative growth.

80

The legacy of great inequality and injustice continues as efforts at land reform have had only partial effect and have often been blocked by the security forces.

The postelection government has not demonstrated the interest or the power to curb the violence and repression of the reactionary elements in the security and paramilitary forces.

A substantial portion of the country is under the effective control of the insurgent forces.

The broad-based opposition continues to be denied any nonviolent channel for dissent.

The United States continues to oppose opportunities to resolve the conflict via direct negotiations as offered by the FDR, Mexico, and other countries and insists instead on following what essentially is a military-cum-elections strategy.

U.S. Policy and Critique

THE REAGAN POLICY

The general outlook of the Reagan policy in regard to El Salvador may be conceived as follows:

Contain Soviet influence and expansionism in the hemisphere, particularly as exercised by its surrogates, Cuba and Nicaragua.

Stop the spread of insurrection/insurgency in Central America and the Caribbean Basin.

Prevent another Cuba or Nicaragua from arising in the hemisphere.

Support, albeit reluctantly, the existing regime in El Salvador, however authoritarian or repressive it might be, as the only viable alternative to a pro-Soviet, anti-American totalitarianism.

The particular policy actions directed toward El Salvador have been the following.

Reliance on the government as the political Center and the principal building block for pursuing a settlement of the conflict.

Provision of military assistance.

Provision of training to military personnel to enhance the capability of security forces in order to stop insurgency and to professionalize the armed forces in order to eliminate involvement in, or support of, repression.

Reliance on elections as the appropriate mechanism to achieve a democratic political solution.

Support for the agrarian reform program of the junta as decreed in March 1980.

Provision of economic assistance.

Support through "quiet" diplomacy to influence the actions of the government, relying more on "carrot" incentives than "stick" sanctions.

Work with neighboring countries to isolate Nicaragua and prevent the inflow of arms and other support to the insurgents in El Salvador.

CRITIQUE OF THE REAGAN POLICY

The Reagan administration's strategic vision emphasizes that the conflict in El Salvador is part and parcel of the East-West conflict. This one-eyed perspective lacks depth, vastly inflates the significance of external support for the opposition, misperceives the significance of the internal, historical causes of the conflict, and prevents the construction of a solution that will serve the national interests of both the United States and El Salvador. The Reagan policies have had a number of damaging consequences.

The Reagan administration's unqualified support for the preelection junta was a major obstacle to a peaceful, long-term settlement; continuing such support for the current regime contributes to further polarization and a deepening of civil strife.

The prime emphasis the United States continues to place on the military aspects of the solution—rhetoric notwithstanding—contributes to increasing polarization; discourages the military from seeking a negotiated settlement; needlessly implicates the U.S. government in the torture, murder, and repression; and opens up the possibility for the Soviet Union to increase the very influence this country fears. The East-West view, which defines the opposition in El Salvador as "the enemy," creates the image that the source of disorder and violence is leftist insurgency. Yet the evidence is that most of the violence, particularly violence against people as opposed to violence against property, has come from the Right. Violence by security and paramilitary forces cut off the possibility of peaceful political discussion in 1980, forcing even moderate groups toward armed resistance as the only viable alternative. And even today the overwhelming proportion of the violence is attributable to the Right. Nonetheless, U.S. policy continues to emphasize stopping the leftist insurgency and rarely addresses the issue of violent right-wing repression. In fact, according to State Department testimony to Congress in December 1981, the United States seeks to "make sure that our friends have the means to defend themselves"; this is the first item in U.S. strategy.

By supplying its "friends" in El Salvador with weapons and support the United States has committed four serious errors. First, the United States placed the means of repression in the hands of many of the repressors under the apparent assumption that only the "good" guys in the security forces would have access to the supplies, equipment, etc. Second, the country cloaked those elements in a mantle of legitimacy, thereby actually reducing their incentive to end their role in the violence or to support structural reforms. Third, in effect the United States indirectly encouraged violent opposition as the only viable alternative to an armed, repressive, rightist force. Finally, this nation helped solidify a situation in which the Soviet Union may be able to increase its influence in the hemisphere.

Viewing immediate elections as the only option and unconditional negotiations as an unacceptable alternative has been counterproductive: it has both undermined U.S. international credibility as a champion of real democracy and hindered movement toward a political solution. Because a major obstacle to a political settlement in El Salvador has been the security and the paramilitary forces, the most positive result of elections might have been the leverage conferred on the winners to bring the military under control, abolish the death squads, continue to pursue social and economic reforms, and open the political arena to dialogue with opposition groups. The election results had belied the wishfulness of this position. Even the inclusion of a few Christian Democrats in the new government has not hidden the fact that they are even less powerful than before to tame the security forces and death squads. The power has shifted further to the right and even to the ultra-right, as was evidenced by the selection of Roberto D'Aubuisson as president of the Constituent Assembly.

That elections were not the most appropriate mechanism to address the particular problems in El Salvador was foreseeable and had been pointed out by many observers. The lessons of history should have made it clear that meaningful, legitimate elections require certain conditions. First, participation must be open to the entire society. The greater the proportion of the population that is excluded or that does not participate, the less the elections perform the crucial function of honestly legitimatizing the results. Second, participants must be assured that they and others with whom they are associated will not be subject to abuse or attack as a result of the positions they articulate or support during the campaign. Third, participation must be understood as active involvement in the entire electoral process: the determination of electoral procedures; the articulation of issues; the presentation of programs; the nomination of candidates; the conduct of the campaigns; the casting and counting of ballots; and the acceptance of, and support for, the results. Fourth, there must be ample and relatively equal access to media to communicate with the electorate. Fifth, there must be guarantees that the casting of ballots will allow for the free exercise of choice without reprisals. Sixth, there must be some basis for believing that the outcome will be respected and followed.

Even a cursory examination shows that these conditions did not exist in 1981 or 1982 in El Salvador. Quite the contrary, threat, intimidation, and assassination were rampant long before the elections. The murder of centrist and leftist political leaders in 1980 and 1981 sent most of the opposition—even the moderates—underground or into exile. The current civil war, itself the result of the closing of nonviolent alternatives for democracy and social

83

reform, severely limited the freedom to campaign. Even in more "secure" urban areas, right-wing forces made it impossible for any candidate proposing national reconciliation and taming of the security and paramilitary forces to campaign and live. The exclusion of so much of the opposition, the continued violence inflicted by the security forces on citizens who opposed their rule, and the long history of electoral fraud and violations by the military made it clear that the conditions for a democratic electoral process did not exist. To focus attention and judge the "success" of the elections on the particular events surrounding the casting and counting of ballots—the stuffing of ballot boxes, the miscounting of votes, the threats to voters by the insurgents or by the Right—and to ignore the significance of the emasculation of the electoral process that is essential to making the choices at the ballot meaningful is to perpetuate a cruel and eventually transparent hoax on both the American and the El Salvadoran people. Even the most secretive of ballots or honest counting of votes has not changed the fundamental character of the elections. The very undemocratic, if not antidemocratic, character of the electoral process resulted in a Pyrrhic victory for democratic forces.

Uncritical acceptance of the electoral process by the United States as a legitimate alternative to negotiations makes its commitment to democracy look hypocritical and hollow not only in El Salvador but also in other developing countries where it ought to stand as a moral alternative to the Soviet Union. Further, negotiations with those groups excluded from the elections are essential for the creation of a viable national political community in El Salvador.

The current agrarian reform program has been blocked by the very oligarchy and military that current U.S. policy has supported. The agrarian reform program has failed both to build adequate political support for the current government among the peasants and to isolate the guerrilla forces. Lackluster administration, inadequate support, and corruption have seriously hindered the implementation of the program. Security and paramilitary forces remain a major obstacle, even to limited implementation. The power gained by the Right in the elections further diminished the reforms. The opposition of these forces led to the cancellation of Phase II and the near-shelving of Phase III.

The U.S. East-West perspective and U.S. opposition to broad negotiations among the major power groups including the FDR undermines U.S. relations with important allies. Our European allies have questioned the wisdom of the U.S. approach in El Salvador. France and Holland openly recognized the FDR as a legitimate party to any solution. Support by the German Social Democratic Party for the FDR has been a source of some tension with the United States. Mexican support for the FDR threatens to increase tensions with Mexico at a time when the need to resolve joint concerns over issues of migration, trade, investment, and energy is growing increasingly important.

Considerations for a New Policy

A positive U.S. policy response to the situation in El Salvador must be based on the following considerations.

A recognition that current U.S. policies have failed. Despite a rhetorical emphasis on elections, the United States has been following essentially a unilateral military strategy that has virtually precluded a political solution to the conflict. It has contributed to a situation that not only is worse for the vast majority of the El Salvadoran people but also is damaging to U.S. long-range national interests. By continuing to give millions of dollars to support a military solution, the United States is contributing to what, at best, will be a temporary solution, forcing this country to continue to confront instability in the region. Worse, U.S. policy is helping to enlarge and polarize the opposition, indirectly encouraging it to seek violence as its only alternative; this country is undermining the confidence of important allies and is fostering conditions under which the Soviet Union could enlarge its influence.

A recognition that a strategic vision that peers at the world through an East-West optic is wrong. Such an improper understanding has the following effects.

—It blinds U.S. policymakers to the internal roots of the Salvadoran conflict. Any effort to address the problems in El Salvador must take into account the unfortunate legacies of violence and electoral fraud as well as the inequitable political and economic structures that have excluded the vast majority of the population. The assistance given to the Salvadoran insurgents by Nicaragua and Cuba—much exaggerated by the Reagan administration's view—is not the major factor in promoting or sustaining the conflict. Treating the issue as primarily an East-West one helps create a self-fulfilling prophecy, actually transforming it into that kind of problem.

—It wrongly classifies the FDR as a Soviet proxy and paints the distorted picture that the only U.S. alternative to Soviet-controlled communism is support for the current regime, regardless of how bad it is. Quite the contrary, the FDR is a broad, center-left coalition composed of major elements of the Christian Democratic party who have defected, Social Democrats, professional organizations, trade unions, peasant organizations, popular organizations, and important elements in the Catholic church, as well as the guerrilla groups. The FDR is controlled by highly nationalistic pragmatists. Its participation in a new government need not necessarily pose a national security threat to the United States.

—It assumes that any Marxist presence automatically means subservience to the Soviet Union and consequently constitutes a serious threat to U.S. vital security interests. This country has learned in other historical situations that it can work with nationalist governments. Yugoslavia is a good example. What is critical is that the society observe internationally recognized rules of

85

nation-state behavior: engage in no external aggression, pose no threat to the security of the United States or other countries, respect treaty obligations, honor financial commitments, etc.

A recognition that the preeminent emphasis must be given to pursuit of a political, not a military, solution to the very serious problem of the breakdown of the national community in El Salvador. Such a political solution must not be merely rhetorical: insisting on inappropriate mechanisms (like elections) which cannot resolve the conflict at this stage is to clothe a losing military strategy in political garb. There is no cohesive national community in El Salvador today. The society is highly polarized, conflict ridden, and split into multiple fragments. Those who make public demands for even the most minimal conditions of a functioning national community—an end to repression by death squads and security forces, civilian control over the military, fredom of the press, freedom to speak and assemble, an equitable and reasonably independent judicial system—risk their lives.

The central question faced in this situation is what kind of steps will generate a process that will begin to open dialogue, build trust, guarantee personal safety and civil rights, and develop institutions to allow factions to work out their differences through discussion and compromise rather than the use of force. Elections are simply not the first step. They are a very effective mechanism to demonsrate the will of the people within the context of a national community, but they are not the appropriate mechanism to *recreate* a national community torn apart by differences that cannot even be expressed, much less resolved, in the current political arena. What is essential now is to build the context in which elections would be a meaningful way for the population to express its will. The appropriate mechanism to create the conditions to construct a minimal national consensus is some form of dialogue or negotiation. This type of activity allows all major parties to clarify their own positions and to begin sorting out where compromise is or is not possible. Tragically, a policy of insistence on elections prior to this step exacerbates the differences, further reduces the possibility of a political solution, increases the likelihood for continued slaughter, and makes a truly free and fair electoral mechanism even more difficult to develop.

While there is no guarantee that negotiations or dialogue will solve the crisis, we can be sure that a continuation of the present military-cum-elections strategy will fail. Negotiations will not succeed quickly: the problems in El Salvador are complex and not amenable to rapid solution. The legacies of violence, electoral fraud, and inequity were created over a number of decades and will take time to overcome. Violence is likely to continue for some time, even under the best of circumstances, but taking the risk of following a policy of *protracted negotiations* is far better than pursuing a policy of guaranteed *protracted conflict.* Even if the process is a protracted one, dialogue and/or negotiations have a much better chance of success, and the costs are much less in terms of the destruction of human life, destruction of the economic infrastructure, and continued breakdown of the national community.

A recognition that a solution in El Salvador must incorporate the vast majority of the population into the political and economic life of the country. Because the FDR coalition is the opposition's most important voice, no viable solution to the conflict is possible without its participation. Likewise, other coalitions that may emerge must be encouraged and permitted to participate. U.S. efforts to impose a solution are certain to fail. The appropriate role for the United States, along with its Latin American neighbors, is to assist in designing and implementing policies to help create the conditions under which Salvadorans may begin to resolve their own problems.

The United States must involve other regional actors who share an interest in such political solutions but who have more influence over the opposition than does the United States. Past United States involvement and the high level of distrust the FDR/FMLN has for the United States gives this country little leverage over the opposition and makes it difficult, if not impossible, for the United States unilaterally to mediate or guarantee any settlement. The United States should strongly support—not ignore or undermine—such efforts as those made by Mexico, Venezuela, Columbia, and Panama and the Catholic church to achieve a political settlement of the conflict in El Salvador and other regional problems.

A recognition that, to stand as a champion of human rights and economic betterment rather than as a co-enforcer of authoritarianism, the United States should do the following.

—*Seek an immediate cessation of all violence against the civilian population and all violations of human rights.* Most immediately, the United States should publicly condemn all violators, especially within the security forces and paramilitary Right, for their acts of terror against civilians, for their incursions into refugee camps, and their crossing of the international border into Honduras. It should pressure the El Salvadoran government to proceed forthrightly with the investigation of all atrocities, paying particular attention to the cases of the four American Churchwomen and the American Institute for Free Labor Development (AIFLD) advisors. It should provide assistance to the victims of violence, grant asylum to political refugees, and provide economic assistance for refugee camps.

—*Seek an immediate cessation of hostilities.* The United States should immediately remove the Green Berets from the Honduras/El Salvador border. It should signal its unwillingness to support such military solutions by opposing the training of any exiles in the United States (Florida, California), Honduras, or any other country. And it should publicly disavow and discontinue the covert operations against Nicaragua that the administration is supporting.

—*Welcome multilateral efforts to solve the conflict peacefully, such as the*

Nicaraguan proposal for joint patrols with the Hondurans along their common border as a way to restrict any arms flow. The United States should also support vigorously the attempts by Mexico, Venezuela, Panama, and Columbia to achieve a negotiated settlement of border problems and pursue seriously the signals from Cuba that Cuba is willing to negotiate its foreign policy toward Central America.

—*Mobilize the already widespread international support, especially of the Mexicans, the European Social Democratic parties, and the Catholic church, to help press for a cease-fire, guarantees against repression of all political leaders and civilians, whether members of the opposition or not, and the implementation of full civil and political rights.*

—*Make continued military aid to El Salvador conditional*. The Dodd amendment requiring that the president certify the Salvadoran government's progress toward stemming human rights abuses and implementing promised reforms was a good first step. The provision of this assistance must require an end to general military repression (not just incidents of violence) and the dissolution of the death squads. The repressive character of the regime can continue to take its pernicious toll without having to resort to the same high level of atrocities committed in previous years. After a certain point, the repressive character of a regime is sufficiently institutionalized so that the population will respond to threats and will be intimidated based on the incidents of the past. Occasional acts of violence are adequate, under these circumstances, to maintain the fear and intimidation. Unless action is taken to eliminate the death squads and end the repression, opposition groups will see no alternative but armed insurgency, and the civil strife and bloodshed will worsen. Insofar as the United States provides assistance that in effect supports these actions, whatever this country's intentions might be, the stains will be on U.S. hands as well.

Conclusions

The construction of a viable alternative policy toward El Salvador is not a matter of some new quick fix, some one new statement or one new action on the part of the United States. It is the entire approach to the problem which must be reformulated. The particular recommendations we make form part of an alternative policy cluster. That policy cluster is based on our analysis that the current, largely military, policy of the United States has failed and that the United States must in fact, and not simply in rhetoric, dedicate itself to a political solution. Such a political solution is not obvious, simple, or guaranteed. New political alternatives have to be created by skillful U.S. diplomacy, drawing on the support of regional actors like Mexico and Venezuela. Creating the conditions for negotiations would be a first step toward finding the kind of political and diplomatic solution that represents the best national interests of both the United States and El Salvador.

6. Honduras: An Emerging Dilemma

Richard L. Millett

Honduras has traditionally been the poorest, the least developed nation in Central America. Two-thirds of its nearly four million citizens live in conditions of poverty. Even during the boom period of the 1960s, the economic growth of Honduras lagged behind that of the rest of the region. The nation lacks health and education facilities, adequate Pacific ports, and experienced civilian leadership. A high percentage of university graduates leave the country, and in recent years a steady stream of unskilled, poverty-stricken refugees have been entering Honduras. Internal transportation costs are immense, and inflation, spurred by the costs of imported energy, is a growing problem. Traditionally exploited by other nations, Hondurans have a strong sense of insecurity and a lack of faith in the future. The military has a long history of corruption and domination of the political process. The economic infrastructure is weak and the economy is highly vulnerable to shifts in prices and demand for a few key commodities.

From 1950 to 1978 the Honduran gross domestic product per capita increased by only 27 percent, the smallest increase in the region and less than one-third of the average increase for all of Central America. This situation was at least partly due to the Honduran rate of population growth, second highest in the Western Hemisphere.

Strengths, however, also exist. The nation still has significant areas of undeveloped land. Urban pressures are less acute than in neighboring republics, a situation explained in part by the relative balance between two major cities, Tegucigalpa and San Pedro Sula. Hondurans prefer dialogue to violence as a means of resolving political disputes, and recent elections have been relatively honest. Extremist groups exist on both the Left and the Right, but they are weak and lack popular backing. There are well-organized labor unions and peasant groups and a surprisingly free press. Perhaps most important,

Honduras lacks the organized, intransigent ruling class that has so greatly contributed to the violence in El Salvador and Guatemala.

Overview

Honduran weakness has provided constant temptation for intervention by more powerful neighbors. Through its history it has been subject to political, economic, and even military interventions from Guatemala, El Salvador, and Nicaragua, all seeking to control Honduras in order to advance their own regional interests. This has aggravated the existing weakness of Honduran institutions and has helped to produce a preoccupation with national security.

The United States has also intervened in Honduras, though not as directly nor for as prolonged a period as it has in neighboring Nicaragua. More important than U.S. government intervention has been the influence of American companies, notably the United Fruit Company and the Standard Fruit Company. For decades they dominated the Caribbean coastal region, owning much of the land, determining wages and employment conditions, and even building and running the nation's railroads. With their total control over the nation's major export, bananas, their support was crucial to the survival of any Honduran government. Their activities also generated considerable local resentment, especially after the crushing of a banana workers' strike in the early 1950s. While not as important today as in the past, they continue to exercise major influence, as demonstrated by their bribing of Honduran President General Lopez Arrellano in the 1970s, an event that ultimately forced the army to remove the general from office.

In 1969 Honduras and El Salvador engaged in a brief war that was brought on by the expulsion of Salvadoran settlers from Honduras. While fighting lasted less than a week, more than eleven years passed before a peace treaty was finally signed. This condition disrupted Honduran trade and set back efforts at industrial development. Further problems were created in 1978 and 1979 by the Nicaraguan civil conflict, which sent tens of thousands of refugees into Honduras. Most returned at the end of the war, but a new wave of refugees, notably exmembers of the Nicaraguan national guard, created problems with Nicaragua's new rulers. Border clashes have been a constant feature of the past two years, with relations growing increasingly strained. At the same time, Salvadoran refugees began to enter Honduras as the internal conflict in that nation escalated. While lacking the ideological component of the conflict on the Nicaraguan border, the presence of the Salvadorans does offer the potential of serious political as well as economic problems. In recent months Guatemalans have joined the flood of refugees fleeing to Honduras, with an estimated fifteen hundred now located in the Department of Copan.

With one brief exception, the military dominated Honduran politics from late 1963 until 1980. The record of this period is an odd mixture of efforts to promote national development, corruption, modest reform programs, and sporadic incidents of internal repression. Perhaps most notable was the beginning of an agrarian reform program, an effort made somewhat easier by the lack of a strong, well-organized domestic landholding oligarchy and by a willingness on the part of the banana companies to divest themselves of some of their properties. While increasingly resented because of corruption, inefficiency, and a lack of progress in resolving national problems, the Honduran armed forces were never, because of their relative lack of brutality and open repression, subject to the degree of popular resentment produced in Nicaragua, El Salvador, or Guatemala.

In 1980, responding to both domestic pressures and strong urgings by the Carter administration, the military began a process of return to civilian rule. This was completed in November 1981 with the election of a civilian president and congress and the promulgation of a new constitution. The elections were won by the Liberal party, headed by Roberto Suazo C. He won the presidency with 54.1 percent of the vote. The Liberals' major rivals, the conservative National party, captured only 41.5 percent of the vote. The Liberals also took control of the congress.

THE CURRENT SITUATION

The Suazo government is confronted with massive problems. The nation remains extremely poor. In 1980 the gross domestic product reached $639 per capita, but economic problems since then mean that it may fall back to near $600 per capita in 1983. Infant mortality is 11.7 percent, the highest level in Central America, and the Inter-American Development Bank's estimate of 40.5 percent literacy for Honduras is the lowest for any Spanish-speaking nation in the hemisphere. Diet and housing are inadequate, and 105 thousand Hondurans have to exist as landless peasants. A population growth rate of over 3 percent and the continued flow of refugees from El Salvador, Nicaragua, and Guatemala make the situation even worse.

While committed to seeking solutions to these massive social and economic problems, the government is severely handicapped by resources that are severely limited. Total GDP for 1982 will be roughly equal to that of 1980, which means a significant decline in constant dollars, especially on a per capita basis. The trade deficit is estimated at $256.7 million. The government is also running a significant budget deficit, which further contributes to inflation. While the official value of the Honduran lempira has been maintained at 2 to the dollar, it has reached 2.8 to the dollar on the parallel market.

The balance of payments gap is being covered by a variety of international lending agencies, including $150 million from the IMF, $77.6 million from the U.S. government ($35 million of which is provided under the Caribbean Basin Initiative), $63.7 million from the Inter-American Development Bank, and $31.3 million from the World Bank. All this contributes to the

91

growing debt burden. The Honduran external debt totaled only $169 million in 1972; estimates are that it will reach $2.137 billion in 1982.

Regional conditions have contributed to this economic disaster. Honduran exports to the rest of Central America totaled $65 million in 1981, but will only reach approximately $49 million in 1982, adding to a negative balance of $32 million in regional trade. Both prices and demand are off for most traditional Honduran exports, with the situation especially bad for coffee, sugar, and bananas. As a result, international reserves have dwindled to practically nothing, creating a crisis for importers as well as for some industries.

As economic conditions have deteriorated, unemployment has risen, reaching 24 percent by the end of 1981, and labor restiveness has increased. Business confidence has also waned; the president of the Honduran Central Bank recently estimated that capital flight since 1979 had totaled $½ billion. The net result of all these factors is that Honduras is currently in the midst of a severe economic depression, a situation that is unlikely to improve significantly for several years.

Two major development projects, a 600-million-dollar hydroelectric project at El Cajon and the 200-million-dollar Olancho pulp and paper complex, offer hope for future economic progress. Both, however, are behind schedule and are experiencing major cost overruns and numerous charges of misuse of funds. Given growing domestic pressures for economic and social progress, coupled with the destabilizing effects of conflicts in neighboring nations, delays in these projects can have serious consequences for the future of Honduras. Lack of a sense of urgency and a mentality of "business as usual" have long characterized both the civilian and the military leadership of Honduras, and there is little evidence of significant change in this in recent months.

Recent U.S. Policies

The policy of the Carter administration toward Honduras stressed the necessity of a return to civilian rule and of rapid progress in confronting the nation's economic and social problems. A conscious effort was made to separate Honduras from any political alliance with the more repressive military regimes in Guatemala and pre–October 1979 El Salvador. Following the fall of the Somoza regime in Nicaragua and the October 1979 revolution in El Salvador, policy changed somewhat. There was increased concern over Honduran internal security and over that nation's relations with the rest of Central America. Military training funds (IMET), which had been reduced in previous years, were slightly increased, and several helicopters were leased to Honduras to aid in its border surveillance. Efforts to promote a settlement of the 1969 conflict with El Salvador were stepped up, reaching fruition in the latter half of 1980.

The Reagan administration has given greater attention to Honduras than did any previous government in U.S. history. The announcement of the president's plan to visit Honduras is only the most visible of a long string of events: the administration has greatly increased economic assistance to Honduras and has placed even greater emphasis on security assistance. Honduras is today second only to El Salvador in Latin America as a recipient of American military aid.

The official rationale for this expanded interest has been "to support the well-being and security of a democratic regime under pressure from external forces."[1] There is at least some element of truth in this. The Reagan administration is concerned about stability and the survival of the elected civilian government in Honduras. Any major increase in internal violence in that nation would significantly complicate U.S. policy efforts in Central America, and the fall of the civilian government, especially through a military coup, would make it more difficult to defend such policies at home and abroad. There are, however, two other reasons for interest in Honduras which appear to carry even greater weight in Washington.

The first of these involves using Honduras to advance administration aims in El Salvador. The major thrust here has been encouraging and supporting Honduran efforts to interdict supplies for Salvadoran guerrillas which reportedly are transiting Honduran land, sea, or air space on their way from Cuba or Nicaragua to El Salvador. This effort is a major justification for increased U.S. military assistance, including the dispatch of numerous mobile training teams. It has also led to increasing problems between the Honduran military and Salvadoran refugees. Charges of military violations of refugee rights and of cooperation with the Salvadoran military in attacks on refugees have increased steadily, as have conflicts between the government and Church groups involved with the refugees.

While the situation on the Salvadoran border remains highly volatile, it has been overshadowed in recent months by the much more dangerous pattern developing along the frontier with Nicaragua. Throughout 1982 charges of U.S. involvement in exile raids from Honduras into Nicaragua became more and more frequent. Early in the year, Don Oberdorfer of the *Washington Post* revealed the existence of an alleged 19-million-dollar fund for CIA-sponsored covert actions against Nicaragua, most of which were to be launched from Honduran territory.[2] This coincided with the mass migration of thousands of

---

1. Prepared Statement of Deputy Assistant Secretary of State for Inter-American Affairs Stephen W. Bosworth before the Subcommittee on Inter-American Affairs, Committee on Foreign Affairs, House of Representatives, 21 September 1982.

2. *Washington Post*, 10 March 1982.

Misquito Indians from Nicaragua to refugee camps in Honduras. The Indians, who were fleeing forced resettlement efforts by the Sandinistas, soon became the focus of intense recruiting efforts by anti-Sandinista leaders in Nicaragua and provided a valuable supplement to existing counterrevolutionary groups, notably former members of the Somoza dictatorship's national guard. Raids across the border increased in number and strength, and relations between Nicaragua and Honduras deteriorated rapidly. While the Honduran foreign minister was presenting an ambitious peace plan to the OAS, accusations were increasing that the Honduran military, with the help of Argentine advisors, was actively training and supporting Nicaraguan counter-revolutionary forces.

As the threat of war grew along the border, so also did U.S. military presence in Honduras. In the last quarter of 1981 there were 8 U.S. military advisors in Honduras. During the first quarter of 1981 that number reached 104.[3] Shortly thereafter the Reagan administration requested fiscal year 1983 funds for upgrading Honduran airfields, announcing that such airfields would be available for U.S. use in "emergency situations." In August the U.S. Air Force helped airlift a battalion of Honduran troops into the Atlantic Coast border area with Nicaragua. Much more extensive joint maneuvers were scheduled for December, leading to reports throughout the region of a possible major effort to topple the Sandinistas during that month.

Efforts to conceal the U.S. role in the Honduran-Nicaraguan border clashes collapsed when *Newsweek* featured the story in its 8 November 1982 issue. *Newsweek* charged that the United States, acting through Washington's ambassador to Honduras, John Negroponte, had carefully orchestrated exile attacks on Nicaragua. A U.S. official is quoted as saying, "It was Negroponte who began dealing with the guardsmen and the Somozistas," while a member of the Honduran military high command is reported to have observed that the commander of his nation's armed forces, General Gustavo Alvarez, "does what Negroponte tells him to."[4]

Ambassador Negroponte and high-placed Honduran officials have denied the accuracy of these and other statements in the article, but there has been a surprising degree of acknowledgment of U.S. involvement with the exiles, including the ex–national guardsmen.

The claim is advanced that the aim is not to overthrow the Nicaraguans, but simply to annoy them and raise the cost of their involvements outside their own borders, but such claims lack credibility. The United States is obviously involved with exile groups and is using Honduras as a base for regional operations, especially against Nicaragua.

---

3. Cynthia Arnson and Flora Montealegre, "Update #7: Background Information on U.S. Military Personnel and U.S. Assistance to Central America," *Institute for Policy Studies Resource* (November 1982), p. 3.
4. "A Secret War for Nicaragua," *Newsweek*, 8 November 1982, pp. 45–46.

There are a few positive aspects to current policies. In the wake of the uproar over the *Newsweek* article, the joint maneuvers with Honduras, set to take place near the Nicaraguan border in December, were postponed. Recent administration statements have placed greater stress on the need for peaceful settlements to regional problems. With strong encouragement from Congress the Reagan administration has supported the maintenance of civilian government in Honduras. It has also increased economic assistance to record levels. While still falling far short of meeting actual needs, this is clearly a positive step and, because of serious internal administrative problems, is close to the level of U.S. support that Honduras can currently absorb.

Critique of Current Policies

The current relatively high level of interest in Honduras is almost unprecedented. It is, however, a largely negative interest, with a focus on the role Honduras can play in supporting administration policies in El Salvador and Nicaragua. Efforts to maintain stability and avoid the internal turmoil so common in El Salvador and Guatemala are seriously handicapped by the administration's view that the major threat to Honduras is external: the encouragement of subversion by Cuba, the Soviet Union, and, at least potentially, Nicaragua. Using this criteria, the Reagan administration has placed its highest priorities on increasing the capacity of the security forces to combat internal subversion and on encouraging Honduras to oppose the Left in El Salvador and to cooperate in operations against the government of Nicaragua.

There are several major flaws to this approach. First, it diverts attention from the growing economic and social problems that actually constitute the major threat to Honduran stability. External forces may seek to exploit these situations, but they do not cause them. The best way to maintain stability is to encourage efforts by the Honduran government to deal with that nation's problems, emphasizing economic, not security, assistance and advocating an opening up of the political process rather than a concentration on the control of domestic dissidents. Current policy also neglects the pressing need for administrative reform and for increased efforts to combat both civil and military corruption within the government.

Current policies involving the Honduran military threaten to upset the fragile civil-military balance existing in that nation. While civilians, through relatively honest elections, have returned to the Presidential Palace, the military has by no means given up power. The new Honduran constitution gives the armed forces a high degree of autonomy. In practice this has meant that the military operates almost independently of civilian controls in border areas and in dealing with problems of internal security. Guarantees of military independence in these areas and of a strong military voice in foreign policy are widely believed to have been extracted from the civilian political leaders by the military in return for its allowance of a free election and a return to civilian government.

Current policy threatens to discredit the newly installed Liberal party government of President Roberto Suazo C. and eventually to increase the chances of a military coup. The first of these is the threat of more immediate importance. While committed to reform, economic development, and respect for individual rights, the new Honduran administration is neither strong nor united. The new president lacks administrative experience and an image of strong personal leadership. The cabinet also lacks strong, able personalities, and conservative military influence remains strong within the new administration. Many of the more aggressively reform-minded leaders of the Liberal party have banded together in the Progressive Liberal Alliance (ALIPO), but this group has been marginalized by the new government. Civilian political institutions in Honduras historically are weak and liable to corruption. The prevailing attitude has been that a public office is a public trough. Failure of the Suazo administration to exercise effective control over the military, to reduce administrative corruption and inefficiency, and to promote economic development and social reform will rapidly erode public confidence in the existing political system and increase support for extremist groups on both the Left and the Right.

Among current Latin American armed forces, the Honduran military is perhaps the most responsive to U.S. influence. In 1981, believing that the United States favored such a course, it even prepared to invade Nicaragua but changed its plans when Washington clarified its signals. Current policy is again moving Honduras toward conflict with Nicaragua. In response to the growing number of exile attacks launched against his nation from Honduran bases, Nicaraguan junta leader Daniel Ortega in July 1982 threatened to "support Honduran guerrillas" if the attacks continued.[5] The recent upsurge of violence within Honduras, notably the "Chinchonero" guerrilla September seizure of the chamber of commerce in San Pedro Sula and the holding of more than one hundred prominent hostages, including two cabinet members, was clearly linked to Honduran involvements in El Salvador and Nicaragua and to the activities of U.S. and other outside advisors, most notably Argentine and Israeli advisors. Before the Falklands/Malvinas conflict Washington seemed to be encouraging the presence of and working closely with the Argentines in Honduras, but in the wake of that conflict the Argentine presence has apparently declined and Washington's ability to influence its activities has almost vanished.

While never as repressive as its Salvadoran or Guatemalan counterparts, the Honduran military has a checkered history. In 1975 two priests and seven

5. Foreign Broadcast Information Service, *Latin America: Daily Report,* 26 July 1982, p. P–9.

leaders of the National Peasants Union were murdered by the military. Two army officers were eventually convicted of these crimes, and human rights conditions showed some signs of improvement until the last months of the Carter administration. Since then, however, conditions have deteriorated. The worst incidents have involved refugees from El Salvador, but domestic dissidents have been increasingly targeted in recent months. These have included priests, union and peasant organization leaders, and officials of left-wing political parties. The increase in domestically inspired incidents is related to perceived signals from Washington that internal security concerns are much more important than human rights. The Reagan administration not only has failed to pressure the armed forces to end human rights abuses, but has steadily increased security assistance throughout this period. This has been perceived as a clear message by the Honduran military: control of dissent is important, human rights are not. This places in jeopardy the current climate of political dialogue and risks creating a trend toward polarization. At a time when U.S. policy should be directed toward reinforcing the fragile democratic system, encouraging dialogue, and providing Honduras with time to address its economic and social problems, these trends are potentially disastrous.

Even more serious are the implications of current policy for relations between Honduras and its neighbors. In order to deal with its internal problems, Honduras needs insulation from current conflict and, ultimately, a restoration of trade with a region returning to peace. It also needs to bring to an end the growing flood of refugees crossing its borders. Current Reagan administration policy is counterproductive in all these areas. It seeks to involve Honduras increasingly in direct confrontations with Nicaragua and in cooperation with the El Salvadoran military against the guerrillas. This reduces trade, risks a major border conflict, and creates a climate of conflict inimical to new economic investment.

A weak, poor, and divided Honduras simply cannot afford involvement in the Reagan administration's confrontational politics in Central America. Such involvement is much more likely to escalate internal conflicts than it is to advance U.S. interests in the region. Administration policies risk transforming Honduras into the Cambodia of Central America, a nation ultimately destroyed by external forces pressuring its military into direct involvement in regional conflicts.

Policy Recommendations

The prime goal of U.S. policy in Honduras should be to insulate that nation from the violence in the region, giving it a chance to develop a viable democratic system. Beyond that, policy should stress support for civilian rule, respect for human rights, and concentration on economic development combined with basic administration reforms. In order to advance these goals five specific policies are required.

Honduran hopes for domestic peace and development ultimately are highly dependent upon the achievement of a regional political settlement, reversing the current trends toward polarization and violence and recreating a climate for expanded trade and investment. In this regard, favorable U.S. response to the Contadora Group's proposals would directly serve American interests in Honduras. A cease-fire and movement toward a negotiated settlement in El Salvador would end the flood of refugees into Honduras and make possible a restoration of trade. In the case of Nicaragua, the United States must end efforts to use Honduras as a launching pad for attacks on the Sandinistas. Instead, Honduras should be encouraged to enter into direct negotiations with Nicaragua to secure the border and prevent the support of either nation for efforts to subvert the other. This could lead to the return of the Misquito Indians to their homes, thereby reducing the refugee burden on Honduras and ending a major source of potential conflict. The United States should also cease all support for the Nicaraguan ex–national guardsmen and instead encourage and support Honduran efforts to break up such armed groups and move the individuals involved away from border areas. As long as the guardsmen continue operating as an organized force, using Honduras as a base for their efforts to return to power in Nicaragua, the possibility of open armed conflict between Honduras and Nicaragua will remain very real.

Nicaraguan-Honduran relations are currently a key to regional peace. Progress here would go far toward stabilizing the region and enhancing the role of Honduras as a moderate force for peace rather than for escalated regional conflict. A peaceful settlement in El Salvador would also contribute to defusing the current tension between Honduras and Nicaragua, as it would remove from the agenda of regional problems the issue of Nicaraguan arms passing through Honduras. At some time, Honduras might also play a role in encouraging a resolution of the dispute between Guatemala and Belize. In all of these cases U.S. policy must emphasize the use of Honduras as a bridge toward peaceful resolution of disputes, not as a pawn for escalated confrontations.

U.S. policy must emphasize its support for the maintenance of civilian government and the respect for individual rights internally. The Liberal party government of President Suazo C. should be encouraged to broaden its base of support, to seek the involvement of labor, peasant, and commercial groups in efforts toward national development. The government must be made to understand that failure to respect human rights will jeopardize U.S. assistance as well as ultimately defeat efforts at national development. In this regard the current activities of the U.S. ambassador seem clearly counterproductive. They divide the nation internally, damage its international image, and even produce growing dissension within the ruling Liberal party. If he does not quickly reverse these actions, the ambassador risks, in the words of a foreign diplomat in Honduras, bringing "the fragile government of Honduras down with him."[6]

Relations with the Honduran military may well present the greatest challenge to policy formulation. Potential U.S. influence with this force is considerable, but it is unfortunately easier to use this influence to produce negative results, such as encouraging confrontations with Nicaragua, than to achieve such positive goals as increased respect for human rights and a reduction in corruption. Internal political realities, reflected in the new constitution, insure that for some time to come the military will play a decisive role in the future of Honduran democracy. It is therefore vital that the United States maintain open contacts with this force and avoid policies that could drive it into the arms of the extreme Right.

Military assistance is one potential avenue for influence with the Honduran military. Currently proposed levels, however, are clearly excessive and tend to exaggerate further the role of the military in society. They also contribute to the climate of confrontation along the Nicaraguan border. They must be reexamined and reduced. Past history and present conditions do give the Hondurans security concerns, and the United States must be sensitive to these. Clear support for the integrity of Honduran territory is important. At the same time, it must be made clear to the Honduran military that true security can only be achieved through accommodation of and negotiation with neighboring states. Continued support of exile groups attacking Nicaragua or of Salvadoran military actions against refugees in Honduras must be ended. The Honduran military must understand that U.S. concern for its security does not extend to supporting it if it deliberately provokes Nicaragua into a border conflict.

Of equal importance, the United States must also stress that all assistance is dependent upon the maintenance of civilian government and the respect for human rights. Whatever reduced security assistance is provided should focus on improving the training and administrative efficiency, not the combat capability, of the armed forces. A long-range goal of U.S. policy should be a reduction in the autonomy and political power of the military, but at the moment the greatest emphasis must be placed on turning around the military's role on the Nicaraguan and Salvadoran borders.

Current levels of economic assistance should be maintained and, eventually, increased. At the moment a greater problem than the level of financing is the use made by the Hondurans of external assistance. Major development projects have been seriously delayed by widespread civil and military corruption. Administrative inefficiency severely limits the government's ability to benefit from economic aid. Any increase in assistance must be conditioned on improvement in these areas, and much of U.S. aid should be focused on

6. "Secret War," *Newsweek*, p. 46.

assisting such improvements, especially in the administrative area. Church and other private groups should be involved in this process. Above all, the United States must do all it can to communicate a sense of urgency in the progress of economic and social reforms. The objective must not be simply a holding action, a series of palliatives designed to keep the lid on social tensions, but rather an effort to move rapidly toward economic development that benefits the mass of the Honduran population. Support for national literacy and health campaigns should be considered. Peasant organizations should be directly aided, and labor organizations should be supported.

Efforts at economic growth must be carefully thought out. Great care must be taken to avoid excessive increases in the debt structure. Short-term exploitation of resources such as timber or expansion of exports such as meat must be balanced against the long-term ecological and social impacts of such projects. The need for a sense of urgency in development must not be allowed to obscure the long-range implications of such efforts.

Every effort possible should be made to involve other nations and multilateral agencies in Honduran development programs. The United States should increase efforts to coordinate its programs with those of other nations in order to produce a coherent, manageable program that Honduras can effectively absorb.

Special attention must be paid to the problems of the refugees in Honduras. The ultimate goal, of course, is to create conditions that will allow them to return home. Until this is possible, the United States, in cooperation with the United Nations High Commissioner on Refugees, should provide increased assistance to these people and should encourage efforts to remove them from the conflicts in their home countries. Without rapid and coordinated external assistance, the refugee burden could produce serious economic, social, and, ultimately, political consequences for Honduras.

Conclusions

U.S. policy toward Honduras is at a critical juncture. Current administration actions run the clear risk of provoking open conflicts between Honduras and its neighbors, ultimately transforming Central America's internal conflicts into a regional war. The fragile balance between the new civilian government and the military is threatened and the existing climate of political dialogue is jeopardized. Under such pressures economic assistance is likely to be squandered and ineffective. There is still time to change course in Honduras, to begin encouragement of positive changes by implementing the policy recommendations outlined here. But time is short and U.S. options are increasingly constrained. An informal policy of promoting domestic development, responsible civilian government, and basic administrative reforms, as well as reducing military influence and increasing respect for human rights, and, above all, a policy of moderation and accommodation in regional affairs will still afford Honduras a good chance of escaping the escalating violence engulfing its neighbors. Failure to pursue such policies, however, could well insure that the United States will soon face a Honduran crisis similar to the earlier Nicaraguan and current El Salvadoran situations.

7. Costa Rica: The End of the Fiesta

Richard E. Feinberg

Overview

Costa Rica has stood proudly apart from the rest of Central America. While its neighbors have suffered under military rule, insecure and short-lived civilian governments, or a family dynasty, Costa Rica has enjoyed nearly uninterrupted democracy. While land tenure and income distribution were highly skewed elsewhere, land holdings were relatively egalitarian in Costa Rica's central valley, and enlightened social welfare policies reduced disparities in living standards. Achievements in literacy, education, and health care delivery compared favorably with the more developed South American countries. Racially and culturally, Costa Ricans considered themselves more European, more advanced, than Nicaraguans or Guatemalans.

The Costa Ricans have attributed their peaceful democracy to their relative tolerance of dissent and to the creation of a welfare state. Channels were open for the expression of a range of views, and ample opportunities existed for ambitious, young individuals to advance within the political system. The generous provision of social services and fiscal subsidies—to business, rural and urban labor, and youth—increased the appeal and legitimacy of the political system. Steady economic growth through the postwar period generated the resources that lubricated this system and made it possible for the living standards of nearly all Costa Ricans to improve.

Relatively wealthy, liberal, and progressive, Costa Rica looked more to London, Washington, and Miami for its sense of identity than to Managua, San Salvador, or Mexico City. Costa Rica seemed an idyllic island that had somehow been misplaced in Central America. But Costa Rica has not been able to escape the economic and political crises that have enveloped Central America since 1979. The Costa Rican economy has proved as vulnerable as

102

the other weak, small Central American economies to fluctuations in the international economy. And political turmoil in Central America has affected the atmosphere in Costa Rica and yielded new directions in Costa Rica's foreign policy and its relations with the United States.

THE RUDE AWAKENING

The economic crisis that struck Costa Rica in 1981 exposed the fragility of Costa Rican prosperity. Export revenues fluctuated with the unstable prices of a few commodities. Government expenditures, subsidies, and social programs had become increasingly dependent upon borrowings from abroad. Costa Rica's industrial plant, not efficient enough to compete on international markets, required a large volume of imported inputs to operate.

The impact of the first round of oil price hikes in 1973 and 1974 was partly offset by a fortuitous boom in coffee prices in 1976 and 1977. Costa Rica was able to increase sharply its export earnings and to maintain the rising volume of imports needed to fuel growth. But coffee prices plunged in 1978, and OPEC again boosted oil prices in 1979 and 1980. Revenues from coffee fell from a record $319 million in 1977 to $248 million in 1980, while the oil bill jumped from $83 million to $186 million. As a result, the trade deficit rose steadily, from $97 million in 1977 to $185 million in 1978 to $315 million in 1979. When the trade deficit peaked at $366 million in 1980, it had reached 27 percent of imports. The trade deficit continued to widen for reasons other than that the international terms of trade had turned against Costa Rica: the demand for imports continued to rise through 1979 as the gross domestic product expanded sharply.

Economic growth was increasingly sustained by the public sector. The public sector deficit rose to over 12 percent of gross domestic product in 1979 as expenditures skyrocketed in order to cover the growing wage bill of public sector employees and the widening losses of public sector enterprises. The public sector absorbed a rapidly increasing proportion of bank credit, so that by 1980, 44 percent of bank credit was being demanded by the government, as compared to only 18 percent in 1970.

But the deterioration of the trade account is only a part of the story. Costa Rica financed its chronic and growing trade deficits with external borrowings. Increasingly Costa Rica's financing needs were being met by commercial lenders. In 1980 total external debt surpassed $3 billion, more than two-thirds of it owed to private creditors. These private credits generally carried flexible interest rates that were adjusted to market conditions. As market interest rates rose, the debt service falling due on an ever-growing body of accumulated debt soared. Interest payments due jumped from $60 million in 1977 to $290 million in 1981—to an astounding $510 million due in 1982.

The combination of a burgeoning trade deficit and high interest payments widened the current-account deficit to $664 million in 1980. To finance an import bill of $1.4 billion, the Costa Rican public and private sectors borrowed heavily, with an increasing portion of the new debt bearing short-term maturities. These borrowings did not, however, suffice to cover imports and debt payments. Costa Rica had to draw on its reserves until they were virtually exhausted.

The bottom fell out of this debt-led growth strategy in 1981, when external lenders simply declined to continue financing such a large current-account deficit. Suddenly frightened by the magnitude of Costa Rica's financial imbalances, foreign lenders sought to reduce their exposure, and Costa Ricans placed their savings in hard currency abroad. Data on capital flight are unreliable, but it was surely large. The inevitable outcome of these cumulative forces was a very sharp drop in imports that in turn forced a dramatic contraction in both consumption and investment. The gross national product fell by 10 percent in 1981 and 1982. The shortage of imported goods contributed to a soaring inflation rate, which jumped from a modest 9 percent in 1979 to nearly 100 percent in 1982. The value of the Costa Rican colon plummeted from nine to the dollar to forty-eight to the dollar. Costa Ricans were shocked at the unanticipated and severe decline in their purchasing power. Average real wages fell some 35 percent, while open unemployment hit 10 percent in 1982; those who were underemployed rose from 7 percent to 12 percent.

Who was to blame for this collapse? "Exogenous factors"—seesawing coffee prices, the higher costs of energy and capital—played an important role. At the same time, the government of Costa Rica first allowed the economy to overspend during the 1976–77 coffee boom and then failed to respond sufficiently when the international environment turned darker. But it would be unfair to point the finger at President Rodrigo Carazo (1978–82). The crisis descended with amazing swiftness, and Carazo lacked the power to contract wages and government spending rapidly enough to balance his country's accounts. Those tax and administrative measures that he did propose were delayed in a parliament afraid to alienate their constituents, who were not psychologically prepared for deep cuts in living standards.

If Costa Rica borrowed too much, its creditors also must share a portion of the blame for having overlent. Since the banks lent too much to many developing countries, the causes must be sought beyond Costa Rica. The banks were under pressure to lend as a result of large inflows of deposits from oil-exporting countries and other sources. They were competing fiercely among themselves for market shares. The banks also misjudged the direction of the international economy: few anticipated the prolonged recession of 1980–82 and its effects on commodity prices and interest rates. Finally, in Costa Rica as elsewhere, neither the government nor the banks were aware of the magnitude of the rapid debt buildup: neither had an adequate mechanism for prompt collection of debt statistics.

The crisis that struck in 1981 had these immediate causes, but it also was the result of longer-term, structural factors. Like many other developing countries, Costa Rica had been pursuing a policy of import-substitution industrialization. The intention was to create jobs in the manufacturing sector and to reduce import dependency. In the 1960s and early 1970s light industry did grow rapidly, but the overall results were disappointing. Industry tended to be capital intensive, so that the number of jobs created per dollar of investment was inadequate to absorb all the new entrants into the urban labor force. And, if dependency on imported finished products was reduced, a new form of dependency arose—dependency on imported machinery, industrial inputs, and technology. Moreover, growing up behind high tariff walls and enjoying captive markets, much of the new industry was relatively inefficient. It could not produce the exports needed to balance its import needs—except to the Central American Common Market. Central America did absorb up to $248 million in Costa Rican manufactures in 1981, but the civil strife and economic contraction that gripped the region by 1982 burst that bubble as well.

Another problem with import-substitution industrialization was that it tended to favor industry over agriculture. While agriculture performed better in Costa Rica than in many other third world countries in the 1960s and early 1970s, food production stagnated from 1973 to 1980. Agricultural imports began to absorb a rising proportion of available foreign exchange.

A second structural problem was the organization of the Costa Rican state. A host of decentralized, semi-autonomous or autonomous agencies and enterprises grew up which were beyond the financial control of the central bank but which could dip into the public treasury. Public firms in oil, electricity, and water began to generate large losses that the central government had to cover. The extensive social security system and other elements of the welfare state developed momentums of their own that seemed beyond the control of the presidency and the parliament.

The third and related fundamental problem was the tax structure. Relying heavily on indirect taxes, the tax system failed to generate revenues sufficient to cover these rising costs. The wealthy elite had been more willing to grant concessions in the form of social benefits and subsidies than to acquiesce in new taxes; the levies on property and income remained light. The revenue problem was compounded when public sector enterprises tended to lag in their adjustment to rising costs. They hesitated to increase politically sensitive prices, even as the depression ate into their revenue base.

Austerity and Adjustment

Adjusting to the shocks emanating from the international environment and correcting deep-seated structural problems will be arduous tasks. Even if

Costa Rica manages to place its financial accounts in order and alters its development model, the 1980s will be austere. Living standards through the mid-1980s at least will be lower for most Costa Ricans than those they enjoyed in the late 1970s.

Costa Rica has entered into a series of agreements with the International Monetary Fund. A two-year standby was signed in March 1980, and when that fell apart, an ambitious, three-year standby, worth $310 million, was signed in June 1981. This program, too, could not be achieved: it proved to be unrealistic in its projections regarding the international economic environment and the ability of the Costa Rican government in a preelectoral period to introduce severe austerity measures. The IMF program was also deficient insofar as it lacked a reasonably detailed investment program of the sort that was supposed to accompany three-year standbys. A more modest standby, worth $100 million, was signed in late 1982.

The basic themes of these IMF programs are similar. Costa Rica has to reduce sharply its external and internal deficits by increasing taxes, cutting some public sector expenditures, raising the prices charged by autonomous agencies, reducing real wages, and regaining some control over credit creation. The external accounts can also be improved by maintaining the real colon near its devalued rate of about fifty to the dollar and by limiting the magnitude of external borrowing from commercial lenders.

It is not only a matter of reducing living standards. The Costa Rican economy must undergo a major restructuring. The foreign exchange shortage will force many industries heavily dependent upon imported components into bankruptcy. This phenomenon is occurring, with varying degrees of intensity, throughout Central America. Over the long run this restructuring could be beneficial if it results in a more efficient foreign exchange–savings industrial sector. But in the short run it will be painful for workers and owners alike. It will also be necessary to restructure portions of the state apparatus. The central government will have to establish greater financial control over the decentralized agencies. Some agencies with overlapping duties and jurisdictions should be merged. Some firms might be spun off to the private sector.

The biggest challenge will be raising the level of investment. As generally occurs in depressions, investment fell very sharply—by well over 50 percent—in 1981 and 1982. Given the depth of the economy's contraction, investment is unlikely to begin to recover substantially until 1985. Investment will have to be generated in greater proportion from domestic savings. Foreign commercial banks are more interested in reducing their exposure in Costa Rica than in extending the long-term credits that investment programs require. Foreign direct investment also fell off in 1982 (from annual rates of around $45 million to an estimated $15 million) as a result of the economic contraction, the foreign exchange shortage, and the political strife spreading throughout Central America. If domestic savings is to rise, Costa Ricans will have to sacrifice their more immediate living standards on the altar of their future well-being.

The burden of serving the accumulated debt threatens to be a major constraint on Costa Rican development. Amortization payments due on principal will certainly have to be rescheduled. During 1981 and 1982 Costa Rica also fell behind in its interest payments, and unless interest payments falling due over the next several years are capitalized or covered by new loans, Costa Rican recovery will be severely hampered, if not strangled. Of course, a decline in market interest rates would help alleviate the burden.

Recovery will also be impeded if conflict in other Central American countries deepens and spreads. Regional strife undermines confidence among investors both in Costa Rica and abroad. Moreover, to the extent that political conflict harms regional economies, potential export markets for Costa Rican goods are reduced.

The Political Challenge

A mechanistic application of the domino theory to Costa Rica would be a gross mistake. The Costa Rican population is much better educated and its middle class is relatively larger than those in other Central American countries. Nor does Costa Rica suffer from the grinding poverty and land pressures that plague El Salvador. It is not riddled with Guatemala's racial conflict. It has not been plagued by a callous, all-powerful ruling family like the Somozas. In marked contrast with those in the rest of the region, the Costa Rican political system, despite signs of stress and even decay in recent years, still enjoys a high degree of legitimacy.

The results of the 1982 presidential elections illustrate the strength of the system and the essentially conservative political instincts of most of the voting population. Despite the fact that the leading candidate of the majority party, National Liberation, was not particularly inspiring, less than 4 percent of the vote went to right-wing or leftist opponents. The National Liberation party also won thirty-three of the fifty-seven seats in the assembly. Most Costa Ricans remained hopeful that the new administration would succeed. A poll taken in March 1982 recorded 54 percent believing there was a great likelihood that the new president, Alberto Monge, would resurrect the nation from the crisis, while 41 percent saw some reason for optimism; only 5 percent were completely pessimistic. But most Costa Ricans are not as sober as Guido Fernandez, an influential journalist, who warned, "We have had a big banquet, and now we have to pay the bill." As it becomes apparent that the recovery will be slow and painful, Costa Rica's democratic institutions and culture will be tested.

Austerity measures will require the government to take on the middle class—the essential backbone of the regime and of the governing party. Economic reforms will place the government at odds with other vested interests, including sectors of manufacturing and finance. The government will need to find ways to implement necessary reforms without resorting to coercive measures. If the government resorts to coercion, Costa Rican political democracy suffers, but if vested interests block reforms, Costa Rican democracy is also likely to lose. Without economic recovery, political decay will surely spread.

If the legitimacy that the Costa Rican political system enjoys is to survive, austerity measures will have to be implemented without gravely worsening income distribution. There is a danger that, in the pursuit of higher levels of savings and investment, the Costa Rican government could cause the structure of income and incentives to become more skewed, and the greater burden of the economic adjustment would fall on the poorer sectors of the population. At the rhetorical level, at least, virtually all Costa Ricans are aware of this danger. For example, the private sector Costa Rican Association of Managers and Entrepreneurs (ACOGE), in its 1982 plan for "The National Effort for Development," warned that "it is in the best interest for the hemisphere, and not only for Costa Rica, that the country's traditional system for promoting social welfare, progress and the equitable distribution of wealth be maintained and strengthened."

Over the medium term, institutional immobility and economic decline might spawn a leftist challenge to the National Liberation party. The more immediate danger to Costa Rica's open political culture, however, seems to come from within that party itself. Monge in particular has blamed labor unrest on an alleged "international communist conspiracy" aimed at Costa Rica. He appears to be playing on the widespread disillusionment with the Sandinistas. Tensions between the Sandinistas and Costa Rica are being flamed by border disputes, by the cross-border raids of anti-Sandinista Nicaraguans living in Costa Rica, and, reportedly, by CIA-inspired anti-Sandinista and anti-Cuban propaganda. So far no "anticommunist" witch hunts have occurred, but the political atmosphere has soured. The more liberal wing of the National Liberation party is unhappy with Monge's rhetoric but seems unable to moderate him. It fears that his rhetoric will increase tensions while arousing fears that could produce a "flight from freedom." Costa Ricans could be led to contract their political liberties in order to save them.

Costa Rica dissolved its army after a brief civil war in 1948. This very lack of an army has been one major reason that Costa Rica has enjoyed the continuity of civilian institutions, even in the face of the economic chaos of 1981 and 1982. The nation relies upon the Organization of American States and the United States to protect its national territory. A very lightly armed civil and rural guard of seven thousand has been in charge of domestic order.

The Costa Rican government is not yet establishing a regular army, but it is upgrading its civil and rural guards. The Reagan administration has allocated $2 million in security assistance, primarily for uniforms, communications, and transportation equipment, in addition to a small training program emphasizing air and sea rescue operations. Venezuela and Israel are providing training and perhaps equipment. The Costa Ricans have also mentioned that they may approach France, Spain, West Germany, Taiwan, and South Korea for security assistance. President Monge has also created a civilian militia, the Organization for National Emergencies (OPEN), whose ten thousand volunteer members are being trained to back up regular security forces in their defense of Costa Rican institutions "against foreign terrorism and subversion." Members of OPEN are politically screened and must be "citizens of proven democratic faith."

Some of this increased emphasis on security is a logical response to the military buildup in Nicaragua and the more general fear that the political strife sweeping the rest of Central America might spill over into Costa Rica. But the dilemma is this: if the political leadership is unable to resolve the economic crisis using democratic means, the instruments are being created which would permit a more coercive approach. There is the further danger that strengthened security forces could decide to take things into their own hands.

U.S. Policy

The United States and Costa Rica have traditionally maintained excellent relations. Many Costa Ricans identify with standard U.S. values—political democracy, a preference for economic liberalism mixed with state welfarism, and a cultural materialism. Like Americans, many Costa Ricans think of themselves as middle class or believe that they have the opportunities to become so. Furthermore, the Costa Rican labor movement has strong ties to the AFL-CIO. President Monge, a former union leader, has worked closely with the AFL-CIO's international arm, the American Institute for Free Labor Development (AIFLD).

Costa Rica has generally been willing to follow the U.S. lead in hemispheric and international affairs. Costa Ricans admire the United States and, with a population one one-hundredth the size, generally accept that relations will be highly asymmetric. The strong nationalism expressed as defiance of the United States that is prevalent in other Central American countries is attenuated in Costa Rica. This may be partly attributed to the fact that the Costa Rican political system, which resembles the American one, enjoys considerable legitimacy. Also, U.S. Marines have not intervened in Costa Rica, and U.S. advisors and weapons have not been used in partisan, civil strife.

This is not to say that Costa Rica has never dissented from U.S. policy. Costa Rica has maintained a policy of granting safe haven to political refugees, and in the 1970s many Chileans and other nationals from South America fleeing U.S.-backed military governments made their homes in San José. More recently, Costa Rica defied the United States when the Carter administration requested the use of an airstrip near the Nicaraguan border during the insurrection that would finally overthrow Somoza. Washington argued that it wanted to place U.S. aircraft there to be prepared to evacuate Americans from war-torn Nicaragua. Some Costa Ricans feared that the United States actually intended to attempt to stem the flow of weapons moving through Costa Rica to the Sandinista rebels or perhaps even to intervene. Permission was denied after a brief, heated debate in the Costa Rican congress. This lilttle-known incident illustrates that, at least in regional affairs, San Jose´ can assert a posture that differs from Washington's.

The Policy of the Reagan Administration

Initially, the Reagan administration paid little attention to Costa Rica. Its eyes were focused on El Salvador and Nicaragua, where the security threat was perceived to be more immediate. Quiet and stable, Costa Rica could take care of itself. Costa Rica, it was recognized, faced a serious economic crisis, but so did many developing countries. The IMF was the institution best equipped to assist countries with balance of payments problems. The administration decided to allow the IMF to take the lead in addressing Costa Rica's financial crisis, and a substantial portion of U.S. bilateral aid was withheld pending an agreement between Costa Rica and the IMF.

Congressional Democrats disagreed with administration priorities and argued that a higher percentage of U.S. economic aid ought to go to Costa Rica. This would demonstrate U.S. support for democracy in Central America. Also, by helping the country to address economic and social problems in their early stages, U.S. aid could help stabilize Costa Rica before an active insurgency developed: U.S. policy could be preventive rather than reactive. Some liberals went so far as to make their vote for aid to El Salvador contingent upon Costa Rica receiving a more substantial share of the aid being authorized for Central America.

By 1982 the administration's own perceptions changed regarding the role that Costa Rica could play in U.S. policy toward Central America. The administration discovered that democratic processes could be stabilizing, even conservative elements. During the 1980 presidential campaign Jeane Kirkpatrick and other Reaganites had argued that Central America's cultural traditions and economic backwardness made authoritarianism virtually inevitable. The U.S. effort to transform ''moderate authoritarian regimes'' into democracies was a naive and even dangerous exercise, they believed. As the Nicaraguan experience had shown, radical elements could take advantage of a power vacuum created by idealist U.S. policies. But, upon close examination of the realities in El Salvador, Honduras, and Nicaragua, the administration concluded that elections could play a useful role in an antileftist strategy. Elections tended to demobilize a population and shift the advantage away from leftist militants and toward more conservative parties or candidates. If the Left refused to participate in elections, it could be accused of being afraid of defeat at the polls; and even if the Left were excluded from elections legally or de facto the administration could argue that the elections, if not perfect, were an important step on the road to building democracy. Democracy, or elections, became a centerpiece of administration rhetoric. The logic of this policy shift required that more favorable attention be paid to Costa Rica.

The administration also found that it was much easier to legitimize a policy of fostering democracy than one of propping up authoritarian regimes. Americans might be willing to tolerate a "lesser of two evils" argument providing that the regime in question stayed off the network news. But when the glare of the media repeatedly focused on the regime's systematic violation of human rights, many Americans tended to dissent. Thus the administration placed great emphasis on the March 1982 elections in El Salvador as proof of that country's progress toward democracy and human rights. The administration recognized that closer collaboration with Costa Rica would buttress its claim that its main objective in Central America was to foster democracy.

Closer association with Costa Rica was facilitated by the election of Alberto Monge as president in May 1982. Monge was willing to work closely with the Reagan administration in Central America, repeating the administration's rhetoric about "international communist conspiracies" having placed Central America in their sights, and serving as frontman and conduit for U.S. policy initiatives. Monge probably acted out of mixed motives. He seemed genuinely alarmed at the antidemocratic instincts of many leading Sandinistas, and he feared that the appeal of the Costa Rican Communist party and other leftist groups might grow as a result of the economic crisis. Monge also apparently felt that the United States would only provide substantial economic assistance if he adhered closely to the administration's policies. Assistant Secretary of State Thomas Enders had reportedly spoken bluntly to Monge, conditioning U.S. bilateral economic aid and U.S. advocacy in the multilateral financial agencies on his support for U.S. iniatives.

Monge spoke out strongly against the Sandinista government and was willing to identify Costa Rica with the Salvadoran regime. In October 1982 Costa Rica hosted a "forum for peace and democracy" that included the governments of El Salvador and Honduras as well as Belize, Colombia, Jamaica, Panama, and the United States, but that excluded Nicaragua. The Costa Ricans reportedly acted at the behest of Washington; the Mexican and Venezuelan governments had just issued a call for a negotiated solution to the Salvadoran civil war and for talks between Nicaragua and its neighbors, and the "forum" provided an alternative posture more in line with Washington's. The Costa Rican government denied that the initiative for the "forum" had come from Washington, but the "Final Act of San José" declaration endorsed several existing U.S. proposals and was signed by the United States. The Costa Ricans are also reportedly working closely with U.S. intelligence agencies in collecting information on leftists—Costa Ricans and others—living or traveling in Costa Rica.

During 1982 President Monge visited Washington twice in search of economic aid. He was undoubtedly pleased when President Reagan decided to visit San José in December 1982 as part of his five-day swing through Central and South America. But the Costa Ricans reportedly balked when the White House suggested that the presidents of El Salvador, Honduras, and Guatemala convene in San José to meet with the American president. Costa Rican identification with the El Salvadoran government had already generated substantial criticism in Costa Rica, and the Guatemalan regime was considered even more unsavory. The Monge government evidently felt that its own image would be too severely jeopardized—that acceding to the U.S. request would make it appear that Costa Rican foreign policy was unprincipled and dictated by Washington. Monge demonstrated that, when pushed to an extreme, he was capable of denying Washington. The Reagan administration backed off, and a meeting was arranged instead with Guatemalan president Ríos Montt during Reagan's brief stop in Honduras.

Costa Rican foreign policy came under further strain in 1983 when Colombia and Panama withdrew from the "forum" in favor of the Mexican-Venezuelan approach to form the "Contadora Group." Concerned sectors within the ruling National Liberation party began to criticize Monge for allying Costa Rica too closely to the Reagan administration and for isolating his country from important regional powers and from their fellow social democrats in Western Europe. Monge showed some signs of discomfort at this censure and publically admitted that the U.S. presence at the San José "forum" meeting had been a mistake. He sought to associate Costa Rica with the Contadora Group's efforts to negotiate peaceful solutions to the region's conflicts. The Reagan administration's policies in Central America were placing Monge in a tough position: he wanted to maintain close relations, but Washington's policies were under increasing attack in the region and among important sectors within his own party.

THE RISKS OF THE REAGAN APPROACH

Reagan administration policy toward Costa Rica is derivative of a broader regional strategy. It is a policy that aims to draw a sharp dichotomy between democratic—or at least "moderate," pro-U.S.—governments and revolutionary regimes, and to build a regionwide alliance of the former against the latter. Just as the administration hopes that "moderate" forces will defeat the Left in El Salvador, so it is attempting to force an alliance that includes Costa Rica and Honduras in its attempt to isolate and eventually unseat the Sandinistas.

Administration policy is based on the assumption that the best way to defend U.S. security interests—and perhaps democratic governments and parties in Central America—is to confront and defeat revolutionary forces. The administration might argue that the Sandinistas, by their example if not their actions, pose a threat to Costa Rican political institutions. Therefore, a U.S. policy that aims to eliminate the Sandinistas and other leftists is also in the best interests of Costa Rican democracy. From this perspective, security assistance to Costa Rica and alliances like the "forum for peace and democracy" are essentially defensive instruments meant to protect democrats against leftist aggression.

This strategy rests on the questionable assumption that a modus vivendi between Costa Rica and a Sandinista Nicaragua is impossible; it seems to assume that Central American regimes can only be at peace with each other if they are politically homogeneous. Furthermore, administration strategy is highly risky. If the policy of confrontation with the Sandinistas and other leftists fails to triumph quickly—a probable outcome—tensions throughout Central America will continue to rise. Mutual suspicions between nations will increase, and the danger of border clashes will become greater. Tensions are also likely to escalate within nations as contending groups abandon compromise for conflict.

Costa Rica will not be immune to the contagion. As Nicaraguan exiles continue to harass the Sandinistas from Costa Rican territory, the danger of border skimishes escalates. An atmosphere of heightened tension and political violence in the region will foster nervousness and perhaps even polarization and militarization within Costa Rica. Certainly a Central America in turmoil will delay economic recovery in Costa Rica, as foreign and domestic investors postpone decisions until uncertainty subsides. These trends are already visible, if still incipient, in Costa Rica.

An Alternative Strategy

A shift in U.S. diplomatic strategy toward Costa Rica requires a rethinking of our approach to the entire region. Similarly, U.S. economic policy toward Costa Rica is derivative of our global economic policies.

Several other countries—France, Spain, Mexico, Venezuela, and Columbia—as well as the Socialist International (a grouping of social democratic parties) and important sectors of the Catholic church have been urging the United States to alter its tactics in Central America. In El Salvador, rather

113

than attempting to defeat the revolutionaries militarily, the United States should participate in a multilateral mediation effort. The objective would be to seek a compromise political solution to the civil war. The United States is also being told that a policy of dialogue and diplomatic correctness is more likely to moderate the Sandinistas than is the current approach of diplomatic and economic isolation and paramilitary warfare. The result of these alternative policies might be regimes somewhat more to the left in their domestic policies than the Reagan administration would prefer. But the continuing influence of these various European and Latin American governments and non-governmental actors in the region, and the overwhelming economic presence of the United States and other Western countries, should provide the means for a diplomacy that safeguards vital U.S. interests. Governments in the region could be expected to at least follow foreign policies of genuine nonalignment, to avoid rhetoric persistently hostile toward the United States, and to continue to be integrated into the global economy.

Adopting these tactics and objectives would alter U.S. policy toward Costa Rica. Rather than trying to embroil Costa Rica in a policy of confrontation with neighboring Nicaragua, the United States could favor diplomatic solutions to the border problems. The United States, perhaps through the OAS, might support an agreement between Costa Rica and Nicaragua to maintain joint border patrols to prevent the illegal flow of arms and people. Neither country would give asylum, training, or other assistance to individuals actively seeking to overthrow the neighboring regime. And, more positively, Costa Rica could serve as a bridge between the United States and other governments and political groupings in the region. In Nicaragua and El Salvador, Costa Ricans should be able at least to assume the role of interpreter between the United States and the political forces at play. Costa Ricans could also help to mediate differences between political factions within countries and help to reduce tensions between nations; an agreement on border patrols between Nicaragua and Costa Rica could serve as a model for a similar agreement between Nicaragua and Honduras.

The return to a more centrist role in regional politics is more likely to stabilize Costa Rican political institutions. If these and other efforts have some success and regional strife is diminished, Costa Rican economic recovery will be facilitated.

Economic Recovery

The Reagan administration has been providing substantial bilateral assistance to Costa Rica, including a record $169 million in fiscal year 1983. But bilateral aid alone cannot compensate for the adverse international environment. Changes in U.S. international economic policy are necessary if the

Costa Rican economy is to recover. Most importantly, the economy of the United States and of other industrial countries must reflate if smaller, developing economies are to prosper. Furthermore, less stringent monetary policies are imperative if market interest rates are to fall, thereby reducing the burden of debt service that threatens to choke off recovery in many developing nations.

The trade preferences that are part of the Caribbean Basin Initiative are unlikely to affect Central America until some measure of political stability is achieved. Investors potentially interested in exporting to the U.S. market are deterred by existing political uncertainty. But in the long run, easier access to the U.S. market could help Costa Rica increase exports in some nontraditional products. Costa Rican exports would probably benefit even more from the recovery of the economies of its neighbors and of the Central American Common Market.

Other reforms in the international economy could benefit Costa Rica. An enlargement of IMF quotas and of the IMF's Compensatory Financing Facility (which provides credits to offset sudden declines in export revenues) are clearly relevant. New regulatory policies that converted the existing "boom and bust" mentality of international bank lending toward a system of steadier, more reliable flows could also help Costa Rica in the future. But to correct for the damage done during the lending spree of the late 1970s and early 1980s, new techniques for debt rescheduling will be required.

In neither the economic nor the political sphere can the United States guarantee the prosperity of Costa Rica. The reform of Costa Rica's political institutions and the restructuring of its economy will require the best efforts of the Costa Ricans themselves. But the United States can help provide the healthy international economy and the secure regional environment that make these tasks easier.

8. Nicaragua: The United States Confronts a Revolution

Lars Schoultz

Nearly half a century ago, U.S. policymakers found a man who could provide stability in turbulent Nicaragua. They installed Anastasio Somoza Garcia as the commanding general of the national guard and then withdrew their marines. Over the course of the ensuing decades, stability in Nicaragua grew out of the barrel of a gun, the majority of Nicaraguans lived in conditions of extreme deprivation, and the Somoza family amassed one of the hemisphere's largest private fortunes. The quintessential banana republic, Nicaragua sat quietly in the backwater of the twentieth century.

When the Somoza dynasty collapsed in 1979, so too did the power of the United States in Nicaragua. Unfortunately, this country bet very heavily on the losing side of a major social revolution. Long the preeminent foreign actor in Nicaragua, the United States watched as all the old, comfortable relationships were destroyed.

Standing in the rubble, President Carter attempted to build a new, more mature relationship with the leaders of revolutionary Nicaragua. Given the difficulty of this task, the Carter administration was remarkably successful in the brief time allotted by the electorate. In stark contrast, during the Reagan administration relations with Nicaragua have deteriorated to the point of open hostility, with the United States conducting a much-publicized "secret war" that threatens to inflame the entire region.

Overview

Many Nicaraguans dislike and distrust the United States. The origin of these attitudes lies not in ideological conflict but rather deeply in the history of U.S.-Nicaraguan relations. With the possible exception of Cuba, Nicaragua

116

has received more attention from the United States than any other Latin American country. The first major U.S. interest in Nicaragua developed shortly after the discovery of gold in California, when Commodore Vanderbilt established the Accessory Transit Company to transport gold seekers across Central America. This commerce served to destabilize the already fragile domestic political system in favor of Nicaraguan conservatives, whose capital of Granada became a major transportation hub on the western shore of Lake Nicaragua.

To counter the growing strength of the conservatives, in 1855 liberal leaders invited an American filibusterer, William Walker, to champion their cause. An adventuresome man with an expansive view of Manifest Destiny, Walker led a band of fifty-eight adventurers who were able to turn the political tide in favor of the liberals. Confounding liberal expectations, however, Walker named himself president of Nicaragua in 1856. He ruled uneasily for a year, until Vanderbilt, Nicaragua's conservatives, and the Costa Rican army forced him to surrender to the U.S. Navy, under whose protection he returned to the United States. After two further invasions of Central America, Latin America's only Yankee president was finally captured and shot by the less tolerant Hondurans.

Walker's arrival in Central America coincided with the awakening of significant U.S. government interest in Nicaragua, particularly among southerners who were seeking to add slave states to the Union. Prior to the U.S. Civil War, U.S. armed forces invaded Nicaragua four times (in 1853, 1854, and twice in 1857); each occupation was brief, but each probably influenced Nicaraguans' attitudes toward this country. One can imagine the feelings of the citizens of San Juan del Norte, for example, when in 1854 their city was destroyed by the U.S. Navy to avenge an insult to the American minister there.

During and after the U.S. Civil War, the United States turned inward, but by the 1890s U.S. policymakers were expressing a renewed interest in the countries of the Caribbean Basin. In 1909 the United States played a major role in ousting Nicaraguan President José Santos Zelaya when U.S. Secretary of State Philander C. Knox referred to him as "a blot on the history of his country" and expelled the Nicaraguan ambassador from the United States. The United States then reinforced its military presence in Bluefields, shielding and supplying the antigovernment rebels until they had gained sufficient strength to capture Managua in mid-1910.

The nearly continuous U.S. military presence in Nicaragua from 1912 to 1933 was highlighted by the marines' unsuccessful campaign to capture Nicaragua's principal national hero, Augusto César Sandino, and their creation of the Nicaraguan national guard. At the same time, U.S. financial advisors directed the nation's fiscal and monetary policy (including the creation of the *córdoba* as the national currency) and in general subordinated the Nicaraguan economy to U.S. and European creditors. This tutelage is unparalleled in the history of U.S.–Latin American relations. As a vassal state, Nicaragua was unable to develop any type of independent political leadership or stable political institutions. Thus, when the U.S. government ended its occupation in 1933, there was no consensus among Nicaraguans on the norms of political behavior. There were no broadly accepted procedures for determining political legitimacy. There was only the national guard. Its power rested on coercion rather than consent.

From 1936 until his assassination in 1956, General Somoza provided the coerced stability that has almost always substituted for popular legitimacy in Nicaragua. He did so, first, by creating large colonies of Nicaraguan exiles in Mexico and the United States, and then by co-opting the remaining opposition leaders. His sons, Luis and Anastasio Somoza Debayle, prolonged the family dynasty for an extraordinary forty-three years, a period punctuated only by the brief tenure of two family retainers in the mid-1960s and an unusual triumvirate in the early 1970s whose principal task was to rewrite the constitution to permit the indefinite tenure of Anastasio Somoza Debayle. During these decades the Somoza family developed a well-documented reputation for avarice and brutality.

Among U.S. policymakers, however, the Somozas were respected for their ability to produce political and economic stability and for their unwavering support of U.S. foreign policy. In return for their support, the Somozas received a broad spectrum of aid from this country. Much of the economic aid ($280 million from 1946 through 1978) was used to enlarge the Somoza family fortune. All of the military aid ($37 million from 1950 through 1978) was designed to increase the coercive capabilities of the national guard, which Somoza personally commanded until mid-1979. Military schooling through the International Military Education and Training (IMET) program was an especially prominent aspect of U.S.–Nicaraguan relations during the Somoza era. Anastasio Somoza Debayle was a graduate of the U.S. Military Academy at West Point.

Given this history of U.S. intervention and support for despotism, it would have been difficult under the very best of circumstances for the United States to establish a satisfactory relationship with the Nicaraguans who toppled the Somoza regime in 1979. Instability was inevitable, for Nicaraguans needed time to create stable political institutions to replace authoritarian rule. Displays of animosity were also inevitable, as Nicaraguans released decades of accumulated hostility toward the United States.

During the Carter administration, U.S. policy toward the new Nicaraguan government was characterized by considerable patience and understanding. President Carter invited Sandinista leaders to meet with him at the White House to underscore his desire to create a constructive relationship. Immediately after Somoza's fall, the U.S. government sent $8 million in emergency relief supplies to Managua and encouraged U.S.-based private voluntary organizations to increase their activities in Nicaragua. The administration also obtained from Congress a 75-million-dollar emergency aid authorization. In the process of convincing reluctant legislators to provide this aid, however, Carter administration policymakers repeatedly used as their central argument the need to contain communism. The day before final congressional approval of the aid package, for example, a White House spokesperson asserted that "the Administration does not intend to abandon the vital Central America region to Cuba and its radical Marxist allies." This argument may have had the positive result of scaring Congress into providing foreign assistance, but it also had the negative consequence of placing policy debates over Nicaragua in a cold war context.

But perhaps that was inevitable, for in 1980 the Republican party platform formally deplored "the Marxist Sandinista takeover of Nicaragua." Since the inauguration of President Reagan, U.S. policy debates have focused on how best to keep the Sandinista leadership, which the administration has insistently characterized as Marxist, from consolidating political power.

The Present Issues

The Reagan administration has repeatedly argued that three issues prevent the development of cordial relations with the Nicaraguan government: the intervention of El Salvador, the militarization of Nicaraguan society, and the destruction of pluralism.

INTERVENTION

On 23 February 1981 the administration published a white paper entitled "Communist Interference in El Salvador," the first page of which contained a map with seven arrows, each indicating a flow of arms from Nicaragua to El Salvador. The administration also provided a set of documents to substantiate the allegations contained in the white paper. Independent investigative reports published in the *Los Angeles Times,* the *Wall Street Journal,* and the *Washington Post* demolished the credibility of the white paper and its documentation. The detailed reports attacked the paper for false and misleading translation, unwarranted insinuations, and unsubstantiated conclusions. The white paper quickly became an embarrassment to career foreign service officers, whose profession was degraded by its publication. Yet aside from the incongruous testimony of the State Department's "Cuban-trained Nicaraguan guerrilla," Orlando José Tardencillas Espinosa, the white paper stands as the only public source to substantiate charges of Nicaraguan interventionism.

If intervention is one of the three basic issues creating the contemporary crisis in U.S.–Nicaraguan relations, and if the United States fears that Nicaragua's actions are, in the words of Secretary of State Alexander Haig, "a prelude to a widening war in Central America,'' then the administration should be eager to present evidence to buttress its case and thereby muster public support. That the administration has not presented this documentation for the scrutiny of the press and congressional investigators suggests that there is no substantial evidence. Operating in a rudimentary society, the Nicaraguan government could never supply more than minimal support for the Salvadoran guerrillas without being detected by the same organizations that assured Congress, not long ago, that they could verify Soviet compliance with SALT II. Certainly the Nicaraguan government is emotionally and ideologically sympathetic to the opposition movement in El Salvador, and it has probably provided the guerrillas with varying amounts of logistical support. But there is little or no evidence to support the allegation of significant Nicaraguan intervention in El Salvador.

Nonetheless, the administration doggedly employs the issue of intervention to justify its policy of hostility toward Nicaragua. To some extent it does so less out of firm commitment than expediency: Nicaraguan intervention is an absolutely crucial component of the administration's integrated explanation for the problems elsewhere in Central America, particularly in El Salvador and Guatemala. The position of the Reagan administration is that turmoil in both of these countries is primarily a result of Cuban adventurism. Yet it is universally agreed that Cuba could not possibly provide support sufficient to fuel one major civil war and another quickly kindling conflagration without logistical assistance somewhere in Central America. If the administration were to admit that its allegations of significant Nicaraguan intervention were not supported by firm evidence, then it would call into question its already tenuous arguments regarding the nature and extent of Cuban involvement in El Salvador and Guatemala. That would lead inexorably to a total recasting of U.S. policy toward Central America, something the Reagan administration is clearly unprepared to consider.

MILITARIZATION

Since mid-1979 there has been a pronounced growth in the size and sophistication of the Nicaraguan armed forces. About twenty thousand Nicaraguans are currently on active military duty, more than double the number of personnel under the Somoza government. In addition to increasing its military personnel, the Nicaraguan government has enlarged and upgraded its military hardware. Press reports indicate that Nicaragua has received several Soviet T55 tanks, has sent perhaps eighty Nicaraguan pilots to Eastern Europe for training, has lengthened and hardened several airport runways, has enlisted the assistance of between fifteen hundred and two thousand Cuban military advisors, and has reached an agreement with France to purchase a variety of arms (including seven thousand air-to-ground rockets, two used helicopters, forty-five trucks, and two coastal patrol boats) valued at $15.8 million. The result is that the Nicaraguan armed forces are now substantially stronger than they were prior to 1979.

How much stronger? Here the data are less clear. While the Reagan administration asserts that Nicaragua's goal is a fifty-thousand-member army and a two-hundred-thousand-member civilian militia, evidence to support this assertion has not been made public. In September 1982 a Nicaraguan military spokesman said that Nicaragua had twenty-five thousand reservists and eighty thousand militia members. These reservists receive three months of active duty military training, but the militia consists merely of civil defense groups that have almost no formal military skills. While it is fairly certain that a significant number of Cuban military advisors were in Nicaragua in early 1982, junta leader Daniel Ortega asserted that fewer than one hundred remained there by August, a figure confirmed by *New York Times* reporter Raymond Bonner.

In mid-1982 a retired U.S. Marine lieutenant colonel, John H. Buchanan, spent a week with the Nicaraguan military under the sponsorship of the Washington-based Center for Development Policy. A veteran of 265 combat missions in Vietnam, Buchanan reported that he was "not very impressed" with the capabilities of the Nicaraguan armed forces. Its Soviet-built T-55 tanks were "nice for prestige," for example, but were unsuitable for Nicaragua's tropical terrain. Despite widespread comments to the contrary, the Nicaraguan air force remained extraordinarily rudimentary as of late 1982: three helicopters and three aged training jets, plus a few old military transports. Nicaraguan officials were quick to indicate that their force compared unfavorably with the U.S.-supplied Honduran air force of about twenty helicopters and at least eighteen modern jets.

In sum, while no data contradict the fact that Nicaragua's military strength now exceeds its might during the Somoza era, neither do the data confirm the Reagan administration's fears of the militarization of Nicaragua.

Given that a modest military buildup has occurred, the most important question is why. According to the Nicaraguan government, increased arms expenditures are necessary for self-defense. From the perspective of Defense Minister Humberto Ortega, "There is a real military danger, and it is our duty and our right to arm our people to defend our nation and our revolution." By whom might the Nicaraguans feel threatened?

First there are the Somocistas—Nicaraguans who work to recreate a society similar to that of the Somoza era—living in exile in Honduras, Guatemala, and the United States. In *Parade Magazine,* the *New York Times,* and ABC News' "Good Morning America," these exiles have been shown receiving military training from Cuban expatriates in southern Florida and California. The Honduras-based National Liberation Army is engaged in open armed conflict with the Nicaraguan government.

Second, there are the military-dominated governments of Guatemala, El Salvador, and Honduras, all of which have expressed profound hostility toward the Nicaraguan government.

Third, and most important by far, there is the United States. The country that has invaded Nicaragua no fewer than fourteen times (1853, 1854, twice in 1857, 1867, 1894, 1896, 1898, twice in 1899, twice in 1910, 1912, and 1926) is now led by an administration that repeatedly issues extraordinarily provocative statements regarding its current intentions. Appearing before the Senate Foreign Relations Committee in March 1981, Secretary of State Haig described Nicaragua as already "lost," then added: "We are clearly going to have to do something in the very near future." In a direct reference to Nicaragua at the December 1981 general assembly of the Organization of American States, Haig asserted that "the U.S. is prepared to join others in doing whatever is prudent and necessary to prevent any country from becoming the platform of terror and war in the region." Since the OAS meeting, the Reagan administration has increasingly emphasized unilateral initiatives to destabilize the Nicaraguan government. "All the countries in the Caribbean are confronted by a growing threat from Cuba and its new-found ally Nicaragua," Secretary Haig told the Senate Foreign Relations Committee in early February 1982. "We will do whatever is necessary to contain the threat."

Looking first at history and then at statements such as these made by U.S. policymakers, any rational Nicaraguan would begin to fear an armed intervention of some sort. By late 1982 it was evident that the intervention involved all three of the mentioned forces in a U.S.-directed covert war waged from bases in Honduran territory. A *Newsweek* cover story in September provided extraordinary details of an integrated program to wage a "secret war" against Nicaragua. Information in the *Newsweek* report was officially denied by the Reagan administration, but a senior member of the National Security Council staff confirmed its accuracy when he explained to a *New York Times* reporter that the goal of the U.S.-directed military activity was to harass but not to overthrow the Sandinista government. According to the NSC official, the clandestine operations were limited to hit-and-run raids along the Honduran-Nicaraguan border and were designed "to keep Managua off balance and apply pressure to stop providing military aid to the insurgents in El Salvador." The Reagan administration's deliberate attempt to creat this fear has seriously misjudged the Nicaraguans' response. What the administration has overlooked is the demonstrated fact that the Nicaraguan government is composed of men and women who participated in long years of bitter armed struggle. The Nicaraguans don't scare; they fight back. Rather than capitulate to U.S. pressures, Nicaragua has prepared to defend itself against a U.S. or U.S.-sponsored invasion. In the United States, the administration refers to Nicaragua's preparation as the "militarization" of that country. To more moderate observers, the preparation reflects a rational policy designed to meet the gravest possible threat to national security: an armed invasion.

PLURALISM

Repression of Dissent

The Reagan administration alleges that the Sandinista-dominated government is engaged in the systematic repression of dissent and that this repression will lead eventually to a totalitarian state. This is an extremely serious charge, and it deserves careful analysis.

Some repression of dissent unquestionably exists in contemporary Nicaragua. The July 1979 Law for the Maintenance of Public Order and Security makes it an offense punishable by imprisonment for ten days to two years to make statements intended to undermine national security, the economy, public order, health, morals, the judiciary, and "the dignity of persons, the reputations and rights of others." The definitions of crimes in this law are imprecise and consequently are open to arbitrary interpretation.

In addition to the public order law, on 9 September 1981 the government decreed a year-long state of economic and social emergency that contains, inter alia, prohibitions on strikes and the dissemination of false economic information. In its 1981 annual report, the Inter-American Commission on Human Rights criticized the decree for its "vagueness, imprecision, and excessive generalization of certain behavior." It is believed that the only charges brought under this decree occurred in October 1981, when three leaders of the principal business organization (COSEP) and four leaders of the Communist party trade union organization (CAUS) were arrested, tried, and sentenced to short prison terms for publishing statements critical of the government's economic policies and, in the case of COSEP, for accusing the government of "preparing a new genocide." The CAUS statement also called for strikes and occupations of factories.

On 15 March 1982 the government declared a state of emergency that temporarily suspended a broad variety of constitutional guarantees and provided for prior press censorship. The premier case of press censorship involves *La Prensa*, the strongly antigovernment newspaper that has been temporarily closed (depending upon how one counts several voluntary protest closings) about ten times. The Trotskyite newspaper *El Pueblo* was permanently closed by the government in early 1980, and the progovernment newspaper, *El Nuevo Diario*, has been closed briefly for referring to the March 1982 declaration of a "state of emergency" as a more drastic "state of siege." The government's own *Voz de Nicaragua* has been forced off the air temporarily for showing disrespect to Archbishop Obando y Bravo, an opposition party's *Radio Corporación* has been sanctioned for criticizing government officials, and the news program of *Radio Católica* has been suspended for broadcasting a biography of a person accused of violent activities against the government. The government has been unable to reach an accord with the archbishop on who should say Sunday mass on the government-owned TV channel, and

123

Radio Amor and *Radio Mi Preferida* have been denied license renewals, ostensibly because their antennas violate zoning laws.

Opposition political parties have experienced considerable difficulty in operating openly. In May 1982 Americas Watch reported that efforts to hold public rallies "have met with refusals by local authorities to issue required permits, government roadblocks (or vehicle checks) and mob action against either the rally or, in at least one case, the party leaders and their homes." But Americas Watch concluded that "there can be no doubt that there is more freedom for political parties in Nicaragua today than under the rule of Anastasio Somoza."

While the threat of repression is clearly present in contemporary Nicaragua, opposition groups nonetheless continue to function openly and vigorously, *La Prensa* conducts truly vehement campaigns against government policies, and opposition elements in the Church and the private sector function openly in a wide range of activities. In short, the accumulated data indicate a situation that is unclear. Thus an overall assessment of the current condition of free expression depends in large measure upon the standards one chooses to employ. Judged by the best standards of North Atlantic constitutional systems, there is repression of the right to free expression in Nicaragua; judged by the standards of a political culture in which respect for free expression has never existed, the current government is probably the least repressive in Nicaraguan history.

Physical Integrity of the Person

On the other hand, there is nearly unanimous agreement that the Nicaraguan government has effectively eliminated threats to the physical integrity of the person. The lone dissenter in this judgment is the Reagan administration, which in its *Country Reports on Human Rights Practices for 1981* issued a carefully worded statement that uses language clearly meant to insinuate that the Nicaraguan government engages in torture. This stands in stark contrast to the 1980 report of the International Commission of Jurists, *Human Rights in Nicaragua, Yesterday and Today,* which stated unequivocally that "torture and ill-treatment as a matter of policy or of systematic practice have been banished from Nicaragua." The 1981 *Amnesty International Report* asserted that AI "has received no convincing accounts alleging systematic ill-treatment or torture of prisoners under the present government." A similar conclusion is found in the 1982 report of Americas Watch, *On Human Rights in Nicaragua,* on page 13 which states:

> We found widespread agreement, even among the Government's strongest critics, that physical torture is *not* practiced in Nicaragua today. . . . The physical treatment of prisoners is not ideal and is, in some respect, unsatisfactory. Nevertheless, we were advised by virtually all persons with

whom we met that, to the best of their knowledge, those forms of torture routinely practiced in some Latin American countries—severe beatings, electric shock, intentional near drowning, and the like—have been effectively eliminated by the Nicaraguan Government. Not one person with whom we spoke reported having been tortured, and those of our sources who observed the operations of Nicaragua's police, security, and prison services told us that torture simply is not practiced or sanctioned by the Government.

The Nicaraguan government's treatment of prisoners has also received widespread attention. In June 1981 the OAS Inter-American Commission on Human Rights issued a *Report on the Human Rights Situation in Nicaragua* which was based upon an on-site investigation made in October 1980. The report is both laudatory and critical; it praises the government for abolishing the death penalty and for establishing thirty years as the maximum prison sentence but criticizes "deplorable" conditions in many prisons and cites the need for better access to appellate processes. The commission also noted improvements: "The penitentiaries, that were always rudimentary, and deteriorated before the fall of Somoza . . . have improved within the economic limitations that face Nicaragua."

The Judiciary

A special concern of virtually all human rights organizations has been the sentences handed down by the nine special tribunals and three special appellate courts that functioned between December 1979 and February 1981 with jurisdiction over crimes allegedly committed by employees of the Somoza government. The tribunals, using procedures that violated a host of established legal procedures, convicted 4,250 defendants. In September 1980 the International Commission of Jurists prepared an untitled private report for the Nicaraguan government recommending improvements in the treatment and processing of national guard prisoners. In June 1982 Amnesty International called upon the government to review the criminal convictions of the 3,174 individuals who remained confined by order of the special tribunals. The government has taken steps to review the sentences imposed by the tribunals. A clemency law adopted in October 1981 provides for an administrative review of each prisoner's case by the government's National Commission for the Promotion and Protection of Human Rights, which has the power to recommend to the Council of State either pardon or commutation of a prisoner's sentence. Americas Watch reported in May 1982 that twenty-one hundred requests for review were awaiting processing.

Since the end of the immediate postrevolutionary period, some accusations of arbitrary justice have been made, but they are few and relate primarily to charges of armed insurrection. In October 1980 thirteen Nicaraguans were convicted of organizing an armed opposition group and planning the assassination of government leaders. They received prison sentences of seven years. In December 1980 eight Nicaraguan businessmen were similarly convicted of conspiring to form an armed group to overthrow the government; they were sentenced to one to nine years imprisonment. In both cases serious questions were raised about the impartiality of judicial procedures.

Civil and Political Liberties

To many observers the most egregious black mark against the Nicaraguan revolution is its failure to provide dissenters with adequate civil and political liberties, including free expression through competitive elections. Retracting earlier statements, the Nicaraguan government announced in mid-1980 that elections would be delayed until 1985.

Two reasons have been identified to explain this policy reversal. First is the siege mentality fostered by opposition groups and the U.S. government. On 10 March 1982 the *Washington Post* reported that President Reagan had authorized the CIA to engage in covert activities aimed at overthrowing the Nicaraguan government. Citing unnamed but high-ranking administration officials, the *Post* story indicated that $19 million had been allocated to build a five-hundred-member paramilitary force to conduct guerrilla warfare from bases in Honduras.

The following day the *Post* editors, certainly no friends of the Sandinistas, published a lead editorial that began with a cautionary remark: "Things are getting out of hand with respect to Nicaragua." After arguing that the United States probably does not intend to invade Nicaragua, the editorial advanced the idea that "the purpose of the CIA's anti-Nicaragua operations is merely to give the Sandinistas second thoughts about their help in Salvador, not to overthrow the regime. But," the *Post* concluded, "you have to be pretty forgetful, or pretty dumb, to buy that argument." Representative Michael Barnes, chairman of the House Foreign Affairs Subcommittee on Inter-American Affairs, commented that the administration's plan, if the *Post*'s claims were true, amounts to "a virtual declaration of war." Six months later *Newsweek* demonstrated conclusively that the CIA's "secret war" was in progress. What Latin American country could prepare for elections while the United States is preparing an invasion force?

An example of how this threatening behavior by the United States has created a climate of extreme insecurity can be found in the conflict between the central government in Managua and the Indian population of the isolated Atlantic Coast. The Reagan administration has used this conflict to excoriate the Nicaraguan government. U.N. ambassador Jeane Kirkpatrick has labeled the government's policy a "campaign of systematic violence" that places Nicaragua "in first place as a human rights violator." At the urging of the

State Department's Bureau of Inter-American Affairs, Senator Robert Kasten's Appropriations Subcommittee on Foreign Operations provided an expatriate Miskito leader, Steadman Fagoth Mueller, with a forum to accuse the Nicaraguan government of killing at least 253 Indians. Secretary of State Haig joined in the criticism by chiding the media for not publicizing a photograph from the conservative French magazine, *Le Figaro*, which he interpreted as evidence of "atrocious genocidal actions by the Sandinistas against the Miskitos." (Following challenges by the French media the editors of *Le Figaro* announced that the photograph in question has been miscaptioned: it had been taken four years earlier, after a skirmish between the Sandinistas and Somoza's national guard.)

As with most conflicts in contemporary Nicaragua, the issues raised by the Miskito Indians defy facile interpretation. The roots of the Miskito problem are buried deeply in Nicaraguan history; they reflect in particular a conscious policy of earlier governments to ignore the existence of Indian groups that populate the least desirable portion of Nicaraguan territory. The central government did not establish effective control over the area until the 1890s, and thereafter the government permitted religious organizations (primarily the Roman Catholic Capuchines and the Protestant Moravians) to provide nearly all social services. The first all-weather road connecting the Atlantic and Pacific coasts was not completed until 1982. Lack of contact with the "Spaniards" of the Pacific region had its advantages, however; it insulated the Indian population from the policies of the Somoza government.

Early efforts by the Sandinistas to integrate the Miskitos and other Indian cultures into the broader Nicaraguan nation were met with a considerable measure of resistance, which culminated in a bloody incident in the village of Prinzapolka in February 1981. This led to the brief arrest of the entire Indian leadership; nearly all of the leaders left Nicaragua following their release.

By late 1981 these historic sociocultural cleavages were broadened immeasurably by geopolitical concerns: anti-Sandinista groups armed and encouraged by the U.S. government, and using the Honduran side of the border as a base, increased the frequency and intensity of their attacks on Nicaragua's Atlantic coast. On 14 December 1981 the government responded by declaring a state of emergency in the Rio Coco region of Zelaya and providing the Ministry of the Interior with legal authority to suspend normal constitutional guarantees. In January and February the government relocated approximately eighty-five hundred Miskitos in four (later five) new settlements about fifty miles to the south.

Two human rights organizations have conducted on-site investigations of this forced relocation. The Americas Watch report of its March 1982 investigation condemns the human agony that the displacement clearly caused, but the report also states that the relocation was not accompanied by the gross violations alleged by Secretary Haig and Ambassador Kirkpatrick: "In our interviews with Miskito men and women who walked the entire way, we heard no allegations of harsh treatment by soldiers during the march, although there were many complaints about the difficulty of the walk through rugged and often muddy terrain.''

In May 1982 the OAS Inter-American Commission on Human Rights also conducted an on-site investigation of the Miskito problem. Upon their return to Washington, the investigators produced a report that, in accordance with standard procedures, was presented privately to the Nicaraguan government. The government, in turn, sent the director of Nicaragua's human rights commission to Washington in late August to negotiate the concrete actions necessary to ameliorate whatever unfavorable conditions the OAS documented in its still-secret report. If (as now seems likely) the government satisfies the commission's requirements, the report will not be made public.

No one can assert with confidence that the Miskito problem and similar conflicts would not have arisen without the aggressive behavior of the U.S. government. But it seems obvious that by its hostile rhetoric and behavior, the United States has encouraged the Nicaraguan government to react to each political challenge as if it were a challenge to the government's survival. In the context of such a struggle, honest and competitive elections simply are not possible.

The second explanation for the delay in holding elections is that Nicaragua needs time to create a genuinely democratic electoral system. There have never been impartial electoral institutions capable of mediating disputes in Nicaragua. The concept of honest, competitive elections is simply unknown in Nicaraguan history. Yet without such institutions, there is no possibility of creating a loyal opposition, for the opposition has no incentive to compete within the rules if the rules are manipulated, as they always have been, by the incumbent administration. In Nicaraguan history, the electoral process has been used only to confer an ersatz legitimacy upon the existing rulers, not to adjudicate political disputes. Thus if it is to have any chance of success, the opposition must be disloyal. And, expecting disloyalty, the government has always been repressive.

It is in this political culture that the Nicaraguans face the formidable task of creating a responsive democracy. Power is presently vested in charismatic leaders, just as it is at the end of any revolution, just as it was at the end of the American Revolution. The overarching task of these leaders is to transfer their power to a set of institutions capable of managing democratically the conflicts inherent in any society. The creation of these institutions is the most difficult political task imaginable. We should not expect it to be completed overnight. In the United States it took a minority of citizens (white males) more than a decade to settle on a workable set of rules, and even then so many citizens balked at the proposed rules that they had to be amended ten times (the Bill of

Rights) immediately upon acceptance. Under the very best of circumstances, it will take a long time to establish a responsive democracy in Nicaragua. Under the threatening conditions created by U.S. hostility, it will take much longer.

But how, precisely, is democracy to be constructed? In Nicaragua the process of creating a participatory society is intimately connected to the process of education. Prior to 1979 Nicaragua ranked last in Central America in nearly every indicator of educational achievement. Logically so, for ignorance facilitates despotism. The 1980 literacy campaign reduced illiteracy from about 50 percent to about 12 percent; in five months of intensive effort, hundreds of thousands of Nicaraguans learned to read and write—rudimentarily, to be sure, but nonetheless they are no longer illiterate. They can read a political party platform. Follow-up programs include no fewer than nineteen thousand popular education collectives to promote adult education, an impressive shift in government expenditures to ensure free and compulsory primary education, and special efforts to integrate the East Coast region. Each of these programs is designed to create informed Nicaraguans who understand the rights and responsibilities of citizenship.

The process of creating democracy is also connected to the process of convincing citizens that the political system can deliver goods and services to people who have historically viewed politics as an apparatus of repression. Health care has been a primary focus. Prior to 1979 the infant mortality rate in Nicaragua was 122 per thousand, the highest in Central America and exceeded in Latin America only by Haiti (130) and Bolivia (168). Life expectancy was fifty-five years, the lowest in Central America. The principal causes of death were all relatively easily preventable diseases that today kill large numbers of citizens only in countries with grossly inadequate public health services.

The current government's popular health campaigns have been designed to eliminate major public health hazards. In 1981 there was a nationwide polio immunization campaign and a malaria-dengue eradication campaign. In early 1982 the government conducted the final phase of its campaign to immunize children and adults against diphtheria, whooping cough, measles, and tetanus. These campaigns encourage mass mobilization: the malaria-dengue campaign, for example, involved fifteen thousand people who first were trained in local workshops and then fanned out into the countryside, destroying mosquito breeding grounds, spraying infested areas, and educating local citizens in further preventive measures.

To U.S. citizens, all this may seem to be an odd way to create democracy. But every political scientist knows that political participation (the prerequisite of democracy) is largely a function of education and self-interest. The Somozas knew this as well, and so they never provided for the education of the population, and they encouraged the belief that participation brings deprivations rather than rewards. The new Nicaraguan government has changed this

129

entire political mentality, but a fully functioning democratic system will not appear quickly. In Nicaragua the creation of democracy will involve patient statesmanship, just as it did in the United States.

While progress has been and will continue to be slow, progress is being made. On 21 October 1982 the Patriotic Front of the Revolution (FPR), a grouping of several political parties that supports the Sandinista government, issued a declaration calling for "formulation of a law governing elections and specifying the procedures to be followed," "the suspension of the Resolution regarding discussion and debate of the law with respect to political parties," and modification of the law "so that all parties be allowed to carry out internal activities." In a clear attempt to foster public political discussion, the FPR proposed "that the Sandinista Television System create a program to be called DEBATE, making available air time to all poltiical parties, labor unions, as well as social and scientific organizations, so that they may present their opinions, proposals and recommendations with respect to the important issues that the Revolution must address." It is too early to determine the government's reaction to this declaration, although it is perhaps significant that the Nicaraguan embassy distributed the declaration on embassy letterhead. At a minimum, the declaration demonstrates a consciousness on the part of revolutionary groups that pluralism is a desirable feature of Nicaraguan society.

In summary, a policy toward Nicaragua that is based upon allegations of interventionism, militarization, and the destruction of pluralism is both unrealistic and ineffective. These allegations are either exaggerated or simply unfounded, and they therefore cannot form the basis of a policy that promotes legitimate U.S. interests in the Central American region.

U.S. Interests in Nicaragua

An effective policy toward Nicaragua must begin with a clear statement of the three basic national interests the United States seeks to protect in contemporary Latin America:

> the physical and military security of the United States;
> fair access to opportunities for trade and investment; and
> the basic civil rights of U.S. citizens engaged in legal, legitimate activities.

The first of these is by far the most important.

The protection of U.S. physical and military security logically begins with a realistic appraisal of precisely what constitutes a threat to this country. During most of the postwar era, there has been very little cost to a facile policy that interprets instability in Latin America as an incipient turn toward communism and, ipso facto, as a threat to U.S. security. After events in Cuba the

United States believed that the danger in this hemisphere lay in delay—in failing to extinguish a fire before it became a major social inferno.

But now times have changed. Increasing global interdependence and the emergence of middle powers as major regional actors have resulted in a dramatic decline in superpower autonomy. As late as 1965 the United States could invade the Dominican Republic with impunity; today this country fully understands that the cost of a similar exercise would be incalculable.

But while the United States recognizes the limits on its power to control instability, it fails to accept the changes that have imposed the limits. It acts instead as if the limits are self-imposed and therefore amenable to self-removal. It seems to believe that the limits can be expanded once again—that it can halt instability in Latin America—by a unilateral exercise of national will. And it is in exercising these beliefs that the United States appears to be on the verge of making a simple fool of itself, running around the Caribbean throwing economic and military aid to any government that panders to the outdated notion of Latin America as nothing more than the U.S. half of the gridiron in an East-West Superbowl.

It is more realistic to recognize, instead, that there are many kinds of instability in Latin America, and that the United States must conserve its limited power for use in those cases where instability clearly becomes a threat to its basic security interests. Is Nicaragua such a case?

One threat from Nicaragua consists of the "Marxist" Sandinistas who dominate the Nicaraguan government. The term "Marxist" is placed in quotation marks because of its very uncertain meaning in contemporary Latin America. It may identify leaders who support a classical dictatorship of the proletariat and the elimination of private ownership of the means of production, but in today's Latin America the term "Marxist" often describes politicians who in Europe would be called "Socialists"—the evolutionary Socialists who currently play leading roles in politics in most of Western Europe. Some of this country's best friends are Socialists. It is one of the great tragedies of our time that the United States permits a reflex reaction to a pejorative label, "Marxist," to make enemies of so many leaders in Latin America before it examines their actual policies. As in the United States, in Latin America *it is invariably more illuminating to watch what politicians do rather than what they say they will do*. This is particularly true in contemporary Nicaragua, where a considerable measure of anti-American rhetoric is simply inevitable.

The more important threat to U.S. security is the external threat of Cuban and Soviet expansion. Here the United States must recognize, first, that in the eyes of many Latin Americans, Cuba is much more than a surrogate for the Soviet Union. The shortcomings of the Cuban Revolution are many, but so too are its achievements. These achievements are closely related to several initial goals of the Nicaraguan revolution. Cuba has created a truly remarkable social infrastructure, particularly in the areas of education and health care. Any Nicaraguan government interested in decreasing illiteracy would naturally adopt at least part of the Cuban approach, for the principal alternative of trickle-down education left 50 percent of the population illiterate. Similarly, Cuba has eliminated most of the public health hazards that Nicaraguans want to eliminate. If the Cuban model works in the area of public health, the Nicaraguans would be foolish to ignore that part of the model. Overall, Cuba's success in addressing a number of the most pressing problems of under-development makes that country a natural ally of similarly committed governments elsewhere in Latin America.

These alliances will naturally increase Cuban influence in Nicaragua, but that does not mean that Nicaragua is on the verge of being ''lost'' to communism and therefore is a threat to U.S. national security unless—and here is the historic opportunity this country is on the verge of handing the Soviet Union once again—unless the United States forces the issue as it did in Cuba two decades ago. In mid-1960 the Eisenhower administration convinced executives of Exxon, Shell, and Texaco not to refine Soviet crude oil in their Cuban refineries. The Cuban government thereupon expropriated the re-fineries and thereafter became totally dependent upon the Soviet Union for oil. In July 1960 the United States cut the Cuban sugar quota (the equivalent of foreign aid in the Nicaraguan case) from 779,000 tons to 40,000 tons for the second half of that year. Standing on the floor of the House of Representatives, Harris McDowell, Jr. (D-Del.), told his colleagues that when ''Cuba's splendid people understand that they must sell their sugar or their economy will be destroyed, they will themselves find a way to deal with the present misleaders and fomenters of hatred.'' Cuba then sold the sugar to the Soviet Union. In January 1961 the Eisenhower administration broke relations with Cuba, and the Kennedy administration then proceeded to pursue a campaign of aggression that climaxed three months later at the Bay of Pigs. The result of these actions? For two decades, Cuba has been perceived as a threat to U.S. national security.

There are startling parallels between U.S.-Cuban relations in the early 1960s and contemporary U.S. policy toward Nicaragua. History indicates that the surest way to make Nicaragua into a national security threat is to push the Sandinistas, as this country pushed Castro, into a corner. The virulently nationalistic Nicaraguans who risked their lives in an armed confrontation with the Somoza regime are not going to capitulate to U.S. pressures. Cut their aid and they will find aid elsewhere or do without; arm and encourage their Somocista rivals and then refuse to sell them arms and they will find arms elsewhere; destabilize their economy and they will reorient it to minimize destabilization; invade their territory and they will fight tooth and nail, in the process accepting as an ally any country that will help defend the Nicaraguan revolution. We have been down this road before, and we know it leads to a foreign policy disaster.

But if we accept the view of Nicaragua as something more than a cold war battleground, then we can begin to see Nicaragua as it should be seen: as a state, like other states, with interests to protect and goals to promote. The task of U.S. diplomats is to protect and pursue U.S. national interests whenever they conflict with those of Nicaragua. There will be many such conflicts: over the role of the United States in El Salvador and the role of Nicaragua in El Salvador, over Cuban activity in Nicaragua and Somocista/CIA activity in Honduras, over fair treatment of U.S. citizens and their property in Nicaragua, over the ownership of off-shore islands, over trade preferences that provide access to U.S. markets, over issues of international relations that arise in the United Nations and the Organization of American States—over the myriad issues that continuously appear in a complex, interdependent world.

Resolution of these conflicts requires not a simple change in tactics from the stick to the carrot, but rather a change in attitude. The United States needs to cease thinking of itself as a quasi-religious crusader—the keystone in the arch of hemispheric freedom—and begin instead to reassert its heritage as a pragmatic Yankee trader. It often forgets that its culture in general and its political system in particular are uncommonly conducive to producing skilled negotiators. It is fully capable of protecting its interests in Nicaragua through civilized negotiation and bargaining.

The first task of the United States is to convince the Nicaraguans that it is willing to accept a nonconfrontational approach to conflict resolution. After forty years of support for the Somoza tyranny and more than a year of hostile rhetoric, it will not be easy to convince the Nicaraguan government that U.S. interest in dialogue is more than a ruse. Certainly this country can begin by halting all efforts to destabilize the Nicaraguan government and by accepting the Nicaraguans' offer to negotiate in good faith on a broad variety of bilateral issues. Given the present tension in U.S.-Nicaraguan relations, it is clearly desirable to use the good offices of a friendly third country to prepare the ground for this rapprochement. The Mexican government has taken the initiative in asking to serve as an intermediary with Nicaragua, Cuba, and the Salvadoran Left. This is a stroke of good fortune that the United States can ill-afford to ignore or, worse yet, to accept half-heartedly in a condescending manner. The United States clearly needs help in Central America, and in this region no country can be more helpful than Mexico.

While trust in U.S. intentions can only develop slowly, it can be encouraged by an open identification on the part of this country with the fundamental goal of the Nicaraguan revolution: a more egalitarian society capable of fulfilling citizens' basic needs. It is difficult to understand what national interest the United States serves by permitting Cuba to become the principal foreign actor with significant commitments to mass literacy, public health, and socioeconomic development in Nicaragua. No significant political group in the United States opposes these goals. There is no reason why this country cannot assist with:

a modest, no-strings program of food aid and technical assistance;

a boost in Export-Import Bank financing;

efforts to encourage private investment with increased insurance from the Overseas Private Investment Corporation; and

trade preferences and other benefits provided by the administration's Caribbean Basin Initiative.

But let the United States move cautiously, taking care not to convert its anticommunist crusade into a similarly single-minded effort to "develop" Nicaragua. There is neither the need nor the desire for another Alliance for Progress. Rather there is the need for patience, understanding, and acceptance of the Nicaraguans' determination to address their pressing needs in their own way. Nicaraguan society is like an abandoned mechanism that, having stood idle for decades, has suddenly been electrified. It creaks loudly, for many of its most important parts are unused to activity; it responds slowly and sometimes makes mistakes. But, in its own way, it works. It works because most Nicaraguans want to make it work. The dead hand of the past has been lifted from the controls in Nicaragua. During the period while the rust is being chipped off and the moving parts are being rebuilt—and while new, inexperienced hands are learning to operate the machinery—there will be considerable instability. The United States probably will be dismayed by some of the Nicaraguans' techniques of rust removal, and many Americans will think of superior ways to repair defective parts. But this country should remember that the current crisis in U.S.-Nicaraguan relations developed from Americans' too frequent refusal to accept the facts that it is the Nicaraguans' society and that Nicaraguans have to identify and solve their own problems. Barring threats to U.S. security or gross violations of human rights, this country should remember that the U.S. goal is to protect U.S. national interests through negotiation, not to dictate the nature of Nicaraguan public policy.

9. Cuba: Going to the Source

William M. LeoGrande

For over two decades Cuba has thwarted U.S. hemispheric policy. Presidents Eisenhower and Kennedy tried to overthrow Cuban Premier Fidel Castro, Presidents Johnson and Nixon tried to break him through economic embargo and covert action, and Presidents Ford and Carter tried to entice him into better behavior with the lure of normalization. All failed. Having resisted the pressures of six presidents, Castro will not be tamed by the seventh.

As unveiled thus far the Reagan administration's policy holds nothing new or innovative. The rising war of words, the renewed effort to isolate Cuba diplomatically, and the tightening of the economic embargo are sanctions refurbished from the 1960s. Having failed then, they are no more likely to succeed today.

It seems incredible that the United States, with its vast economic and military resources, has never found an effective response to the Cuban challenge. U.S. policymakers have spent the better part of twenty years searching for ways to translate their overwhelming resources into real leverage.

But the unpleasant truth is that Castro's decision to align Cuba with the USSR, which agreed to subsidize Cuba's survival, deprived the United States of its traditional ability to dictate the terms of U.S.-Cuban relations. Until America accepts this reality and adjusts its policies accordingly, successive administrations will continue, as did their predecessors, to search in vain for the magic formula that will make Castro behave.

Overview

Relations between the United States and Cuba were strained even before the Soviet Union's patronage made Cuba a focal point of the cold war.

Washington's long and friendly relationship with Fulgencio Batista's dictatorship, the intense nationalism of Castro's revolutionary movement, and Washington's assessment of the new regime as dangerously radical burdened bilateral relations from the outset with deep mutual distrust and suspicion.

These latent tensions became manifest when the United States excoriated the policies of the new Cuban regime: its 1959 agrarian reform, which nationalized substantial holdings of U.S. citizens; its determination to open trade and diplomatic relations with the Soviet bloc; and its willingness to provide sanctuary and assistance to other Latin American revolutionaries. To Washington's objections Cuba offered defiance. The rising spiral of hostile rhetoric took on a dynamic of its own.

Cuba's leaders must also assume a major share of responsibility for the deterioration of relations. But once Washington undertook to strangle the Cuban Revolution economically and subvert it militarily, Havana was forced to find a patron willing and able to defend it. The Soviet Union took on this task reluctantly at first, later with relish. Without Soviet assistance, the Cuban economy could not have survived the severing of U.S. ties; without Soviet arms, Cuba's revolution could not have survived U.S. efforts to overthrow it.

During the 1960s Washington held fast to its policy of hostility, organizing paramilitary attacks and recruiting its allies to join the diplomatic and economic embargo on Cuba. Outside the hemisphere, the embarge met with little success, but among Latin American states only Mexico refused to abide by the sanctions imposed in 1964 by the Organization of American States. Cuba responded to its pariah status by stepping up the export of revolution to its neighbors, even though this policy strained relations with the USSR. To the Soviets, Cuba's strategy was unrealistic as well as detrimental to their objective of fostering peaceful coexistence.

U.S. Policy Comes Full Circle

In the early 1970s U.S. policymakers began to reassess relations with Cuba. The policy of hostility had failed to destabilize the Cuban regime and had not noticeably deterred Cuba's export of revolution. At the same time, the advent of détente made Cuban communism seem less malevolent and Cuba's ostracism less rational. One by one, Latin American states began to abandon the sanctions, and Cuba responded by moderating its revolutionary zeal in favor of normal state-to-state relations. The carrot, it appeared, was a better policy lever than the stick. Within the OAS and even within the United States itself, pressures began building to normalize relations with Cuba.

The Ford administration took several initiatives in this direction. It eased the economic embargo for subsidiaries of U.S. firms operating abroad, voted in 1975 to relax the OAS sanctions, and dropped its demand that Cuba sever its relations with the Soviet Union as a precondition for normalization. Shortly thereafter the United States and Cuba began private discussions on the full range of bilateral relations.

The movement toward normalization ended, however, when Cuba deployed—according to Castro—thirty-six thousand combat troops in Angola to support the Popular Movement for the Liberation of Angola (MPLA). Washington reacted by denouncing Cuba as a Soviet puppet, threatening a military response to any further Cuban adventures abroad, and making the withdrawl of Cuban troops from Angola a precondition for resuming the normalization process.

By 1977 Cuban troops had begun withdrawing from Angola, and so the incoming Carter administration did not regard them as an insurmountable obstacle to improved relations. The new administration negotiated a fishing agreement with Cuba and resumed discussions on a broad range of bilateral issues. Both Cuba and the United States sought to propel the process forward by making a series of minor but symbolically important concessions. The United States halted reconnaissance overflights and lifted the ban on travel to Cuba. The Cubans in turn released four thousand political prisoners, including a number of U.S. citizens. Havana also began a dialogue with leaders of the Cuban exile community, concluding agreements to allow exile visits to Cuba and to permit the reunification of families. These efforts led to the establishment of diplomatic interests sections in both capitals—a move one step short of diplomatic recognition.

Carter's efforts to normalize relations with Cuba, like Ford's, collapsed as a result of Cuba's Africa policy. In 1978 Cuba sent twenty thousand combat troops to Ethiopia, coordinating the move much more closely with the USSR than had been the case in Angola. Over the next few years, U.S.-Cuban relations deteriorated dramatically as a result of successive minicrises: the 1978 invasion of Zaire—which the United States accused Cuba of instigating—by Katangan rebels; the deployment to Cuba of Soviet MiG-23 fighter aircraft, which in some configurations are capable of carrying nuclear weapons; the 1979 controversy over the alleged Soviet combat brigade in Cuba; and 1980 flotilla of Cuban refugees from Mariel.

The Reagan administration has from the outset taken a hard line on Cuba, in part because of Cuban assistance to revolutionaries in Central America. The administration has imposed new sanctions, including tightening the economic embargo, and is attempting to reisolate Cuba within the hemisphere. Administration officials have even warned that the United States is prepared to exercise military options against Cuba unless it halts its arms shipments to the guerrillas in El Salvador. In short, U.S. policy has come full circle. Yet a hard-line policy is no more likely to succeed now than it did twenty years ago.

William M. LeoGrande

Realities or Wishful Thinking?

Cuba remains, after all, a socialist country in which the economy and polity are organized according to values profoundly different from those prevailing in the United States. These differences translate into sharply conflicting policies across a broad spectrum of international issues. Areas of mutual interest between the United States and Cuba do exist—the anti-hijacking and fishing agreements negotiated in the 1970s were based upon such mutual interests. But in light of the deep differences between the two countries, it would be naive to expect that even under the best of circumstances the opportunities for accord and mutual benefit will ever overshadow the occasions for conflict and competition.

The United States must learn to live with this reality unless it is willing to confront the Soviet Union directly. Neither the sanctions applied during the 1960s nor the enticements offered during the 1970s were sufficient to divert the Cuban government from its program of socialist construction at home and revolutionary solidarity abroad. These bedrock policies can be altered only by changing the basic character of the regime itself or by overthrowing it—both unlikely occurrences.

Despite recent economic hardships in Cuba and their attendant political discord, Castro continues to enjoy broad popular support. Unlike some of its East European counterparts, the Cuban regime has responded to discontent with pragmatic reforms. In the past two years, as in the early 1970s, the regime has modified prevailing economic orthodoxy to stimulate consumer production and has rearranged political institutions to improve elite sensibility to mass opinion. Moreover, whereas Polish nationalism is anti-Russian and tends to erode the legitimacy of a Soviet-linked regime, Cuban nationalism is anti-Yankee and tends to bolster a regime in confrontation with the United States. Thus, with or without the propaganda broadcasts of Radio Martí—the U.S.-sponsored station proposed by the Reagan administration—Castro is not likely to face an eruption of mass opposition.

If the Cuban regime is relatively secure from internal upheaval, then only direct, massive military force can change its basic domestic and international orientation. Even in strictly military terms, this option is untenable. Cuba is defended by a well-trained, well-equipped professional army of one hundred thousand people, an equal number of reservists, and a militia of five hundred thousand. To occupy the island would require the United States to strip every other theater of operations, including Western Europe and the Persian Gulf, of conventional forces.

Moreover, an invasion would provoke an immediate confrontation with the Soviet Union. Not only would an invasion place U.S. troops in combat against the several thousand Soviet military personnel stationed in Cuba, but it would also violate the agreement that ended the 1962 missile crisis whereby

138

the United States pledged not to attack Cuba in return for the withdrawal of the Soviet missiles. The Soviet Union, therefore, could not ignore an invasion or any other direct military action, such as a blockade or air strikes.

Nor is there any political exchange that America could feasibly offer the Soviets to induce them to abandon their support of Cuba. As U.S.-Cuban rhetorical exchanges have escalated, the Soviets have repeatedly warned that Cuba is, in late Soviet President Leonid Brezhnev's words, "an inseparable part of the socialist community." A U.S. invasion of Cuba would imperil world peace as much as would a Soviet invasion of West Berlin.

For Washington, then, the challenge is to abandon the hopeless quest for ways to eliminate U.S.-Cuban conflicts and instead to devise a strategy for managing them. The measure of success will be whether U.S. policy modifies Cuban behavior in ways that advance the interests of the United States. Great expectations in this regard would be illusions, but if the United States bases its policy toward Cuba on realities rather than on wishful thinking, some successes are possible.

Outstanding Issues

To design a strategy for managing conflicts with Cuba, the United States must begin to specify the issues in contention and the sorts of Cuban behavior that damage U.S. interests. These issues fall into two categories: strictly bilateral questions between the United States and Cuba, and multilateral issues involving a third country.

Most of the bilateral questions are relatively insignificant. Left over from the deterioration of U.S.-Cuban relations in the 1960s, they could probably be settled if both parties had the will to proceed with negotiations. Compromise would not require either side to relinquish vital interests. The outstanding issues include the ongoing U.S. economic embargo of Cuba, the presence of the U.S. naval base at Guantánamo, U.S. reconnaissance flights over Cuba, immigration, U.S. demands for compensation for property nationalized in 1959 and 1960, and Cuban counterclaims for damage caused by the embargo and by the Central Intelligence Agency's secret war in the 1960s.

With the exceptions of immigration and compensation, none of these issues involves Cuban actions or potential actions that are or have been damaging to the United States. On the contrary, most involve Cuban demands for a cessation of U.S. activities—the embargo, the occupation of Guantánamo, and the overflights. This imbalance may explain why Cuba has generally been more willing than the United States to enter negotiations over the bilateral issues; Cuba has a good deal more to gain from their successful resolution.

Since the uncontrolled exodus of refugees in 1980, immigration has been

139

the main bilateral issue in which the United States has had a significant stake. The flow of tens of thousands of exiles could be resumed at any time, once again making a mockery of U.S. immigration laws and worsening social pressures in Florida. For humanitarian reasons and because of the intense emotions of the Cuban-American community, the United States could do little to halt such an inundation.

The Reagan administration claims it has contingency plans to prevent another exodus, but any plans beyond deploying the Coast Guard to halt the boat lift, as the Carter administration tried to do, are difficult to imagine. In fact, it was candidate Reagan who blasted Carter's efforts to bar the refugees; as president, Reagan could expect similar treatment from his political adversaries.

The key conflicts between the United States and Cuba have never been strictly bilateral. Ever since Cuba adopted socialism and sought safety with the Soviet Union, Cuba's partisan position in the cold war has dictated the terms of U.S.-Cuban relations. Washington has viewed Soviet military assistance to Cuba and Cuban assistance to foreign revolutionaries as threats to the security of both the United States and its allies abroad. As Cuban foreign policy has become increasingly global and more successful, Washington's fear that Cuba acts as the vanguard of Soviet influence in the third world has become more acute.

Cuba's partnership with the Soviet Union and the potential danger it holds for U.S. interests are real, although the relationship has not always been portrayed realistically. If the Cuban-Soviet partnership lies at the heart of U.S. concerns about Cuba's international behavior, then the U.S. response must be premised on an understanding of that complex partnership and on a realistic assessment of the dangers it poses for U.S. interests.

The Cuban-Soviet military relationship has not constituted a serious direct threat to U.S. security since 1962 when the Soviets attempted to place intermediate-range ballistic missiles in Cuba. The agreement that ended the missile crisis prohibits the Soviet Union from deploying offensive weapons on the island. This agreement was extended in 1970 to encompass Soviet nuclear submarine bases and again in 1979 to cover Soviet ground forces. As long as the agreement remains in force, Cuba can pose little danger to the United States.

At some future time of crisis, of course, the Soviets might abrogate this agreement and use Cuba as a forward naval or air station for Soviet action in the Western Hemisphere. The United States can do little about this possibility now other than plan for that contingency. But the chances of such a scenario materializing are remote; a Soviet military initiative in the Western Hemisphere makes little strategic or geopolitical sense. Even if the USSR intended simply to divert U.S. forces from other theaters of operation, a credible threat would divert Soviet forces as well and would bring U.S. retaliation against Cuba, by far the most militarily exposed member of the Soviet bloc.

The Soviet Union is not likely to initiate a superpower confrontation under such unfavorable circumstances for such small stakes. Nevertheless, a confrontation could develop if the United States abrogated the missile crisis agreement, as Ford threatened to do because of Cuban policy in Africa and as Reagan threatens to do over Cuban policy in Central America. A naval blockade or air strike against Cuba would force a Soviet response—if not in Cuba, then elsewhere in the world. Another obvious Soviet option would be to upgrade the Soviet military posture in Cuba in ways currently prohibited. Cuba could then pose a direct security threat once more to the United States.

Other Cubas?

In the absence of such a threat, the United States has been preoccupied with Cuba's third world initiatives, in Angola, Ethiopia and Central America, and the Non-Aligned Movement. Washington has interpreted Cuba's actions—whether diplomatic, economic, or military—as gambits in the cold war, aimed as much at advancing Soviet interests as Cuban ones. The extreme version of this interpretation reduces the Cubans to mindless proxies of the USSR with no autonomy or interests of their own.

Such a view is not supported by the historical record. Despite the support Cuba has received from the Soviet Union, relations between the two have been complex and volatile. During the late 1960s Cuban leaders openly criticized the Soviet Union for sacrificing proletarian internationalism on the altar of peaceful coexistence. Cuba cited the willingness of the Soviets to do business with rightist regimes in Latin America, their capitalist trade relations with the third world, and their inadequate defense of North Vietnam. The Cubans, in contrast, sought to create a new revolutionary international at the 1966 Tricontinental Conference in Havana and to forge a militant third force with Vietnam and North Korea within the socialist camp.

Such differences, however, have diminished since 1970. Cuban and Soviet world views now correspond closely, making possible a variety of cooperative ventures abroad—in Angola, Ethiopia, and South Yemen. If this partnership remains intact, most Cuban foreign policy successes will have the effect, intended or not, of advancing Soviet interests. But the sharp disagreements of the past should demonstrate that the current Cuban-Soviet partnership is neither inevitable nor interminable.

Even in the 1970s there have been significant discrepancies between Cuban and Soviet policies. In Angola Cuban troops helped the late President Agostinho Neto's moderate faction of the MPLA defeat the 1977 coup attempt

141

by Nito Alve's pro-Soviet faction. In Ethiopia Cuba has refused to send its troops into combat against Eritrean rebels. Instead, it called for a negotiated settlement despite the Soviet Union's initial preference for a military solution to the insurgency.

The most important difference between current Cuban and Soviet foreign policies concerns the quest for a new international economic order. As the 1979–82 leader of the Non-Aligned Movement and a self-described member of the third world, Cuba has long been in the forefront of demands for change in the international economic system—including advocating that all developed countries, capitalist and socialist alike, expand development assistance to the third world. Castro's speech before the 1979 U.N. General Assembly on behalf of the nonaligned countries explicitly called on the socialist states to contribute their share of the burden. The Soviet position on the new international economic order has been unenthusiastic at best.

Other Cuban foreign policy initiatives seem to be of little concern to the Soviet Union, among them Cuban policy in the Caribbean region. Although the Soviets have not, as far as is known, tried to restrain Cuban behavior, they have shown remarkably little enthusiasm for creating other Cubas in the region. The Soviet Union has refused to underwrite the expenses of socialist construction in such countries as Jamaica (under former Prime Minister Michael Manley) or Nicaragua. Even the Salvadoran Communist party's modest request for arms was met with reluctance in Moscow. The Soviet economy can ill afford to finance any more Cubas in the Caribbean, especially because they would provide only a marginal strategic gain over the existing partnership with Cuba itself. Indeed, the next major disagreement between Cuba and the Soviet Union could come over Soviet unwillingness to shore up a faltering Nicaraguan economy.

Hostility or Engagement?

As U.S. policymakers seek to formulate responses to Cuba's international activism, they must look beyond the Manichaean rhetoric about Cuban puppets and mercenaries. Cuban-Soviet agreement and cooperation varies from region to region. For the United States to assume that Cuban behavior comes at Soviet behest is foolish and dangerous.

It is equally dangerous to determine U.S. policy toward regional conflicts by looking at Cuba's posture rather than the realities of the conflicts themselves. Current U.S. policy in Central America, for example, is hostage to Washington's animosity toward Cuba. Washington cites Cuban assistance to revolutionary movements in the region as evidence that Cuba created these movements and that therefore their leaders are implacable enemies of the United States. The idea that these insurgencies may be authentically indigenous and that there may be no solution to the region's crises without the insurgents' participation is lost in the cacophony of anti-Cuban rhetoric. Washington ignores the real source of insurgency in Central America—decades of economic inequality and political oppression.

Indeed, Central America offers a perfect example of what has been wrong with U.S. responses to Cuban initiatives abroad. By treating Cuba as the source of Central America's problems, the United States loses sight of regional dynamics, focusing only on the East-West dimension of local conflicts. The United States would respond more effectively to Cuban initiatives by focusing on the regional conflicts themselves, seeking solutions that deprive Cuba of political advantage. As Angola and Ethiopia demonstrate, Cuba's opportunities for major gains are greatest when regional conflicts erupt in violence and become internationalized. When negotiations resolve conflicts, as they did in Zimbabwe, Cuba—and the Soviet Union—are prevented from extending their influence through military aid.

As they contemplate how best to manage the conflicts between the United States and Cuba, U.S. policymakers face a choice between two broad sets of policy options. A policy of graduated hostility, on the one hand, is a coercive strategy aimed at forcing Cuba to cease activities objectionable to the United States by punishing Cuba for undertaking them. At the heart of this strategy lies the premise that no significant improvement in America's relations with Cuba should be undertaken until it fundamentally alters its foreign policy.

A strategy of gradual engagement, on the other hand, seeks to induce changes in Cuban behavior by positive reinforcement. This strategy is based on the premise that an improvement in U.S.-Cuban relations could serve U.S. interests even if Cuba did not change its basic foreign policy positions. This strategy does not, however, rule out such change as a long-term objective of U.S. policy. To embark on this strategy, the United States would have to make a decision to offer inducements to Cuba and, if they are met with a positive response, to follow them with additional inducements. The United States can, of course, introduce some punitive measures into an overall strategy of engagement. What is critical is the decision to test the possibility of improving relations.

The specific components of the strategy of hostility range from a relatively passive stance of malign neglect to active policies of diplomatic isolation, economic embargo, paramilitary attack, or even direct military assault. During the 1960s U.S. Cuban policy sought to overthrow Castro or, failing that, to raise the cost to Cuba of pursuing a socialist path of development in partnership with the USSR. By making the survival of the Cuban Revolution as difficult as possible, the United States hoped to deter other Latin American countries from following the Cuban model.

Washington achieved some success. The sanctions did damage the Cuban economy and force Havana to divert vast resources from economic development to national defense. Cuba's subsequent economic difficulties and its dependence on the USSR are by no means enviable. And in at least two instances—Angola and Nicaragua—revolutionary governments, despite an ideological affinity with socialism, have tried to maintain mixed economies and good relations with the West in the hope of avoiding Cuba's difficulties. Ironically, the Cubans themselves have apparently encouraged these governments in this course.

But if the United States succeeded in making Cuba a negative example, it failed to overthrow the Cuban Revolution. Moreover, the overall effect of the sanctions on bilateral relations was not salutary. The full range of sanctions, excluding only direct military attack, failed to modify Cuban behavior in ways favorable to the United States and actually seemed to make Havana more belligerent. And although the policy of isolating Cuba from Latin American countries and the other Western states damaged the Cuban economy, it also forced the Cubans to rely more heavily on the USSR for economic and military aid. Thus the central problem as perceived by Washington—Cuba's relationship with the USSR—was exacerbated.

If the Reagan administration is indeed intent upon returning to the strategy of hostility, it will encounter the same problems with this strategy that existed in the 1960s, without the attendant benefits. No one can now expect diplomatic and economic isolation to endanger the Castro regime's survival. Cuba today is much less economically dependent on the West than it was twenty years ago.

In fact, the effect of graduated hostility might be precisely the opposite of what it was intended to be. Cuba's most assertive international posture came in the late 1960s—the period of exporting revolution—when U.S.-Cuban relations were at their worst. Moreover, Cuba can now strike back in ways that it could not before; Castro could unleash Cuban troops in Africa—in Zaire, Somalia, or Namibia—or Cuban refugees from Mariel.

On balance, a strategy of graduated hostility offers so little leverage that it is unlikely to alter Cuba's foreign policy except perhaps for the worse. It promises no more than a continuation of the status quo both in U.S.-Cuban relations and, more important, in Cuban-Soviet relations.

In contrast, a strategy of gradual engagement advocates the progressive establishment of links between the United States and Cuba to enhance the ability of U.S. policymakers to exert leverage on Cuban behavior in the future. There is some historical precedent for such a strategy in the Ford and Carter administrations' efforts to begin normalizing relations. Cuban involvement in Angola and Ethiopia, however, clearly demonstrated that Cuba was unwilling to make major foreign policy concessions in exchange for normal relations with the United States. This fact has become the principal argument against a policy of engagement.

But this argument has force only if the main justification for a U.S. policy of engagement is the prospect that Cuba will give up its entire foreign policy—its relationship with the Soviet Union and its support for friendly governments and revolutionary movements abroad—in exchange for relatively minor concessions by the United States. Such unrealistic expectations explain why U.S.-Cuban relations have been stalemated for so long.

The Cubans, however, are not as intransigent as the Reagan administration would have us believe. In the spring of 1982 they expressed an interest in opening discussions with the United States over the crisis in Central America. Both publicly and through diplomatic channels, the Cubans offered to begin talks regarding the role of external powers in the region and the need to reduce the danger that Central America's conflicts might escalate into a wider international confrontation. The Reagan administration refused to respond to these initiatives, preferring to maintain the fiction that the Cubans were bent on exacerbating the regional crisis.

A strategy of gradual engagement would entail seeking out the most pliant issues for both Cuba and the United States and negotiating agreements with balanced concessions from each side. Negotiations no doubt cannot resolve some issues in isolation, and the two countries will have to examine those issues as part of a broader package. But more important for success would be the U.S. acknowledgment that compromise must be mutual.

In the short term such a policy has a number of advantages. The United States and Cuba could resolve most of their bilateral issues, leading to economic and diplomatic relations that would give Washington at least some leverage on other issues. The United States could probably persuade Cuba to mitigate its denunciations of Washington in such international forums as the Non-Aligned Movement and the United Nations. More significant, a less confrontational relationship would diminish the credibility of Cuba's efforts to build its prestige in the third world on the image of an embattled David confronting the Goliath of U.S. imperialism. In addition, an improvement in U.S.-Cuban relations would eliminate Cuba as a potential flashpoint of superpower confrontation. Improved relations might also begin to free U.S. policymakers from the tendency to react reflexively against every Cuban initiative abroad, regardless of the circumstances.

In the long term a policy of gradual engagement would allow Cuba to reduce its military and economic dependence on the Soviet Union. As long as U.S. hostility persists, Cuba's ties with the Soviets remain essential to Cuban national security. The Cuban-Soviet relationship will not, however, wither away in short order. Cuban soldiers have been trained with Soviet arms, and Cuban factories are filled with Soviet equipment. Soviet economic and military assistance to Cuba is indispensable, and no Western nation would be prepared to assume these burdens, even if the Cubans were looking for a new patron.

Nevertheless, Castro has always been one of the most nationalistic

145

leaders in the socialist bloc. Whenever circumstances have allowed, he has tried to reduce Cuba's dependence on the Soviet Union, especially by attempting to create a Cuban constituency in the third world. This strategy is not so different from that pursued by Yugoslavia, although Cuba's nonalignment is less neutral. If Cuba is to have any prospect of striking out on a more independent course, it must have the economic and military breathing space to modify its relationship with the Soviet Union. Only the United States can create that opportunity by moving away from the policy of hostility which leaves Cuba no option but to hold fast to its Soviet patron. For years the United States has sought to encourage East European states to distance themselves, however slightly, from the Soviet Union, and several—Romania, Hungary, and Poland—have done so. Surely the prospects for such a development are greater in the case of Cuba, despite its reliance on Soviet aid, than they are in Eastern Europe.

A realistic assessment of the advantages to the United States of pursuing a strategy of gradual engagement with Cuba shows that limited gains, particularly on bilateral issues, are fairly certain, whereas major gains, such as changing Cuban foreign policy significantly or rupturing Cuba's partnership with the Soviet Union, are at best long-term possibilities. Such gains may not be impressive, but they are nevertheless superior to the results achieved over the past two decades by a policy of hostility.

10. Brazil: The Case of the Missing Relationship

Albert Fishlow

Introduction

Brazil has emerged as one of the key targets of the Reagan administration's newly crafted policy for Latin America. Central America remains the principal preoccupation, to be sure, and an anticommunist ideology the dominant conceptual basis. But in dramatic fashion, responsive to the emerging debt crisis of the largest countries of the region, in the fall of 1982 the United States at least temporarily upgraded its attention to those countries and refocused on economic problems. The change was long overdue.

In particular, recognition of the importance of Brazil did not require subtle reasoning. Brazil, after all, is the principal military power in South America and sits astride the sea lanes of the South Atlantic that carry petroleum from the Persian Gulf and strategic minerals from Africa. Its technological sophistication has made possible increasing exports of arms—estimated now to be in the range of $2 billion. It is the eighth largest market economy in the world, with a gross product of around $250 billion. Brazil has rapidly increased its integration into international markets in the last decade: since 1973 its exports have quadrupled and its debt has increased by a factor of about five.

Equally to the point, Brazil is undergoing far-reaching internal changes. The economic miracle and authoritarian stability no longer exist. Brazil is experiencing its worst economic downturn since the Great Depression, with a negative growth rate of almost 4 percent in 1981, and a larger decline in industrial production; 1982 was stagnant, and 1983 will likely again show negative results. This recession has been imposed by the need to shore up a vulnerable balance of payments that remained in deficit in 1982 on current account by some $14 billion, even though exports had nearly doubled between

1978 and 1981. From 1973 to 1980, despite world recession and ever-larger oil imports, Brazil managed through reliance on external finance to sustain a growth rate of almost 7 percent. Now its economic prospects, at least in the near term, are more clouded.

At the same time, a transition from authoritarian rule has gained speed. The direct elections for governor planned for November 1982 took place as scheduled, providing the first opportunity for a popular vote for that office since 1965. A new congress was chosen at the same time under a multiparty system that has only recently supplanted the formerly mandated two-party structure. The results, on the whole, registered significant gains for the opposition, and only a precarious margin for the government in the electoral college. While few speculate that an opposition candidate could gain the indirectly elected presidency in 1985, talk of a possible civilian successor has verbally monopolized early discussions. The military seems prepared fully to return to the barracks.

In subsequent sections, I first examine briefly the evolution of U.S. policy toward Brazil before the Reagan administration took office; I then consider the economic problems now confronting Brazil and, on the brighter side, the accomplishments of, and prospects for continuing, political opening; I next analyze the bases of the initial Reagan policies toward Brazil; I conclude by asking whether the reversal in the fall of 1982 will prove to be durable or prove to be another mere transitory flurry of U.S. attention.

Antecedents

The Reagan administration began by fundamentally misreading the history of the postwar U.S.-Brazilian relationship.[1] The pre-Carter years were never quite so harmonious and the relationship was never quite so beautiful as Roger Fontaine, now on the National Security Council staff, once postulated. Very early on, after World War II, Brazil discovered that the United States, promises to the contrary, was not about to commit significant public resources to an ambitious Brazilian project of economic development.

Only after the military intervened in 1964 was there a brief interval in which the dominant Brazilian economic development objectives and the preeminent U.S. security concerns were almost fully congruent. The new military government was fully anticommunist and had justified its revolution on those grounds. Washington's response was immediate and financially generous.

That golden age did not last out the decade. As Brazil accelerated its

[1]For a fuller discussion, see my earlier "Flying Down to Rio: Perspectives on U.S.-Brazil Relations," *Foreign Affairs,* Winter 1978/79.

economic growth and became integrated into the international economy after 1967, the alliance progressively eroded. Brazil gained access to private capital in quantities that far exceeded the availability of public loans. The United States was dispensable. Moreover, a new economic capability promised to underwrite a more assertive and independent Brazilian international role. The generals who came to power after 1967 were neither committed constitutionalists nor cosmopolitan internationalists. In place of junior partnership they visualized *grandeza*. While Brazilian foreign policy would continue to be staunchly anticommunist, it no longer needed to ratify U.S. positions.

The 1973 oil crisis was the decisive turning point. It exposed a Brazilian vulnerability—Brazil was the third largest oil importer in the third world—that was at odds with the perceptions of emergent power. In its time of troubles, Brazil found little consolation in its relationship with the United States. The help that was forthcoming came from international financial markets. Indeed, the United States became an active antagonist in 1974 and 1975 in three respects: nuclear fuel, trade, and human rights.

The U.S. decision in July 1974 no longer to guarantee processing of fuel for nuclear reactors then under construction by Westinghouse was a hard blow to a country seeking to expand its nuclear capacity as a substitute for high-priced oil. That the decision applied universally, because of limited U.S. capacity and potential domestic demands, did not help. On the contrary, it drove home the absence of a special relationship and the reality of continuing dependence.

During 1974 the United States also found Brazil at fault in a countervailing duty action brought by American shoe manufacturers. To compensate for export subsidies, Washington imposed a customs surcharge. The decision placed at risk the entire subsidy system—an important component in Brazil's new drive to export manufactured products. Brazil filed a formal diplomatic note of protest.

Finally, as human rights violations acquired wider public notice in 1975—evoking a determined effort in Brasilia to regain control over local military authorities—the United States was drawn increasingly into an adversary position. Congressional interest pushed the State Department into a more active stance than it wished to take but a less active stance than the U.S. embassy in Brasilia counseled was needed. Inevitably, the Brazilian military government was sensitive to external voices joining the rising internal criticism.

As the relationship was buffeted by these obvious tensions, both the United States and Brazil sought to obscure the realities. The United States wishfully elevated Brazil to a new moderate third world leadership role it no longer could or wanted to play in its weakened economic circumstances; Brazil's strategy was much more flexible and self-serving. Brazil pressed for an explicit "special relationship" in an effort to extract the utmost in its bilateral dealings with the United States, although appreciative that there was precious little to gain. Indeed, one of Foreign Minister Antônio Silveira's objectives was ratification of the more independent and flexible policy he was already following. The professions of a century-old friendship and recognition of Brazil's status as an emergent power in the 1976 memorandum of understanding concluded during then Secretary of State Henry Kissinger's visit were no longer to the point.

The new Carter foreign policy initiatives magnified the latent tensions in the relationship. By giving priority to a global solution of issues like nuclear proliferation and to universal rules in international trade and other economic matters, the United States stripped the "special relationship" of even its limited function. At the same time, the Carter administration's emphasis on an industrial-country cooperative economic recovery strategy pointedly excluded Brazil: emergent powers need not apply. A more aggressive human rights policy downgraded both the traditional economic and the security bases of modern U.S.-Brazilian relations and directly threatened the military's role. At the same time, it secured for the United States a much more favorable image with the independent rising domestic opposition to the authoritarian regime.

Quite apart from early tactical errors of the Carter team, there were thus accumulating substantive differences that finally cracked the facade of amicability. Neither a ceremonial presidential visit in 1978 nor the diplomatic success of a negotiated phaseout of export subsidies in exchange for exemption from countervailing duties ever served to put the official relationship back together again.

The new administration pledged to try. But its initial guiding principle of restoration of the status quo ante was inadequate. Not only did it resurrect U.S. security concerns of the cold war at the expense of traditional Brazilian economic development objectives, it also was seemingly blind to the profound internal transition Brazil is undergoing. A policy for the 1980s cannot ignore the Brazil of the 1980s.

Brazil Today

Brazil now faces a set of interlinked economic problems whose full gravity has finally become apparent. Part of the present difficulties can be traced to the quadrupling of oil prices at the end of 1973 and beginning of 1974 and, again, to the 1979 price shock, subsequent high international interest rates, and slowing of world trade. But they are not the only factors. Internal distortions also derive from the "miracle" years: a lagging domestic agricultural supply; a rising and competitive participation of the public sector in investment; an inability to sustain private profit margins through limited wage gains that, while positive, still were smaller than productivity increases and did not make significant inroads upon income inequality; and a very high elasticity of import demand that was financed by increasing reliance on foreign debt. In a favorable external market of cheap oil and cheap money, these problems were more easily confronted. After 1974 petroleum was no longer cheap. And after 1978 neither was money.

Brazil initially compensated for much greater oil costs by borrowing under relatively favorable terms in international capital markets. That, in conjunction with restrictive import limitations, helped to sustain a relatively high growth rate even as the world economy slowed. But this performance was achieved at the expense of increased external vulnerability as debt and attendant repayment obligations mounted. The counterpart was an increased internal vulnerability as larger public subsidies to the private sector and mounting state investment were financed by higher inflation.

The alternative of slower economic growth to restore balance was faced only sporadically. When Finance Minister Mario Henrique Simonsen once more advocated credit and fiscal restrictions in 1979 to remedy accelerating inflation and deteriorating external balances buffeted by a new oil price shock and rising interest rates, he was dismissed. Instead the government opted for a more optimistic prognosis of the architect of the original post-1968 economic miracle, Antônio Delfim Netto. Rapid economic growth could produce more for domestic and foreign markets, thus simultaneously lowering inflation and putting the balance of payments into equilibrium. His unorthodox 1980 policies of cheap credit and firm government controls on exchange rates and internal price indexing to lower inflation produced no miracle this time. In the new setting of domestic excess demand and very large international indebtedness, economic growth was sustained, but at the expense of a doubled inflation rate and a foreign exchange liquidity crisis. As a consequence, Delfim, a convert to orthodoxy since late 1980, was forced to opt for a severe recession. A continuing decline in industrial production occurred throughout 1981, and unemployment mounted to a tangible concern, particularly in São Paulo and other industrialized centers.

Prospects in 1982 were no more favorable. Continuing recession in the industrialized countries began to take their toll in shrinking markets for exports and declines in commodity prices. The modest balance of payments improvement registered in 1981 as a result of a record growth in exports and compression of imports could not be sustained. That meant continuing restriction on domestic demand was required: in order to finance current account deficits of close to $15 billion and roll over mounting amortization on past debt, external credit markets had to be satisfied.

The size of the Brazilian floating debt subject to variable interest rates translated into foreign exchange needs that could only be satisfied by more loans, not by more exports. Despite a very favorable trade performance after 1978, debt service and oil imports together more than exhausted export earnings in 1981, and the situation in 1982 was worse.

The international capital market thus became the decisive and harsh arbiter of domestic policy. It registered its insistence on orthodox restrictive policies through higher spreads on loans to Brazil and limited access to new loans. The recession on which Brazil embarked in 1981 was fashioned in New York rather than Brasilia. The foreign constituency dominated the wishes of those who might have preferred more expansion in anticipation of the elections in November 1982. As *Business Week* headlined in its 26 October 1981 issue: "Brazil's Money Pinch Pleases the Bankers."

With unanticipated suddenness, even the restrictive domestic policies were to prove inadequate. Mexico in August 1982 announced it could no longer service its $80 billion debt. Argentina, still reeling from the economic effects of the futile South Atlantic war, was in a similar situation. As a consequence the continuing bank finance required by Brazil to meet *its* obligations was simply not to be found in nervous money markets. Reserves were drawn down but did not avert near-illiquidity of the Bank of Brazil, whose short-term inter-bank borrowing had been shoring up the shaky finances of the government for several months. Despite the brave front of the economic managers and the presentation of a new and rigorous austerity plan designed to restore the confidence of external creditors, it was almost a foregone conclusion that Brazil would have to announce agreement with the IMF or a formal stabilization program as soon as the election had been held.

And so the Brazilian government eventually did, bolstered by bridging finance from the Bank of International Settlements and the United States. The application to the IMF was approved in record time, providing access to a combined total of some $5 billion from the compensating facility and quota trenches over the next three years. More important still was the IMF's indispensable assistance in requiring the banks to roll over loans coming due in 1983, to restore short-term trade and inter-bank credits, and to provide an additional $4.4 billion in new money needed even by the austerity plan. Indeed, where the IMF formerly satisfied itself with imposing conditions on the country, it now imposed them on the banks. As the full magnitude of the successive liquidity crises in the fall of 1982 began to be perceived, dramatic institutional changes were occurring without plan. The period of free and buoyant international financial markets has ended, at least temporarily, and perhaps forever.

The IMF financial transfusion has not restored the health of the economy, even prospectively. First, resources have been made available grudgingly, as regional banks unhappy with their exposure have sought to avoid renewal of old commitments, let alone establishment of new ones. Brazil has been forced countless times to cajole and threaten in a vain effort to obtain compliance on the restoration of inter-bank credits. Second, the amount of finance is not large enough. The projected 6-billion-dollar surplus on merchandise account is an ambitious target, even as the dominant—perhaps sole—policy objective in 1983. The export decline of 15 percent in 1982 cannot be easily reversed even with moderate recovery in the industrialized countries, and imports have been much compressed for several years. Help from lower oil prices and declining interest rates is welcome, but it is not sufficient to prevent Brazil from running out of money before year's end, even with the economy closely reined. In February 1983, in an effort to bolster trade performance, the government undertook a maxi-devaluation of 30 percent—making clear how far the performance of the external accounts and external pressures determine domestic policy.

The focus on managing the immediate crisis has obscured the continuing future burden of the external debt, now set at the end of 1982 by official sources as $83 billion, and by others as closer to $90 billion. The likely sacrifice Brazil will be called upon to make is not merely of one more year of slack performance added to the previous two. Limited finance in a world of sluggish trade growth implies continuing adjustment costs of lowered and even negative growth to cope with debt service that claimed, in 1982, including short-term rollover, much more than the total value of export receipts. While a dismal 1983 can be weathered, the prospect of a similar 1984 and 1985 has begun to evoke mounting domestic resistance to the government's present strategy of fully meeting its obligations.

It is not a situation that favors a constructive opposition. While it is easy to point out the high costs of current policies, and their modest potential benefits, the external vulnerability is real. This explains the central role that opposition leaders have accorded to renegotiation of the debt, unilateral if necessary, as the solution. In so advocating, they rely upon the preference of the international banking community, influenced by governments, for a major restructuring rather than a formal default, which could shock the world financial credit structure. It is a doubtful approach. At best, the immediate burden might lessen, but at the price of foregoing the additional net capital inflow necessary to service past debt and finance imports. Renegotiations rarely give adequate room to maneuver, especially when private debt dominates. Only if conducted under the auspices of the IMF, or in conjunction with other large debtors, could such a policy be effective. The latter now seems unlikely, and the former is what we now, for all pratical purposes, have. By its nature it cannot provide the relief from the painful costs of adjustment that many seek. That is not the same as denying the need, and even inevitability, of some major reformulation of present debt service obligations. There are now too few degrees of freedom for government policy to achieve an efficient, medium-term adjustment.

The government is resistant even to discussion of such modifications. It seeks to reestablish its now tarnished claims for a monopoly on technocratic competence as well as to avoid still another implicit confession of past mismanagement. Yet increasingly it becomes clear that political and not merely technical decisions will affect economic outcomes. This influence is possible only because Brazil has experienced a far-reaching transformation in popular participation in the last decade.

Since 1974 Brazilian military leadership has sought to devise and implement an extrication strategy consistent with political stability. President Ernesto Geisel's "decompression" policy between 1974 and 1979 was conceived and managed by General Golbery do Couto e Silva, the éminence grise since 1974 of the military faction committed to a conservative, limited, and managed democratization. Golbery's delicate objective was to retain the substance of the post-1964 accomplishments and the scope for executive authority while introducing more open procedures.

Decompression, however, was forced increasingly to contend with new and independent forms of civil response. The Church, initially a pillar of support for the regime in 1964, became converted to more vocal opposition to repression and human rights violations as these became more frequent after 1968. Intellectuals, and particularly lawyers, became more bold during the Geisel presidency and insisted that, in the absence of subversive opposition to the regimes, censorship could be lifted and legal processes restored. Entrepreneurs joined in criticism of the arbitrariness of the government in executing economic policy: *estaticização,* state intervention, became the rallying cry of a conservative opposition based in São Paulo that found the technocracy overbearing and too powerful. Workers reacted to accelerating inflation by demanding larger wage gains and the right to organize. New labor leaders of a post-1964 generation emerged; the most prominent was Luis Inácio Silva, popularly known as Lula. He led the successful, albeit illegal, strike of the metallurgical workers' union in 1978.

Decompression thus became simultaneously a strategy against the military hard-liners *and* the perceived civil political opposition that might otherwise obtain a leading role. Tactics responded to the particular enemy that seemed most threatening at one or another time. Increased repression after the electoral defeat of the government in 1974 was followed in 1975 by dismissal of the commander of the Second Army, based in São Paulo, where violations had been the most open and defiant. The elections of 1978, conversely, were permitted to take place only under new rules that modified the political process by favoring the government. Earlier, in April 1977, dictatorial powers were invoked to close the congress in order to decree the new conditions. Authoritarianism—the continuing right to reformulate the rules—was exploited in the service of an eventual return to the rule of law. Indeed, Brazil's sharp response to the Carter administration's nuclear proliferation and human rights policies was an integral part of this pattern of domestic political management. Government opposition should not therefore be interpreted fully at face value. But it would be equally wrong to ascribe a large part of the progress toward political participation to the human rights policies.

Geisel, despite signs of restlessness in the military as civil society reasserted itself, persevered in his program of reform, even at the cost of dismissal of his war minister. His personally chosen successor, President João Figueiredo, was selected because of his commitment to the program. General Golbery was retained as chief civilian (though he was hardly a civilian) advisor to oversee the continuation of a process that had subtly transformed itself into *abertura,* a genuine opening to broader participation. The character of the regime has decisively changed. In recognition of the central importance of legal norms, Institutional Act No. 5, the basis for extraordinary powers decreed in December 1968, was repealed and the right of habeas corpus reestablished; judicial authority was accepted as an increasingly independent counterweight to the executive. The rights to know and to criticize were conceded. The government abolished formal censorship of the press, if not of more popular media, and resigned itself to manifestations of popular dissent. Finally, the government broadened the prospects for a civilian political process in which eventually new parties and former popular leaders, including those banned from Brazil after 1964, might compete for real power.

Abertura has proved surprisingly resilient. The political opening has thus far survived the 30 April 1981 bomb explosion at Riocentro in which elements of the armed forces seemed clearly implicated, requiring a government cover-up. It has persisted after Golbery's unexpected forced resignation in August 1981, which initially provoked anticipations of a harder, military-imposed line. It has continued despite the heart attack of President Figueiredo in September 1981 and his absence from office until November. *Abertura* still continued intact despite the government's November 1981 package rules that changed voting procedures to require party-line balloting in an attempt to build upon the strong edge in local organization which the government party enjoys. That decision made clear that the capacity to change the rules is one of the rules of the transition.

The election, and the campaign leading to it, were a final and decisive confirmation. Opposition political speeches were measured in their rhetoric and proposals; they neither challenged authority nor advocated radical policy alternatives. Electoral results were mixed: neither the government nor the opposition won a clear victory. Aided by its new rules that give less weight to the polls in the most populous states, the government emerged with a narrow majority in the electoral college that will select the next president. It did so by retaining control of more state houses and legislatures, even while the opposition gained the industrial heartland of São Paulo, Minas Gerais, and Rio de Janeiro. In the Congress, the government enjoys a commanding lead in the Senate, but only a plurality, 235 out of 479 seats, in the Chamber of Deputies.

This successful transition is all the more notable in view of the persistent suggestions that the economic crisis might disrupt the electoral process. In fact, it may have helped to guarantee it. The demise of the economic miracle, and with it the myth of technocratic omniscience, have accelerated the demands of civil society for direct participation. Broader popular involvement has progressively transformed the political opening from a paternal dis-

155

pensation to a semi-autonomous process with its own momentum. It cannot easily be disrupted, nor is there evidence of significant opposition. The supposed invincible alliance of interests among the state, national capital, and foreign investors that was posited to underlie authoritarian rule is not in evidence.

Politics and economics come together now in another way. The newly elected Congress can be expected to compete with the formerly all-powerful executive in the arena of economic policy. The economic record that once legitimized the military regime is now a magnet for critical scrutiny. Enhanced congressional debate, although with limited binding effect, will weaken further the false dichotomy between technical economic management and political compromise. It will also tilt toward policies that are more inward-looking and expansionist just when the IMF is insisting upon the opposite.

In the states, particularly the most industrial states, the challenge of austerity will also elicit a response. Newly elected opposition governors will be under popular pressure to alleviate the misery of the unemployed and the low-income recipients to whom they appealed for votes. At the same time the states face severe constraints on their expenditure, especially now that external borrowing is limited and concentrated in the hands of the Central Bank. The frustration of futility may reduce the effectiveness of policy coordination between the states and the central government and increase the level of political criticism.

These internal dynamics, reinforced by increasing attention to the presidential succession, assure a continuing debate on the appropriate form and extent of integration into the world economy. The current crisis has made the external environment a central part of the broader question of longer-term economic strategy. The government remains optimistic that economic growth can be regained through trade and borrowing and believes that it is the best and only way to improve the well-being of the poor. The opposition, on the other hand, calls for structural reform and attention to the internal market and an economic model that is more oriented to distribution.

Yet there is a subtle convergence that should not go unnoticed. On the one hand, the former faith of government supporters in international economic integration has lessened. On the other, the opposition is increasingly cognizant of the role of exports as a necessary condition of autonomy. This convergence adds up to a Brazilian foreign policy that is potentially even more independent and driven by economic objectives than that in recent years.

U.S. Policy

These far-reaching changes in Brazil, already under way and apparent when the Regan administration took office, were of little import to the design of U.S. policy. Rather, this country's relationship with Brazil was restructured in accord with the new principles underlying U.S. foreign policy as a whole. Four of those principles are central. First, the dominant concern of the United States is its strategic capability vis-à-vis the Soviet Union. Second, North-South issues have their solution in free trade and free flows of capital, both of which are to be exclusively determined by market forces. Third, political stability in Latin America not only contributes to faster economic growth by attracting private resources but also is necessary in order to deflect a new potential wave of Soviet- and Cuban-inspired subversion. Fourth, diplomacy is to concentrate on matters of bilateral concern, with only nominal support for multilateral procedures and even less for the substance of global issues like nuclear proliferation, the law of the sea, and the international economy.

From these axioms the specific corollaries of the Reagan administration's initial policy posture toward Brazil can be deduced. Brazil was important to the United States not because its economic development requirements and size pose an opportunity and a need to devise rules to ease the potential tensions of interaction with the already industrialized countries or because its political opening is a general model to be encouraged for the Southern Cone of Latin America or because its political opening is a general model to be encouraged for the Southern Cone of Latin America or because it is a central and potentially influential actor in resolving a series of multilateral questions still outstanding, including those of North-South relations. Brazil was important, rather, as a potential ally against Cuba and the Soviet Union, as a bulwark of stability in a seemingly less tranquil Latin America, and as a developing country committed to a larger role for the private sector and thus affording new opportunities for U.S. exports and investment.

Not surprisingly, priority was attached to enlisting Brazil more actively in the East-West struggle. Assistant Secretary Thomas Enders, in the major speech of his visit to Brazil in August 1981, stressed four elements that tied the two countries together. One was concern for the destiny of other countries in the hemisphere, i.e., the foreign intervention in the Caribbean Basin. Another was a common interest in preserving the security of the South Atlantic, i.e., the Soviet and Cuban involvement in Africa. The third was preoccupation with the Soviet invasion of Afghanistan and Soviet pressure on Poland. The fourth, the common challenge to promote world prosperity, was the single deviation from a conceptual framework designed in cold war terms. Vice-President George Bush's subsequent visit similarly emphasized a more energetic anti-Cuban, anti-Soviet collaboration.

The Pentagon hoped to go even further. For it, an explicit South Atlantic Treaty Organization bringing together Brazil, Argentina, and South Africa, and greater military cooperation, probably remain central objectives. The State Department was hard pressed to limit the pitch to just more active Brazilian diplomatic engagement.

157

The specific benefits Washington offered to Brazil were a closer, revitalized, bilateral special relationship. Frictions dating from the Carter years were to be eliminated. Most significant, the United States pledged to become again a reliable supplier of nuclear material, still impermissible under current U.S. law that requires more rigorous inspection standards than Brazil accepts. In the interim, Washington has permitted Brazil to purchase fuel from Urenco (a consortium of German, Dutch, and British companies) for its Angra 1 reactor without being subject to the multimillion dollar fine provided in the original Westinghouse contract. Human rights, of course, no longer disturb the relationship, and had not done so even before the Reagan administration's demonstrated downgrading of their priority. Publicly the administration expressed support for *abertura,* while privately it was sensitive to the needs of the regime to retain control of the process. In the area of trade policy, the administration accepted the new export subsidies imposed in 1981 in violation of the 1978 agreement to phase them out. In the end, only five products were required to pay compensating countervailing duties.

While these problems were solved through bilateral efforts, the Reagan administration succeeded in creating new and more serious ones. Most important in practical terms is the continuing adverse consequence of high interest rates. Since 1978 these rates have increased not only in nominal terms, but relative to inflation. Reaganomics, a mix of tight monetary policy, tax cuts, and military spending increases, is necessarily a high real interest rate policy. Because of the size of the Brazilian debt, a change of one percentage point in nominal interest rates produces a 500- to 600-million-dollar effect on Brazil's balance of payments. That is about the impact of a 2-dollar change in the price of oil per barrel, with one significant difference: instead of being able to cut back its use of higher-priced money, Brazil is required to borrow even more to offset the larger deficit. This is by now an old story to U.S. officials; all our allies are upset. But one might have expected more sympathy for the plight of a Brazil experiencing a serious recession because of its international payments problems. Instead, Paul Volcker, during his trip in September 1981, apparently stressed the need for greater Brazilian discipline. Only later did the realization of the dimensions of the problem sink in.

What the United States has offered to Brazil through its endorsement of free trade, and hence the market access vital to Brazil's development prospects, it threatens to take back by insisting on Brazil's graduation from special preferential benefits that its developing-country status has so far bestowed. In 1981 three Brazilian export categories were removed from the list of products eligible for tariff-free import under the generalized system of preferences. This executive decision—along with removal of twenty-five other categories primarily affecting Hong Kong, Taiwan, and South Korea—was justified as necessary to forestall congressional action depriving these newly industrializing countries of preferences altogether. This bilateral determination affects Brazilian exports only marginally, but it is a worrisome omen. In addition, Brazil has been singled out, along with European exporters, in the steel complaint before the International Trade Commission. Potentially even more serious is a strong U.S. move to deprive Brazil (and other middle-income countries) of access to concessional loans from the World Bank on grounds of its increased per capita income. While the current recession postpones that day of reckoning for some time, the intent is unchanged.

The content of this policy could not carry the burden of the revitalization of the relationship the administration sought. Brazil does not share the fundamental East-West perspective on global problems the United States tried to impose. Brazilian suspicion of detente because of Brazil's fear that the great powers together might seek to freeze power—as in the Nuclear Non-proliferation Treaty—does not translate into an automatic and virulent anti-Sovietism. Brazil's commercial mission to Moscow in 1981 and failure to participate in the grain embargo showed otherwise. Brazil's continuing break in diplomatic relations with Cuba does not mean it will exert itself to remove Cuban troops from Angola or to involve itself in Central America or the Caribbean, as the United States would like. Indeed, a Brazilian high-level commercial mission from the private sector pointedly visited Cuba in January 1981 to examine the possibility of resuming trade—even while Secretary of State Alexander Haig was railing against Cuban intervention as a proxy for the Soviet Union. Brazil's ties with Angola and black Africa are well established and assist growing exports. There is minimal concern for the safety of the South Atlantic, and no interest at all in a military treaty to defend the area. Harsher U.S. actions are more capable of tilting Brazil toward greater hostility to potential American intervention than of rallying more support.

Anti-Sovietism could work in 1964 in the flush of a military revolution to rid Brazil of a subversive threat and because there was a large direct economic payoff in the form of development assistance. Neither factor was relevant before the emergency and in the fall of 1982. Even the hard-line military, preoccupied with the transition from authoritarianism, perceives the threat as internal, not external. And it also saw little economic advantage to be gained.

In its zeal to reconstruct and revitalize the special bilateral relationship through a shared perception of the security threat, the Reagan administration thus misrepresented reality. First, there is no such shared perception, nor is there likely to be, whether the United States successfully promotes closer relationships with the Brazilian military or not. Economic development remains the prime Brazilian objective, and in that area this country was insensitive and even in active opposition. Second, U.S. policy was completely unresponsive to the significant changes under way in Brazil and their implications for this relationship. Third, Brazilian enthusiasm for closer bilateral relations was quite limited. Brazil has had a steady dose of lowered expectations throughout most of the postwar period. Symbolic visits are no longer an

159

adequate substitute for substance, as President Figueiredo's May 1982 trip to Washington underlined.

Final Observations

While these dissonant circumstances intruded into the relationship, they went largely untreated until the fall of 1982. Then the seriousness of Brazil's debt crisis provoked a change. President Reagan put together a hastily scheduled visit in November that was the occasion of announcing an emergency interim loan to tide Brazil over its immediate liquidity problem. The U.S. Treasury and Federal Reserve played, and continue to play, an active role in encouraging continuing private lending, as well as counseling IMF flexibility and support. Shortly after Reagan's Brazilian trip, the United States reversed its opposition to expansion of IMF quotas and espoused the case for them, urging their adoption as quickly as possible.

These actions eloquently confirmed what was wrong with earlier U.S. policy. They struck a responsive chord in the Brazilian government, which was eager for assistance with its payments problems. They came to grips with the primacy of Brazil's economic objectives. In appreciation, Brazil softened its opposition to U.S. initiatives at the GATT ministerial meeting in November and seemed to hold out the promise of closer ties and a more supportive foreign policy.

Can this newfound relationship, vaguely reminiscent of the golden age of 1964–67, long endure? I think not, precisely because it hearkens to a lost past. Temporary economic advantage cannot long divert the independent objectives of Brazil's foreign policy. Brazil—needing oil, external capital, and markets—will necessarily pursue a pragmatic and narrowly self-serving strategy that precludes automatic support for the United States on a continuing basis. It sees itself less as a responsible emergent power and more as a victim of external circumstances which is justified in its subsidies, import controls, and other interventions, as well as in its stands on international issues.

The Reagan administration errs anew if it believes that the financial assistance it has provided to Brazil, and may continue to give, is adequate to achieve its still paramount security objectives. President Figuereido gave public notice of this discrepancy on his recent visit to Mexico when he endorsed that country's peace-making efforts in Central America. Brazil may stop and search Libyan aircraft, but it is not persuaded of the validity of U.S. policies in the region. The basis of a successful bilateral relationship lies in a workable and productive economic interdependence rather than in an illusion of strategic congruence.

In the last analysis, the administration understates the importance of the international economy in setting its foreign policy. For many, if not most, countries, the global economic environment has principal weight. Yet the Williamsburg communique gave little sense that President Reagan is willing to abandon domestic objectives in favor of global goals, and certainly not where the developing countries are concerned. The U.S. commitment to the debt problem goes to the treatment of crisis symptoms and to faith in the power of global economic recovery. But the issue is deeper and not merely short term. The present flows of private bank finance are potentially inadequate to support the economic growth Brazil could, and must, sustain. Brazil does not stand alone, moreover. The question is one of broad policy toward the third world, not bridging loans for one country. The agenda encompasses not only debt, but also trade; not only the rhetoric of free markets, but also domestic economic policies that facilitate U.S. competitiveness. Finally, a more sympathetic stance implies recognition of the legitimate interests of the developing countries in global issues like the law of the sea, arms transfers, nuclear proliferation, and other noneconomic questions.

The administration has come part of the way in the last several months. But that part is easiest because few fundamental changes have been required. The future will require more. Only a different conceptual framework, and continuing concrete actions, will succeed in channeling Brazil's independent pragmatism in less conflictive directions and serve U.S. interests more effectively.

11. Argentina: Rebuilding the Relationship

Gary W. Wynia

Argentina has seldom attracted much attention in the United States. But that is hardly surprising, given its location, its cultural ties to Europe, and its disinterest in being the object of American concern. That changed suddenly on 2 April 1982, when the Argentine army landed on the Falkland/Malvinas Islands, beginning a tragic saga that was reported episode by episode to a baffled world until it ended in Argentina's humiliating defeat by the British military three months later.

Bewilderment about Argentine behavior is nothing new. The country has always been inexplicable to most; it is a nation that is endowed with substantial natural wealth and human capital but persistently plagued by economic emergencies and political debacles. Yet, even now, only the most defeatist persons write Argentina off as unsalvageable, for beneath the veneer of apparent self-destructiveness there lives a sophisticated people known for their ability to survive in relative comfort while constantly flirting with disaster. Whatever their adversities, few Argentines have suffered the deprivations common to Bolvians, Peruvians, and Guatemalans.

Argentine is economically troubled and politically divided today, just as it was before the Falklands/Malvinas war. In 1976 the nation's armed forces took control of a nation shocked by terrorism and economic disorder. They persecuted suspected terrorists along with anyone else who resisted their authority, promising to maintain order, restore economic confidence, and then supervise the creation of some form of constitutional government. But after seven difficult years it become clear that the armed forces had failed, and that Argentines longed for a government of their own choice, whatever the risks.

U.S. officials should make a special effort to assess the forces at work within Argentina carefully and realistically as they respond to events in the months ahead. If they do not, they will undoubtedly repeat many of the embarrassing errors they made during 1981 and 1982. The Falklands/ Malvinas war and its interruption of Argentine-U.S. cooperation has given American leaders an unexpected opportunity to start anew, putting the lessons learned in 1982 to work in the formulation of policies more in line with the interests of the citizens of both countries.

Overview

If anything characterizes Argentine politics, it is the military's habit of evicting civilian presidents only to allow them back into office some years later. After the turn of the century, the middle-class Radical party rose to challenge the conservative oilgarchy's monopoly of public office. But in 1930, after fourteen years of Radical party rule, the oligarchs brought the democratic experiment to a halt, evicting the Radicals in the midst of the world depression with the help of the military. Nothing has occurred since to break the habit of military intervention. What did change later was the primary source of political division within the nation.

In 1943 nationalistic officers turned against the oligarchs, evicting them from office and allowing free elections two years later. Little was the same afterwards. General Juan Domingo Peron was elected president in 1945, ruled for a decade, was overthrown and fled into exile in 1955, returned to become the country's president again in 1973, and died after one year in office. Built primarily on the shoulders of organized labor and the urban poor, the Peronist movement counts from 40 to 60 percent of the Argentine electorate among its constituency.

Whether to allow the Peronists to govern has been the major preoccupation of an Argentine military that turned against Peron in 1955. Three men were elected president after 1955: Radicals Arturo Frondizi in 1958 and Arturo Illia in 1963 in contests from which Peronist candidates were excluded, and Juan Peron in 1973. None completed his term. Frondizi and Illia were removed by the armed forces not long after each had let the Peronists compete in congressional elections, and Peron died two years before his wife and successor, Isabel, was deposed by the military.

Political divisions are reinforced by intense disputes over economic affairs. Disagreements over how to promote the nation's development have split political parties, businessmen, farmers, and labor leaders into two camps: nationalists, who favor a highly protected industrial economy backed by an interventionist government, and internationalists, who are convinced that protection is self-defeating, preferring instead that Argentina rely on agricultural and industrial exports for its growth. Neither group has monopolized policy for long. Instead, the country's economic direction has shifted frequently from determined efforts to achieve the objectives of one approach to

163

equally intense campaigns to apply the dictates of the other. The result has been an unstable, cyclical policy process that has taught enterprising Argentines to hedge their bets against inevitable shifts in official policy.

The most recent policy change came when the military removed the Peronists in 1976. After Peron's death the Peronist movement was torn apart by bitter infighting; at the same time, the country's establishment was frightened by unprecedented terrorism and the country's economy was shaken by record inflation. The military's intervention surprised no one, although the brutality of its antiterrorist campaign did. Once in place, General Jorge Videla and the junta turned the direction of the economy over to civilians from the internationalist camp.

Minister of Economy Jose Martinez de Hoz's prime objective was to make Argentines live by the rules of the marketplace, securing their individual and corporate gains where the laws of supply and demand dictated. Specifically, this involved the gradual opening of a highly protected economy to foreign competition, the reduction of state ownership and economic regulation, and the displacement of "weak" private firms by those able to withstand price competition. Simultaneously, officials sought to reduce a rate of inflation that had soared to over 400 percent in 1976.

In early 1980 Argentine officials and their friends abroad boasted that despite some minor setbacks Martinez de Hoz had worked a miracle of sorts, eliminating price and wage controls, reducing tariffs substantially, lowering inflation to around 100 percent, and raising the country's dollar reserves, from $555 million in 1976 to $9 billion in 1979. But only one year later what was striking was not the government's achievements but how quickly they had vanished. Economic crisis and investor and consumer dispair, not order and growth, plagued the nation. Real gross domestic product fell by 6 percent and manufacturing fell by a shocking 14 percent in 1981. Nothing could have been more embarrassing to an autocratic government that, having eliminated the terrorist threat, justified its rule by claiming a unique capacity to restore order and prosperity to the nation.

Then came the invasion of the Falkland Islands, the European Common Market's five-month blockade of trade with Argentina, Argentina's defeat, and financial panic. Martinez de Hoz's reliance on an overvalued exchange rate in 1979 and 1980 combined with the world recession in 1981 and high interest rates abroad to cause the Argentine foreign debt to soar from $8 billion in 1975 to a record $37 billion at the time of the invasion. Simultaneously, the Argentine peso collapsed, going from twenty-four hundred pesos per U.S. dollar in early 1981 to fifty thousand at the war's end. With the GDP declining by 7 percent in 1982, the postwar government was destitute and its creditors were frightened by the possibility of massive defaults. As the year ended, negotiations between the Argentine government and its creditors, and between both of them and the International Monetary Fund, seemed to be the last hope for bringing the debt problem under control. But no one, in either the military or the political parties, forecast a speedy recovery for the Argentine economy, even under the best of circumstances.

Argentina's economic woes were accompanied by political problems with which the military proved unable to cope. They began as General Roberto Viola replaced President Videla as scheduled in March 1981. From the outset he contended with the rising protests of businessmen upset about the high cost of credit and the threat of foreign competition brought on by lower tariffs. Officials had anticipated that many of the weaker Argentine firms would go under as the economy opened up. But the bankruptcy of some of the country's largest companies and the collapse of sixty financial institutions during 1980 and 1981 was too much. At first Viola acknowledged the protestors, promising to slow tariff reduction and provide subsidized credit to ease short-term debt burdens. He also sought to placate them by inviting delegates from entrepreneurial associations to assume posts in his cabinet. The result, however, was not a new unity, but a divided cabinet that prohibited the formation of a coherent program.

The pleas of political party leaders for the restoration of competitive politics also haunted Viola. Though both he and his predecessor had promised to restore constitutional government, neither was anxious to launch the process. Taking advantage of the government's economic woes and rising editorial criticism of its competence, political party leaders, led by Peronists and Radicals, pressed for the adoption of a program leading to national elections within three years. Viola responded by meeting with individual leaders; he recognized the legitimacy of their pleas but refused to concede to the demand for a restoration schedule. He knew that immediate concessions to the parties might provoke hard-line officers who still distrusted the parties. Yet he also recognized that without the cooperation of these well-entrenched organizations the creation of a legitimate government was impossible. Viola chose the middle ground, but in doing so he neither placated military hard-liners nor satisfied party leaders.

General Viola was forced into early retirement by a frustrated junta only eight months into his term. He was succeeded by General Leopoldo Galtieri, who promised to get the economy's liberalization back on track, but before Galtieri's economics could be tested he launched the invasion, hoping that a swift victory would bring him and the armed forces the popularity and power that had eluded them in the past. Instead, he took his nation to defeat and humiliation. And, like the colleague he had removed eight months before, Galtieri was forced out; General Reynaldo Bignone was brought out of retirement to replace him. With the defeated armed forces in disarray, Bignone scheduled national elections for October 1983 and started the restoration process by announcing a new political parties statute in August 1982. Soon thereafter the Peronists, Radicals, and other parties began registering their members and preparing the way for candidate selection, confident that they had the military on the run, yet quite aware that there was nothing inevitable about the restoration of constitutional government or respect for it after its creation.

U.S.-Argentine Relations

Argentina and the United States have never been close diplomatically, but hostility between them has been minimal and infrequent. Only during World War II did Argentina assume a strategic importance to the United States, and then the United States was given no special access because Argentines claimed neutrality until just before the war ended. Until recently the two countries have gone their separate ways since neither required the help of the other to accomplish its primary foreign policy objectives.

Trade between the two countries is significant, though it is not essential to the technology-hungry Argentines as long as European and Japanese supplies are available. Many U.S. manufacturers have plants or outlets in Argentina, but Argentina is less important to most of them than either Brazil or Mexico. Of more importance to the Argentines is the fact that they compete with the United States in the international grain market. Since the late nineteenth century Argentines have depended on the sale of grain and beef to finance the country's economic development. Today Argentina is the world's fifth largest exporter of grain, selling 10.1 million tons in 1980. Though industry accounts for a larger share of the gross national product than agriculture, reliance on grain exports remains quite high because they supply the foreign exchange needed to purchase capital goods, technology, and raw materials essential to industry. It was this dependence on grain sales and not the Carter administration's human rights policy that led the Argentine government to ignore President Carter's call for a boycott of grain sales to the Soviet Union in 1979. Trade with the Soviet Union after its invasion of Afghanistan was never a matter of dispute in Argentina as it was in the United States. Despite its anticommunism at home the military regime was compelled by economic self-interest to trade with the Russians. U.S. human rights policy was simply irrelevant to this decision. Only by guaranteeing Argentina an equivalent market could the United States have forced a reconsideration of its trade policy.

Argentina must trade with other communist countries as well. Again there is little that the United States can do. Argentina trades with Cuba, for example. The exchange was begun by civilian presidents and is sustained by military ones who have repressed the political Left in their own country. Argentine firms, including some that are American owned, are eager to expand their markets in Cuba and Eastern Europe. Instead of discouraging them, the Argentine government, by following an economic policy that aimed at lowering production costs at home in order to increase sales abroad, tried to promote industrial exports. A central objective of post-1976 economic reform was to increase the country's competitive position. Tariffs were lowered and the peso was overvalued in order to reduce the cost of imported consumer goods that in turn were to induce Argentine industrialists to lower their costs and increase their efficiency, eventually leading to a cheaper product that was competitive in international markets. The strategy is not unique to Argentina, but because of years of protectionism and high labor costs, it is more painful there. For it to work Argentina had to secure new markets abroad against stiff competition from countries like Taiwan, Korea, and Brazil which have been increasing their industrial exports for some time.

In their foreign relations Argentine leaders also have been guided by a tradition of independence from the major powers. This is most evident today in the country's nuclear energy policies. Argentines have refused to sign regional agreements aimed at limiting the proliferation of nuclear weapons. They argue that they have no intention of arming themselves with nuclear weapons but refuse to have their policies circumscribed by treaties with neighbors or the major powers. Traditionally, they have used foreign policy to gain a respect abroad that their domestic woes seemed to deny them. They are sophisticated people who believe they deserve better. Thus to appear to be little more than the instrument of a major power was thought to undermine their independence and with it their self-esteem.

And though U.S. officials might wish otherwise, the Argentine military is not dependent on the United States for its weapons or training. Obviously the armed forces welcome the opportunity to purchase sophisticated weapons from the United States, but this desire can seldom be used by American officials as leverage over the Argentine military establishment. As in the past, the Argentine armed forces can purchase what they need from suppliers in Europe, Israel, and even Brazil, and they can manufacture much at home. The sale of arms to Argentina by the United States gains income for the American arms industry but little diplomatic leverage.

Finally, there is the issue of human rights. The Videla administration was singled out for criticism by President Carter, international organizations, and private groups for the way official and paramilitary forces seized, tortured, and killed the many citizens they suspected of subversion. Disappearance and imprisonment are markedly reduced today, but the government has not relinquished the power to seize anyone it wishes. It is this condition that makes human rights still a major issue in Argentina. The armed forces must also deal with the issue of the "missing ones," those seized since 1976 but still unidentified by the government. Demands for an accounting have grown during the past year and have led to divisions within the military over how to deal with the issue. Some officers want to publish the names and close the books, but others fear that their publication would provoke hostility and retribution from the country's future leaders. For the time being the issue has been excluded from the presidential agenda.

The Reagan administration tried to distract attention away from the issue of human rights, but it will not be turned away. In April 1981 the issue returned to the front pages in the United States with the publication of exiled Argentine editor Jacobo Timerman's account of his imprisonment by the Videla administration. Timerman's moving tale, as well as his presence in the U.S. Senate hearing room, gave human rights activists and congressmen an effective instrument in their successful efforts to block the appointment of Ernest Lefever to the human rights post in the State Department. It also served as a reminder of the loss of human liberty under autocratic rule. Timerman indicted Argentine officers not only for their deprivation of his constitutional rights but also for their anti-Semitism. The latter charge became the subject of intense controversy in Argentina as well as in the United States. Argentines acknowledge the presence of anti-Semitism among some officers and paramilitary groups but disagree on the threat it poses. Yet, whatever the truth, the fact that anti-Semitism and human rights are still the subject of debate in this country is sufficient to require that the Reagan administration confront both issues directly and publicly.

Past U.S. Policy: An Exercise in Self-Defeat

Little good comes from war, and the battle between the Argentines and the British over the Falkland/Malvinas Islands was no exception. It did, however, accomplish one thing: it brought to an end the short-sighted and self-defeating policies of the U.S. government. Their abrupt halt was certainly not welcomed by American officials; had there been no invasion and war, these policies would have been continued as long as conditions permitted.

Policy toward Argentina should aim at protecting U.S. security and promoting trade and other exchanges between the peoples of the two countries. How to achieve those ends is naturally the subject for dispute. Recent experience offers lessons that should inform the discussion in the months ahead. Should they be ignored, past mistakes will probably be repeated.

The Reagan administration's policy within the hemisphere was derived from its bestowal of highest priority to the East-West struggle. To execute its strategy it sought to forge alliances with Latin American governments of like mind which would assist in the suppression of forces considered hostile to U.S. interests and/or favorable to those of the Soviet Union. Argentina was to become a major contributor to the scheme.

Previously reluctant to assist in the execution of any U.S. plan for the hemisphere, the Argentine armed forces, bitter about having been castigated by President Carter for their brutality, welcomed the Reagan administration's shift in priorities. In return for the embrace given them by the new president, Argentine officers offered to assist the United States in Central America. Emboldened by their defeat of terrorists at home, they supplied technical assistance to their colleagues in Honduras and El Salvador in 1981. They also listened sympathetically to U.S. requests for collaboration in increasing U.S. military presence in the South Atlantic, which was to be made possible through American use of Argentine naval or air facilities.

In their eagerness to take advantage of Argentina's sudden receptivity to their plans, American officials lost sight of the superficiality of the entire arrangement. Had the military conflict not undermined the American initiatives, the forces at work within the Argentine political process no doubt would have done so, for the entire effort was based more on wishful thinking about Argentine sympathy for the administration's program than on an accurate understanding of how fickle the military would be as a result of its precarious position within Argentina. More specifically, U.S. policy can be faulted for its inappropriateness, its unattainability, and its perverse political consequences.

First, its inappropriateness. A notable example was the decision to seek an agreement aimed at the use of a military facility in the South Atlantic. What would the United States gain from such a base, or even from the close cooperation of the Argentine navy and air force along the country's southern coast? Very little, it seems. The most critical sea lanes in the area are on the eastern side of the Atlantic, out of reach of the Argentine navy and air force with their limited refueling capabilities. Moreover, given their intense nationalism, it is doubtful that Argentine officers would tolerate the construction of a large U.S.-controlled facility. A small base, on the other hand, would at best only have given the U.S. military a symbolic presence that would do little to deter the Soviets or other U.S. rivals but would do much to irritate the proudly independent Argentine people.

The administration's policies can also be faulted because they were not sustainable, even had there been no war. One should not be deluded by the appearance of Argentine enthusiasm for the Reagan administration's initiatives. Undoubtedly the junta was relieved by the cessation of the Carter human rights policies. Its sudden friendliness cannot be explained from a bilateral perspective, however. The U.S. initiatives came at an unusual time in Argentina, a time when the contenders for power, both military and civilian, were trying to use their recognition by foreign government, business, and academic leaders to reinforce their importance and legitimacy internally. This is rather ironic given the country's tradition of independence from foreigners, but it is not really that strange. Foreign authorities became minor instruments in an internal struggle. This is why Peronist leaders as well as junta members were visiting the United States and making speeches wherever they were invited, from the Council of the Americas to the Harvard Center for International Affairs. Eventually they discovered the diminishing returns of such visits; meanwhile many Americans mistook their actions as evidence that they had suddenly risen in Argentine esteem.

Argentina's new relationship with the United States also aided the military's defense of its extravagant consumption of resources. Even by Latin American standards, it was gorging itself with weapons, subsidies to military-run public enterprises, and additional fringe benefits. After 1976 the regime's fiscally conservative civilians had met with no success in halting the growth in military expenditures, but Galtieri's new minister of economy, Roberto Alemann, extracted the president's pledge to accept substantial cuts in the military budget in 1982. As they often do, the service chiefs cried foul, claiming that their increased foreign obligations, ranging from defending the country against a possible invasion from Chile to working closely with the United States in the South Atlantic, prevented their compliance.

Last but certainly not least were the adverse political consequences of U.S. policy. The Argentine public did not share Viola's and Galtieri's enthusiasm for the Reagan administration and its objective in the region. Political party leaders in particular resented both presidents' attempts to gain credibility outside the country at a time when their power was declining at home. But by reinforcing the military's claim of a strategic mission, the U.S. government gave the Argentine presidents another excuse for treating their civilian opponents as threats to the nation's defense rather than as the legitimate critics that they were. Increasingly at a disadvantage because of the economy's decline, the junta was desperate in 1981 to justify its failure to recognize civilian demands for the immediate restoration of constitutional rule. New external obligations gave the junta one justification, while the invasion of the Falklands/Malvinas provided another.

The Falklands Invasion

Predictably, it was the belligerent Argentine generals and not the Reagan administration's congressional critics who forced the administration to face reality and recognize the naivete of its belief in Argentine dedication to the Reagan agenda for the hemisphere. On 2 April 1982 the Argentine armed forces invaded the Falkland/Malvinas Islands, taking possession of the British-ruled territory over which they had claimed sovereignty since the British had occupied it in 1833. No one, except perhaps the British foreign secretary, was more startled and confused by the Argentines' boldness than Argentina's friends in the Reagan administration were.

Since 1966, when United Nations Resolution 2065 had instructed the Argentines and the British to decolonize the islands, the two countries' diplomats had failed repeatedly to resolve differences between Argentina's claim of complete sovereignty over the islands and the islands' eighteen hundred British citizen-residents' demand that the territory remain under British rule. Argentine governments had threatened invasion in the past but seldom had been taken seriously by procrastinating British governments that did not want to risk the domestic political repercussions of islanders protesting against turning the territory over to the Argentines. When the invasion was finally launched, not even the persuasive power of President Reagan, in a last-minute telephone call to Argentine President Galtieri, could hold back the Argentine armed forces.

Refusing to reward the invaders by acquiescing to their conquest, the Thatcher government sent its fleet to the South Atlantic, hoping to combine military force with hard bargaining in order to secure the eviction of the Argentine troops and the renewal of negotiations over the fate of the islands and their residents. However, when the conflict proved irresolvable through negotiations, a very disappointed U.S. government found itself in the midst of a war between a trusted old ally and an unreliable new one.

U.S. policymakers can learn a great deal from careful study of the invasion and its aftermath. The most obvious lesson is how a desperate military regime can easily misinterpret the intent of a superficial friendship constructed hastily by a new U.S. president. Argentina's claim on the islands merited a more sincere effort to resolution than was made by Labor and Conservative governments in Britain during the 1970s and early 1980s. It is also a popular cause, being embraced by every Argentine from childhood; civilians and military are equally committed to it. But the decision to invade in April was motivated by more specific needs of the Galtieri administration. Some were largely internal. Foremost was Galtieri's need to diffuse rapidly rising public protests against economic austerity. Mass demonstrations against the government, unknown since it took power in 1976, rocked it one week before the invasion. Argentine officers and technocrats, convinced that petroleum will be found near the islands, were also interested in offshore drilling rights. And it is conceivable that some officers welcomed the invasion as a means of resisting Minister of Economy Alemann's attempt to reduce the military budget.

It is on the external front, however, that Galtieri made his most costly miscalculations, some of which were encouraged inadvertently by the Reagan administration's policies. When it invaded, the Argentine military was convinced that the world would accept its conquest as an accomplished fact. The Russians, dependent on Argentine grain, were expected to veto the predictable British-sponsored U.N. Security Council Resolution censuring Argentina for the invasion; instead the Russians abstained. The third world countries were supposed to cheer Argentina's attack on colonialism; however, most of them, plagued by their own border disputes, gave only token support. Great Britain, deep in an economic crisis, was expected to scream loudly, but reluctantly to accept its fate. And, finally, the Argentines' North American ally, though publicly displeased, was to work behind the scenes to calm the British and discourage its European friends from taking reprisals against Argentina. Not surprisingly, Argentina's politically insecure but belligerent military leaders assumed that in exchange for their enthusiastic contributions to U.S. security in Central America, they had earned U.S. toleration of their regional political and security claims, even if their actions were distasteful to a U.S. ally. Here too they miscalculated, though it is easy to understand why, given the Reagan administration's persistent public defense of the Argentine generals.

The invasion should also remind Americans of what unreliable allies Argentina's military rulers can be. The armed forces govern a nation that resents their methods and their inability to learn from their mistakes. Moreover, the Argentine junta was never fully committed to the Reagan administration's anti-Soviet objectives, for, though it was anticommunistic at home, it needed the Soviet grain market for economic survival. The foreign exchange and financial crises the junta faced after the war only increased its dependence. This does not mean that the Argentines will ally themselves militarily with the Soviets, as some were predicting when U.S.-Argentine relations turned sour during the war. What it means is that when matters within Argentina necessitate setting out on nationalistic adventures disapproved of by the United States, the Argentine military will do so. In short, Argentines are not natural enemies of the United States, but neither are they about to be close allies, especially when they are governed by officers who have no means to sustain their authority other than physical force and emotional nationalism.

The Political Future

It is essential that a distinction be made between what is transient and what is enduring in Argentine politics. This is especially so at a time when Argentines are trying to chart a course leading to constitutional government that will be neither smooth nor guaranteed of success.

Argentine politics have never been simple. The military does not view itself as the ally of a small rural oligarchy, but rather as the restorer of order and discipline to a society plagued by political conflict. It has been frustrated by civilian politicians and frightened by terrorists, and it is tired of the country's economic troubles. But its approach to the nation's governance has proven too rigid, cruel, and simplistic. Convinced that competitive politics are destructive, the military believes that its duty is to offer something else. Yet repeatedly it has been forced to face the fact that it cannot ruthlessly wipe the slate clean and start anew. Sooner or later disappointed service commanders always discover the impossibility of their task and make their way to the nearest exit, albeit temporarily. The Argentine regime created in 1976 has endured longer than its predecessors, but its rule has been more disastrous to the country and embarrassing to the military itself than that of its predecessors.

The principal opponents of military rule within Argentina today are not terrorists, but the political parties that have governed the country during the past thirty years. In 1976 Argentine party leaders accepted the need to defeat terrorism militarily; they knew that they had as much to lose from a terrorist victory as did the military. But they parted company with President Videla when repression was extended to party leaders, journalists, and many others who had no association with terrorism. Nevertheless, parties like the Peronists and Radicals had little choice but to wait until the military undermined itself before reasserting themselves in 1981. When they did, they were ready to engage once again in the familiar but precarious game of negotiating the military's withdrawal from office.

Argentine political parties must share some of the blame for the country's economic and political condition. They and the military, along with labor leaders, businessmen, and farmers, are intense competitors, and each has contributed to the country's malaise. But the parties remain a major force and will not go away, as the armed forces repeatedly discovers. In June 1981 the five largest parties, led by the Peronists and Radicals, formed a united front dedicated to persuading the president to restore constitutional rule following a schedule leading to open elections in 1984. Six months later they took the unprecedented step of issuing a declaration of principles, promising a moderate course in economic and social policy once the constitution is reinstated. A move toward unity that might seem normal in most democracies was a major achievement in Argentina. Peronist and non-Peronist political parties, long bitter rivals, had at last discovered the virtues of a common agenda and the necessity of working with rather than against each other. Anything less, they now acknowledge, would be self-defeating.

It is the survival of the political parties that made the Reagan administration's approach to Argentine politics appear so deficient and its initiatives so inopportune. Ambassador Jeane Kirkpatrick's visit to Buenos Aires in 1981 was just one of many examples of this. By refusing to talk with party leaders who were already discussing their views with Argentine government officials and the staff of the U.S. embassy, she conveyed a message, even if unintended, of the Reagan administration's opposition to them. Ignoring party leaders was strange behavior, especially by a U.S. official who has argued so intensely for recognition of the fact that one of the attributes that distinguishes an authoritarian government like Argentina's from a totalitarian one like Cuba's is the ability of the former to achieve the coveted goal of redemocratization.

Nothing conveyed the growth of opposition to military rule better than the criticism expressed by the leadership of the Roman Catholic hierarchy. The traditionally conservative Church leaders had tacitly supported the Videla government in 1976. The support was withdrawn five years later when they publicly called for the restoration of democratic government and the rule of law. One might accuse the political parties of being motivated by nothing more than narrow self-interest in their drive to restore constitutional rule, but this is hardly true of the clergy. In July 1981 Church leaders called for national reconciliation, and in December they held a much publicized meeting with the parties in the national front. The message that the bishops sent the military was clear: the war against terrorism was over, the time had come to allow other Argentine patriots the opportunity to govern the nation.

The Argentine people emerged from the war confused, demoralized, and bitter, eager to blame others for their fate. Disgust with their military's conduct was common, and the denial of any means for punishing the military for its misdeeds only increased public frustration. Much of the Argentines' wrath was directed at the British and their American allies, no doubt in part because of the need for scapegoats. But the Argentines were also convinced that the British victory was made possible by American supplies of fuels and other materials. The necessity of American loyalty to its British ally was generally understood, but that did not make accepting the Reagan administration's abrupt shift in policy early in the conflict any easier to accept.

But despite a bitterness that will linger for some time to come, the impact of the war on Argentine diplomacy will not be as great as was feared at the war's end. Argentines have no choice but to maintain normal relations with the nations of Western Europe and the United States. Argentina's unfortunate economic dependence and vulnerability dictates cooperation. To be sure, if elections are held, nationalistic rhetoric will be heard, and the new government, whether Peronist or Radical, will reverse some policies, giving higher priority to protecting national enterprise against foreign competition and compensating those who suffered from economic liberalization. But it is no longer a simple matter (if it ever was) of Argentina versus the rest of the world. If current party platforms are to be believed, party leaders are aware of the nation's plight and recognize the limits it places on their nationalistic ambitions.

A New Realism

The time for wishful thinking is over. Argentina must be dealt with as it is rather than as American strategists would like it to be. The Falklands/Malvinas debacle has, it is to be hoped, made that clear. Argentina cannot be made to serve as an instrument of U.S. foreign policy, as was hoped a few years ago. It must be regarded as a nation without any natural enmity toward the United States but one that will be an unreliable ally as long as its domestic politics is plagued by deep divisions that make consistent policy impossible.

To begin with, American officials should give up hope of enlisting the Argentine military to help them achieve their strategic objectives elsewhere in the hemisphere. Clearly little is gained from such adventures, and at worst they merely tie the United States to an insecure armed forces that enjoy using their foreign obligations to justify the repression of their opponents at home. Second, the United States should do nothing to discourage the restoration and operation of civilian rule, no matter how removed from the center stage U.S. actions might seem to be. Civilian governments may not prove to be compliant with American wishes, but they offer the only route to a humane, civilized political life for this troubled nation.

Third, the United States can play a constructive role in the postwar era. Though it can hardly function as a mediator between Britain and Argentina, it can help advance the process of negotiation in the United Nations or some other appropriate body. A long-term solution to the Falklands/Malvinas matter is needed, and the United States, even if it has to work through other parties, has the clout required to start serious discussions. Understandably, English intransigence will delay progress, but that is no reason for procrastination. To save face, the Argentines cannot start the discussion, and obviously the English will do nothing to reopen the issue for the time being. But the desire is there on the Argentine side, along with the hope that the U.S. government will discreetly assist in the effort.

Life is not easy for Argentines or for the foreign governments that deal with them. But there is no reason that U.S. officials should make it any more difficult by lending their support to Argentina's autocratic rulers in the hope of achieving ill-conceived and illusive security objectives.

12. Chile: From Democracy to Authoritarianism

Arturo Valenzuela and Robert Kaufman

The U.S. presidential campaign of 1980 was followed as avidly in Santiago, Chile, as it was in any American city. Officials of the government of General Augusto Pinochet hoped that a Ronald Reagan victory would help normalize relations with the United States after several years of antagonism over Chile's human rights record. By contrast, prominent figures of Chile's civilian political groups, including the late former President Eduardo Frei, looked to a possible Reagan victory with foreboding. They feared that an end to U.S. concern for human rights not only might lead to greater government abuses, but, more fundamentally, might set back efforts to return the country to democratic politics and the rule of law.

During the Carter years relations between Chile and the United States were cold and tense. Arms sales to Chile were cut off and bilateral aid was reduced to a trickle. U.S. representatives of multilateral lending institutions were instructed to vote against loans to Chile. After the Chilean government was implicated in the assassination in Washington of former Chilean Ambassador Orlando Letelier, Export-Import Bank credits were banned.

Upon his election to the presidency, Ronald Reagan moved quickly to reestablish closer ties with the military dictatorships of the Southern Cone, significantly changing the tone and direction of U.S.-Chilean relations. The restrictions on economic credit and arms sales imposed by the Carter administration were lifted. Reagan emissaries, including General Vernon Walters, United Nations Ambassador Jeane Kirkpatrick, National Security Advisor Roger Fontaine, and Undersecretary of State Thomas Enders, have visited Chile to engage in high-level conversations with Pinochet and top officials of his government. Career foreign service officer George Landau was replaced by conservative academic James Theberge as United States ambassador to Chile.

After the war over the Falkland/Malvinas Islands in which Chile took a neutral, if not openly pro-British stance while most Latin American nations supported Argentina, the Reagan administration once again signaled its expectations that ties with Chile would be strengthened. In July 1982 a joint seminar, organized by the U.S. embassy and the Chilean Superior Academy of National Security, was attended by high-level U.S. officials including Fontaine and Assistant Secretary of State Everett E. Briggs. In a widely publicized speech, Briggs praised Chile as a "model of free-market economics," noting that Pinochet's "program to return to a real and long lasting democracy arouses the interest and solidarity of President Reagan's administration."[1]

At stake for U.S.-Chilean relations is an issue that has been extant at least since the early 1970s: the presumed conflict between a U.S. commitment to human rights and democracy, and the defense of American security interests. Reagan officials argue that their friendlier approach to regimes such as Chile's reflects a more pragmatic adaptation to a number of realities that were ignored by Carter's emphasis on human rights. These perceived realities include: the inherent tendency toward authoritarian politics and governments in Latin America; the importance of anticommunist dictatorships as bulwarks against external Soviet threats to the hemisphere; and the viability of authoritarian regimes as the only real alternative to internally based Marxist movements supported by the enemies of the United States. According to the administration a policy based on such realities will safeguard U.S. security interests and at the same time encourage democracy and achieve more human rights gains through quiet diplomacy.

It is our contention, however, that the Reagan foreign policy toward the Southern Cone countries, and more particularly toward Chile, has lost touch with the situation and is most detrimental to the long-run security interests of the United States. In the first place, the policy misreads the profoundly democratic character of Chilean politics prior to the 1973 coup. Second, it misconstrues the character and stability of the military government led by General Pinochet. Third, and most seriously, it adopts a short-sighted and counterproductive view of political alternatives to the Chilean dictatorship, alternatives that include the reestablishment of democratic politics.

The stark reality is that the longer the Pinochet government remains in power, the more difficult it will be for democratic sectors to effect such a transition, and the more likely that Chilean politics will be characterized by significant instability. Indeed, during Reagan's first year in office human rights violations increased substantially and were aimed primarily at centrist

---

[1]Everett E. Briggs, "Bilateral Foreign Policy: The United States and Chile," mimeo presented to the Seminar on Foreign Policy sponsored by the Chilean National Security Academy, U.S. Embassy, USICA, Santiago, Chile, 20–22 July 1982, p. 2.

political forces committed to democratic politics. The paradox of the Reagan administration policy is that it is encouraging the very outcome it seeks to avoid. What is being sought with so little success in El Salvador today—a responsible centrist alternative to the extremes of the political process and strong institutional structures capable of conducting public policy in a fair and democratic manner—is still possible in Chile. However, it is being undermined daily by the repressive tactics of a regime that is intent on destroying moderate political alternatives in order to ensure its own survival.

Increased repression is but a sign of the substantial weakening of a regime that is presiding over a catastrophic economic situation in which the banking system has virtually defaulted and much of domestic industry has been decimated while unemployment has risen to close to 30 percent. By attempting to cling to power in view of broad-scale dissent, which now extends to most of the business community, the government is encouraging further polarization of the political process and is paving the way for a highly unstable political future in which elements bent on revolutionary warfare may gain a measure of influence, to the detriment of hemispheric and U.S. interests. While the United States cannot necesssarily control events in a country such as Chile, its actions are closely monitored by key groups that can be encouraged or discouraged in their policies by effective U.S. action. This is particularly the case in a situation of extreme economic vulnerability. By ignoring political leaders and opposition forces that may very well constitute the core of a future government, the Reagan administration is simply fostering suspicions and misunderstandings which might make it difficult to establish viable relations in the future.

Overview

An important presupposition of the Reagan claim to "realism" in its South American policies is its skepticism about the viability of democracy in that part of the world. In an article that brought her to the future president's attention, Jeane Kirkpatrick provides the most articulate public rationale of the current administration's position. The Carter human rights policy was a form of "misguided moralism" based on the naive American assumption that it is "possible to democratize governments anytime, anywhere, under any circumstance." But "most governments in the world are, as they always have been, autocracies of one kind or another." Consequently, in framing U.S. policy, it is important to distinguish between relatively benign "authoritarian" regimes that are passive, friendly to U.S. interests, and not systematically repressive, and the more malevolent, generally pro-Soviet "totalitarian regimes" of the Left. Since democracy is elusive, the United States should support the first type in order to avoid the second.[2]

[2]Jeane Kirkpatrick, "Dictatorships and Double Standards," in Human Rights and U.S. Human

178

What is striking about this analysis is how inconsistent it is with Chilean reality, and thus how irrelevant it is as a basis for U.S. policy toward that country. Chilean political institutions prior to the Pinochet government were among the most democratic in the world. By the same token, the Pinochet government fails to accord to the stereotype of a relatively unobtrusive but stable authoritarianism that can be safely tolerated, if not encouraged, for want of better options.

As early as the 1840s, some twenty years after independence from Spain, elected presidents shared authority in Chile with a strong national legislature and an independent judiciary. By the 1870s suffrage had been expanded and active political parties with grass-roots support had begun to establish themselves on the political scene. Before 1973 constitutional stability was disrupted only twice, setting Chile apart not only from its Latin American neighbors, but from most European countries as well. In 1891 there was a brief civil war that pitted the legislature against an intransigent executive, and in 1924 and 1932 the military became directly involved in politics, disrupting constitutional practices for several weeks. Before Pinochet no Chilean president had ruled without the mandate of a free and competitive election. Indeed, if Pinochet lasts until September of 1983 his will become the longest tenure of any chief executive in Chilean history.

One of the principal characteristics of Chilean politics in the twentieth century was its strong party system, which spanned the ideological spectrum, giving Chile a political coloration strikingly similar to that of France or Italy. The Right consisted of the traditional Liberal and Conservative parties, which in 1965 merged into the National party, commanding about 20 percent of the vote. Leaders of the Communist and Socialist parties gained parliamentary seats in the early part of the century, and those parties had representation in the left-of-center Popular Front Government elected in 1938. The Communist and Socialist parties gradually increased their voting strength so that by the early 1970s they had close to 40 percent of the vote. The Center in Chile was occupied by the middle-class Radical party, which gave way in the 1960s to Chile's largest party, the Christian Democrats, with approximately 30 percent of the vote.

It was to the Christian Democrats that Chileans turned in 1964 after years of frustration with economic stagnation, high inflation, and social inequality associated with the centrist governments of the 1940s and 1950s and the conservative government of Jorge Alessandri in the early 1960s. Under the leadership of President Eduardo Frei (1964–70), and with massive support from the United States, which viewed Frei as the best answer to Fidel Castro in Latin America, the Christian Democrats embarked on significant reforms.

Rights Policy: Theoretical Approaches and Some Perspectives on Latin America, ed. J. Wiarda (Washington, D.C., American Enterprise Institute, 1982), pp. 11, 26–27. This article originally appeared in *Commentary* 68, no. 5 (November 1979).

However, for many Chileans the reforms were too few and too late. For others, many of whom supported Frei in 1964 to avert the election of Salvador Allende, the candidate of the Socialist and Communist parties, the reforms went too far. In the 1970 presidential election, contested by candidates of the Center, Right, and Left, Allende achieved a plurality of the vote. He was confirmed as president by the Congress after the Christian Democrats obtained his written commitment to respect democratic institutions and procedures. Attempts by the Nixon administration to bribe the Christian Democrats to oppose Allende's election in Congress and to induce the Chilean armed forces to overthrow the government proved unsuccessful.

The Allende government sought dramatic changes in the socioeconomic organization of Chilean society. Its policies plunged the country into a severe economic and political crisis. It can be argued that the reforms sought were too far reaching; that the economy was seriously mismanaged; that the coalition government of six parties was chaotic and unworkable; that Allende was too soft on the extreme left fringe of Chilean politics and that he needlessly provoked the profound antagonism of domestic opponents and the United States. On the other hand, many of Allende's policy objectives (such as land reform and a strong state role in the economy) were shared by a majority of the electorate and, in whole or in part, by many opposition elements. All parties in the Chilean Congress, including the conservative National party, voted in favor of the Allende initiative to nationalize the American-owned copper mines. And though elected as a minority president, Allende commanded a substantial and growing support within the electorate during his three years in office.

For all the serious difficulties Chile faced during the Allende years, it must be underscored that the country continued to be a vigorous democracy. Few countries in the world have had as free and active a press with such a range of opinion. The political opposition adamantly opposed the government from its majority position in the congress. The courts continued to function, often reversing government initiatives. Full rights of assembly and debate extended across the political spectrum and elections continued to be held on schedule. Nor did the economic and political crisis lead a majority of Chileans to conclude that a deviation from constitutional procedures was the only solution to the country's difficulties. In the March 1973 congressional elections the government parties gained seats as voters denied opposition parties the gains in Congress that would have allowed them to impeach the president. Shortly before the coup, polls conducted by the opposition showed that a substantial majority of the population opposed a military coup.

Despite the efforts of courageous leaders on both sides of the political divide, Chile's political elites were not able to bring about a democratic solution in time to prevent military intervention. Allende became an increasingly lonely figure, resisting the cries in some quarters to arm workers even as evidence mounted that a coup was imminent, while fearing a compromise with opposition parties lest he be further isolated from his own supporters. When compromise proved elusive, Allende resolved to call a plebiscite on his government as a constitutional way out of the impassse, a measure that only led the military conspirators to accelerate their timetable for the violent overthrow of the government in which Allende was the most prominent victim. Large sectors of the middle class welcomed the coup as a way to overcome the chaos and uncertainty of a regime that they felt was leading the country to ruin.

"It may not be always easy to distinguish between democratic and totalitarian agents of change," comments Kirkpatrick in her 1979 article, "but it is also not difficult. Authentic democratic revolutionaries aim at securing governments based on the consent of the governed and believe that ordinary men are capable of using freedom, knowing their own interests, choosing rulers."[3] The reasons for the military coup that overthrew Allende are complex and include the mistakes of his government. Yet Allende was not a totalitarian agent of change. The breakdown of democracy in Chile was the result of extreme polarization of Chilean politics which undermined the strength of traditional institutions and destroyed a balance of power among contending groups that historically had resolved their differences through consensus and compromise.

The Pinochet Government as a "Traditional Military Autocracy"

The government of General Pinochet did not seize power with the intention of correcting the abuses of the politicians and then turning the country back to democratic rule. Confounding many of its early supporters, the military government has turned out to be the most revolutionary in the nation's history. With brutality unprecedented in Chile, thousands of persons were arrested, killed, and tortured, and countless others were forced into exile. The Chilean congress has been shut for nearly nine years, and will be shut for another seven according to current plans. All political parties have been disbanded. Many of the country's top political leaders (along with thousands of others) have been exiled. Labor unions have been purged and their leadership has been harassed, exiled, or killed. Universities dismissed thousands of students and fired hundreds of faculty members including, in recent years, those who opposed the Allende government. Chile's once proud universities continue to be governed in a highly authoritarian manner by military officers appointed directly by the president. Government policies

[3]Ibid., p. 28.

have led to strong confrontations with Chile's Roman Catholic cardinal and a majority of the bishops, as the Church has sought to safeguard basic human rights, academic freedom, the right to free expression, and a return to democratic practices.

The Chilean regime is best described as a personalistic military dictatorship. In most recent Latin American military regimes presidential authority has been rotated among different military leaders, but Pinochet has managed not only to remain in power, but also to consolidate further his authority through a skillful manipulation of military promotions.

The constitution of 1980, adopted in a national plebiscite that gave few guarantees of impartiality and fairness, ratifies Pinochet's personal rule for the next sixteen years. Its provisions grant him authority to declare a state of emergency, relegate people to internal or external exile, forbid public assembly, and censor all publications. In sharp contrast with Chile's 1833 and 1925 constitutions and legal traditions, the new constitution eliminates the right of habeas corpus under emergency rule. While serious violations of basic human rights such as indiscriminate killings and disappearances have declined, they have not been eliminated. In 1981 and 1982 arrests increased, as did incidents of external and internal exile; several cases of brutal torture were documented. This reversed a trend toward amelioration of the worst human rights abuses during the last years of the Carter administration.

Nine years after the coup the government continues to censor publications, prohibit assembly, ban political parties, and outlaw elections. A curfew is still in effect in Santiago, and emergency measures continue in force. Ironically, the continuation of these repressive policies, rather than indicating the success of the government in consolidating its authority, is an indicator of its continued instability. Pinochet's effort to create new institutions that would make the traditional political institutions and political parties obsolete has proven so far a resounding failure. Political parties formed in the nineteenth century and early twentieth century have survived, though their leadership has been severely hurt and their organizational capacity has declined. New rules and procedures aimed at breaking the back of the traditional labor and student movements have failed to create new and depoliticized organizations, as opposition elements identified with traditional parties have succeeded in garnering most leadership positions. The few labor leaders who supported the coup have now joined the ranks of the opposition and are working actively with labor leaders of the proscribed parties. Even in the country's professional associations, such as the College of Medicine, many of whose members also supported the coup, opposition slates have been elected despite enormous official pressure. The fact is that the military authorities so far have not succeeded in dismantling the essential elements of Chilean civil society which had evolved over so many years. The authoritarian and arbitrary procedures followed in setting public policy, which has excluded organized groups from the decision-making process, have contributed to a growing resentment against the authorities. Pinochet is weaker today than he has been at any time since the coup.

The collapse of Chile's vaunted economic model has only aggravated the regime's political poblems. While government economic policies did succeed in the short run in bringing down inflation, balancing the national budget, accumulating sizeable reserves, and reducing the balance of payments deficits, they also left the economy extremely vulnerable to an international recession.

A much too drastic reduction in tariffs for Chile's overprotected industry led to a significant weakening of the country's industrial base as local companies found it difficult to compete with foreign importers. At the same time, the freezing of the Chilean peso in relation to the dollar, though helping in the fight against inflation by making foreign goods cheap, made it difficult for Chilean exports, which gradually lost whatever comparative advantage they had. Furthermore, the concentration of wealth in the hands of a small group of individuals who, with the aid of massive foreign loans, were able to set up banks and financial institutions to purchase bankrupt industries and industries sold by the state, led to rampant speculative increases of domestic investment.

The first signs of serious difficulties with the Chilean economy came late in 1981, when the government was forced to take over eight bankrupt financial institutions that had close to 20 percent of deposits in the private banking sector. This action deviated sharply from the government's previous commitment to free-market economic policies and presaged the takeover in 1982 of additional financial institutions, including Chile's largest private bank, the Banco de Chile, owned by the second-largest industrial conglomerate in the country. Though the state has covered for the difficulties of the banking system, the weakness of Chilean industry (reflected in an unprecedented number of bankruptcies) and its inability to pay off debts has meant that Chile has had to renegotiate its foreign loans, which now amount to over $18 billion. This is a staggering debt for a country with a population of eleven million. In 1981 Chile used well over two-thirds of its exports of goods to pay off the service on the debt, and the debt service ratio has worsened in 1982.

The severe economic recession has aggravated the plight of the poor, who never benefited much from the military regime, even when the economy seemed to be improving in the late 1970s. By the end of 1982 real wages had declined again to below the 1970 averages and unemployment reached depression levels.

The economic downturn has transformed the rising stream of criticisms of the government into a raging river. Many businessmen and farmers are now arguing that Chile is much worse off today than it ever was under Allende. In response, Pinochet attempted to bring into his cabinet a representative group of domestic businessmen who were critical of his extreme free-market economic policies. However, when the business leaders argued for a political relaxation as well as economic changes, the president reacted angrily, entrusting the government to individuals who had no visible societal support. The government is now extraordinarily isolated; Pinochet makes most of the fundamental decisions himself, and in an increasingly arbitrary fashion. To the criticism in business circles can be added a sharpening of criticism from labor leaders and a renewal of open forms of dissent, particularly in the universities. Growing numbers of military officers are also questioning the wisdom of government policies and the government's long-term viability.

Implications of the Pinochet Regime for Redemocratization and Long-Term Political Stability

Ambassador Kirkpatrick has argued that a U.S. policy of open criticism of dictatorial regimes only weakens them, raising the possibility of a totalitarian rather than a democratic alternative. But such an analysis is far too simplistic. While it may be true that democratic regimes seldom emerge from totalitarian ones, it does not follow that authoritarian regimes are highly conducive to democracy. In fact, by clinging to power through a deliberate destruction of moderate political groups and forces and through wanton disregard of constitutional rules and procedures, authoritarian regimes thwart incipient democratic institutions and undermine old ones. This is clearly the case in Chile, where Pinochet's personal ambitions are the major obstacle to a reinstitution of stable democratic politics. As Kirkpatrick notes, "The longer the autocrat has held power, and the more pervasive his personal influence, the more dependent a nation's institutions will be on him. Without him, the organized life of society will collapse like an arch from which the keystone has been removed."[4] The longer Pinochet and the military stay in power, the greater the process of societal and political disintegration, the greater the personalization of the regime, and the lesser the likelihood of the stable democratic outcome which the Reagan administration professes to be the ultimate goal of its policies; conversely, the more likely a situation of continuous unrest and instability in which extremists of both the Left and the Right with no democratic conviction would dominate the political process, as they do in much of Central America today. The best guarantee against totalitarianism is not authoritarianism but stable democracy. As Juan Linz has noted, authoritarian regimes are more likely to become leftist totalitarian ones. No democratic regime has gone that route without direct external military intervention.[5]

[4]Ibid., p. 13.
[5]Juan J. Linz, *The Breakdown of Democratic Regimes: Crisis, Breakdown, and Reequilibration* (Baltimore, Johns Hopkins University Press, 1978), p. 15.

Because it seeks to retain power by destroying Chile's democratic institutions, the Pinochet government has taken aim at a range of moderate organized civilian groups, including professional associations, community and religious groups, and labor unions. Above all, repression has been directed toward Chile's traditional political parties, the institutions most capable of promoting the return to democratic institutions, basic political freedoms, and the rule of law.

The government has dealt harshly with Chile's largest party, the Christian Democrats. As the party of the. Center and the party with close ties to the Roman Catholic hierarchy, the Christian Democrats are in a position to play a key mediating role with both the Left and the Right. They have outstanding leaders and technocrats with significant government experience, particularly in the economic field. They also enjoy considerable support within the armed forces and among sectors that strongly opposed the Allende government.

For these reasons the military authorities seem to feel threatened by the Christian Democratic party and have made it difficult for the party to survive and function. Its newspaper was closed, its leading magazine has been periodically confiscated, its radio stations have been silenced or severely curbed, and several of its books have been banned. Key leaders of the party have been exiled without the possibility of judicial appeal. They include two former party presidents, Renan Fuentealba and Andres Zaldivar, both of whom held high positions in the Frei administration. More recently, former Minister of Justice Jaime Castillo, a prominent leader of the party and founder of Chile's Human Rights Commission, was exiled for signing a letter in support of several labor leaders (including the Christian Democratic president of the country's largest federation) who were imprisoned by government authorities for "illegally" representing workers. In January 1982 Castillo, Zaldivar, Fuentealba, and Claudio Huepe, a former congressman, were barred from entering the country when they flew to Chile to attend the funeral of former president Frei, who had become the most prominent opponent of the military junta and who continued to enjoy enormous popular support until his death. Another Christian Democratic exile, former Minister of the Interior Bernardo Leighton, a highly regarded leader with close personal ties to pollitical leaders in all parties, was shot in Rome.

The Christian Democratic party is the same party that the United States strongly supported in the 1960s as a counterforce to Cuban communism. Support included extensive covert subsidy of party activities and electoral campaigns, at times without the knowledge of party leaders, and extraordinary amounts of foreign assistance for Chile when the party held the presidency.

The Reagan administration has committed itself to backing the Christian Democrats in El Salvador with a similar rationale while lamenting their weakness and the weakness of democratic forces in a country polarized between an insurrectionary Left and right-wing groups. It is ironic that at the same time the United States government is tacitly supporting the destruction of

185

the far more important and influential Chilean Christian Democrats. By turning a deaf ear to their plight, and that of other centrist forces in Chile, the United States runs the serious risk of contributing to a further polarization of the political process which could lead the country down the same tragic path that El Salvador has followed.

And if the Christian Democrats have been severely hurt by the Pinochet government, their moderate counterparts on the Left have been dealt an even more serious blow. As late as December of 1981 leaders of the small but influential Christian Left party, an offshoot of the Christian Democrats, were arrested and severely tortured. Their "crime" consisted of sponsoring, along with other democratic parties of the Left, a series of meetings about the future of Chilean democracy and the unity of the noncommunist Left. These parties are committed to Chile's historical tradition of democratic procedures and institutions and have strongly repudiated extremist sectors calling for armed insurrection. The noncommunist Left in Chile, including the Socialist party, commands an important following in the country, with between 25 and 30 percent of the electorate, and would play a crucial role, along with the Christian Democrats, in any effort to move back to constitutional government.

But the Pinochet government has no interest in allowing any constructive political dialogue to prosper. Few of the leaders of Chile's leftist parties are in the country. When Jaime Castillo, the head of Chile's Human Rights Commission, was exiled, he was joined by three other prominent leaders of the moderate wing of Chile's Socialist opposition. Included in the group was Carlos Briones, the highly respected minister of the interior in Allende's last cabinet. Briones, the universally respected long-time former head of Chile's social security administration, was never imprisoned by the military, though he was detained for a time under house arrest. By exiling him, along with Alberto Jerez, a former senator of the Christian Left party, and Orlando Cantuarias, a former senator of the middle-class Radical party, the government further reduced the number of prominent leaders of Chile's Left who were committed to democracy.

And, in an ominous development, Tucapel Jimenez, a prominent labor leader, was assassinated in late February 1982 by elements apparently connected with the security forces. Jimenez, the long-time head of the National Association of Government Employees and one of the few labor leaders to support the coup, had become publicly critical of the military government. He was actively working with labor, business, and political leaders for unity of the moderate sectors of the opposition. His death recalls the attempt on Bernardo Leighton's life in Rome and the assassination of former Chilean Foreign Minister Orlando Letelier in the streets of Washington and the murder of General Carlos Prats, commander in chief of the army during the Allende years, in a residential neighborhood of Buenos Aires. All were prominent and moderate leaders of the opposition.

Ironically, by repressing the Christian Democrats and the moderate Left, the authorities are playing directly into the hands of the isolated and numerically insignificant forces of the revolutionary Left. They are also playing into the hands of the strong Chilean Communist party, which recently issued a declaration advocating, for the first time in its history, the violent overthrow of the regime. Unlike the democratic parties, which function in the open and have been schooled in the art of electoral appeals, the extreme Left and the Communist party have the organizational capacity and will to create underground organizations capable of surviving repression and expanding their base among discontented sectors of the population. It is premature to evaluate the consequences of the strategy being pursued by the Communist party. There is evidence of bitter disagreements in party ranks over the call to arms, with most of the opposition coming from leaders in Chile itself who are skeptical of orders sent by party leaders in Moscow. It is clear that the repression of moderate political leaders of the democratic Left has the effect of strengthening the hand of those within the Communist party who argue that the time has come to create an armed insurrectionary movement.

In sum, in confusing its own survival with the long-term interests of the country, the Pinochet government is seeking to eliminate the very elements that would make possible a transition to democracy and stable representative government. Democratic forces view with alarm a policy that curbs their ability to maintain an organizational presence as political institutions capable of channeling demands and controlling societal forces in an orderly and just fashion. The weakness of moderate forces simply adds to the political uncertainty of any transition process and makes more likely a future racked by instability—which can only give comfort to totalitarian elements.

This alarm is shared by important elements committed to democratic politics on the right of the political spectrum and by much of the big business community, most of which supported the coup and the Pinochet government in its early years. It is also understood by moderate elements within the government itself which have been pressing with little success for a liberalization of the regime. They have argued that the image of the regime has been severely hurt by indiscriminate violations of human rights and the government's refusal to expand civil and political rights. They urged the adoption of a more moderate constitution and a more rapid transition to civilian rule, only to be overruled by Pinochet.

Many former members of the National party, proud of Chile's tradition of democratic politics, worry that by postponing a civilian opening, the regime is making the transition to democracy more difficult. They also worry that the longer the regime stays in power, the more difficult it will be for National party members to find a place in a democratic political system. If the parties of the Center and the Left have been severely curbed, at least they are struggling to maintain an organizational presence. The National party, by contrast, has simply gone out of business and runs the risk of being overwhelmed by the opposition unless it has a chance to reestablish itself as an organization with a mass constituency in the near future. Prominent business leaders are already attempting to mend fences with the Christian Democrats as the economic situation worsens and they find no organized dissenting voice to the regime on the political Right. And there are signs that the Christian Democrats are picking up support among small business elements and women voters who used to vote for the Right.

A few outstanding conservative political figures have shown considerable courage in working with the opposition parties. Some, for example, labored for months on the Commission of Twenty-Four, which was organized by the Christian Democrats and is composed of representatives of all parties, to draft an alternative to the Pinochet constitution. And a former senator of the National party joined other critics of the regime in speaking for the Right at the recent funeral of Eduardo Frei, which turned out to be the first massive antigovernment political demonstration since the 1973 coup.

Despite government actions, it is still not too late to structure a democratic civilian government in Chile. Because of its democratic past, Chile's parties possess impressive leadership and organizational skills that are rare in most of Latin America. The bitter experience of the Allende government and its dictatorial aftermath has had a sobering effect on most of the country's political elites, who seem intent on avoiding the mistakes of the past. In the face of serious odds, efforts have been made to build a consensus and a genuine spirit of conciliation to guarantee stable democracy in the future. The Christian Democrats seem to be a logical center force that is seeking to bridge the gap between disaffected elements in the business community and sectors on the Left in an attempt to bring about a coherent and unified policy. The problem in Chile today is not the accumulated difficulties of the stormy past, but the inability of Chile's first real authoritarian regime since independence to open up the political process.

Foreign Policy Implications of the Chilean Case for the United States

U.S. foreign policy must take into account the realities of a complex and imperfect world. It cannot be held captive to an idealism that neglects the fact that as a world power the United States must deal with regimes that do not respect human values and democratic freedoms. But neither can it be guided by preconceived assumptions that under the guise of "realism" are incompatible with U.S. values and U.S. basic security interests. By viewing most of the third world, and Latin America in particular, as "traditional autocracies" the United States neglects to consider the vast differences from country to country. By conceiving U.S. options as a simple either/or choice between supporting a friendly anticommunist ally and "installing a government hostile to American interests and policies in the world," in Ambassador Kirkpatrick's words, the United States ignores the fact that many authoritarian regimes are responsible for the lack of stable democratic alternatives.[6] More often than not these regimes are the problem, not the solution.

By adopting a policy toward Chile that neglects consideration of human rights, the United States is siding with the repressive policies of the Pinochet government against moderate political forces; it is also siding with one faction of the government against other factions that have advocated further liberalization.

During the Carter presidency U.S. pressure contributed to the extradition of Michael Townley, the Chilean agent who confessed to the assassination of Orlando Letelier. By contrast, Reagan administration policy, with its emphasis on normalization of relations with Chile, has yielded no concessions in the human rights area on the part of Pinochet and has encouraged his ambitions to perpetuate his rule. The State Department's review of human rights in Chile during 1981 makes it clear that human rights violations increased significantly during the first year of the Republican administration. Indeed, Human Rights Commission President Jaime Castillo and the three leaders of the moderate Left were expelled from Chile only days after Ambassador Jeane Kirkpatrick made a much publicized visit to Santiago, illustrating the fact that "quiet diplomacy" among friends does not work.

Strong pressure from the United States for liberalization of the regime, particularly in view of the deterioration of support for the government and the serious collapse of the Chilean economy, would contribute to the strength of those sectors that are genuinely committed to stable democracy and that are seeking an early return to constitutional rule.

A U.S. policy of pressuring the Chilean government to liberalize would not conflict with the need to coordinate U.S. policy in concert with its neighbors. The Pinochet regime has few defenders on the continent, even among military regimes, which are critical of the excessive personalization of military rule. Pinochet has not been visited by any foreign head of state during his long tenure in office, and his hosts in Brazil and Argentina deliberately downplayed his visit to those countries. Pinochet's position of tacit support for Britain in the Falklands/Malvinas dispute only contributed to his isolation on the continent. Finally, most neighboring countries, including Argentina, Brazil and Uruguay, are now joining Peru and Bolivia in a transition process back to democratic rule which will leave Chile as one of the few military regimes on the continent.

A concern for national security questions, such as the accessibility of the

---

[6]Kirkpatrick, "Dictatorships and Double Standards," p. 9.

sea lanes around Cape Horn and of Chilean ports in the event that the Panama Canal was closed, as well as the implications of war with Argentina over the Beagle Islands, further underlines the importance of restitution of a stable civilian regime. The behavior of the Argentine military in the Falklands/ Malvinas war revealed how erratic and unpredictable a closed regime with limited societal accountability can be, particularly when it has little support and faces mounting problems.

U.S. interests are best served by an early return to democracy in Chile. While maintaining correct diplomatic relations with the Pinochet government, the United States should make it clear that it is unhappy with the prolongation of arbitrary rule. This means, of course, that the Reagan administration should refuse to certify that Chile has made progress on human rights and should threaten to rescind its decision to renew economic and military aid and government-backed credits. Because of the vulnerability of the Chilean economy, the United States should also insist that it will vote against Chilean aid by multilateral agencies and that it is prepared to consider a policy of discouraging loans to Chile by private banks unless the military government gives genuine proof of its willingness to respect political and human rights.

In meeting these objectives, the Pinochet government should be prepared to institute an amnesty for the thousands of Chileans who were exiled without trial. It should discontinue arbitrary arrests and torture and should allow political parties to exercise their rights of assembly and free speech. Finally, and following the recent example of the Argentine military junta, it should announce its willingness to institute a timetable for return to civilian rule within the next year or so, after a period of consultation with the country's political forces which would provide guarantees to the military authorities against retribution for past actions.

Chile provides an opportunity for a bipartisan U.S. foreign policy to state unequivocally its concern for moral and democratic principles and provide genuine support for those in other countries, even small countries, who share and believe in those principles. Such a policy is compatible with the basic values of this nation, but, more importantly, such a policy, by contributing even in small measure to the establishment of a stable and legitimate regime, will stave off the threat of endemic political instability which has caused so much concern elsewhere.

III

U.S. Policies and Latin American Issues

13. U.S. Economic Policy toward Latin America: The Deepening Problem

Richard Newfarmer

Coping with the Inexorable Squeeze

The economies of Latin America entered the 1980s in precarious condition. Steep new jumps in the price of oil in 1979 and 1980, on top of the lagged adjustment to earlier energy price increases, acted to produce a cumulative wave of balance of payments deficits. Then interest rates soared to historical highs because of the monetary and fiscal policies in the industrialized countries, raising the cost of private debt, the principal mechanism Latin America had used to cushion and delay the adjustment to the initial oil price increases. As the 1980 recession in the United States was followed by a minirecovery and new recession in 1981 and 1982, demand for commodity exports from Latin America slumped and their prices fell. By 1982 the region was caught in an inexorable squeeze between rising debt service payments and stagnant export earnings.

These events made 1982 the worst year for Latin America in the postwar period. According to the United Nations Economic Commission for Latin America, the region's economic growth rate was negative 1 percent, or negative 3 percent in per capita terms, the lowest in thirty-five years. This was down from 1.2 percent in 1981 and 5.8 percent in 1980. Inflation averaged nearly 80 percent, higher than any year except 1976. The region's current account deficit was $34 billion in 1981—in the red for the second straight year with little prospect for improvement in 1982. Its external indebtedness has quadrupled since 1977, approaching $300 billion by the end of 1982. The shock of this performance was all the greater because it followed a decade of growth rates consistently above 5 percent.

Most countries had also performed poorly in 1981. In Central America,

193

El Salvador's production fell by almost 9 percent for the second successive year. Costa Rican production fell by 1.5 percent. The Guatemalan and Honduran economies showed no net gains. Nicaragua grew by 6 percent, but production was still well below the level of 1977. Jamaican production was also stagnant, and still below 1973 levels. In Argentina, GDP dropped by 3 percent and inflation was over 90 percent. The Chilean economy slid into deep recession at the close of the year. The Brazilian economy contracted by 3.5 percent. Only Mexico and Peru recorded adequate growth in 1981, with 8 and 4.5 percent, respectively.

But even these bright spots dimmed in 1982. Growth rates in Argentina, Brazil, and Mexico were negative in 1982. The El Salvadorean economy contracted by 4.5 percent, and all Central American countries had negative growth except Panama. Chile registered the largest decline, with 13 percent.

The squeeze caused by rising debt service payments and slowly growing export earnings is part of a much larger set of strains in the international economic system. In international finance, overlending and overborrowing during the 1970s led several countries to the brink of default in the 1980s. With so many countries unable to pay their debt service, the international finance system appeared fragile, scaring many smaller lenders out of the market and thereby further destabilizing the system. But the strains extend beyond finance, to trade. The recession in the industrialized countries, in addition to causing a downturn in the demand for exports from developing countries, created new demands for restrictions on imports to protect domestic jobs, resulting in a round of new protectionist measures in the late 1970s and early 1980s. Latin America's newly industrializing countries, with sizeable manufactured exports and heavy debt—principally Brazil and Mexico—found themselves caught at the center of a mushrooming crisis in finance and in trade. Debt service was rising while protectionism threatened to cut off export earnings that represented the only way out.

The socioeconomic problems of the region, however, go far deeper than the crisis of the early 1980s. With wealth highly concentrated, unemployment and underemployment at persistently high levels, and poverty still the way of life in most areas of Latin America, growth has provided a safety valve permitting a few of the most assertive and fortunate of the poor to climb onto the bottom rung of the consuming middle class. When growth turns to stagnation, latent social discontent not infrequently is translated into demands for political change.

The objective of U.S. economic policy toward the region is to assuage the current crisis and help create the conditions for sustained, broadly shared growth—conditions that often require social reforms as well as changes in government policy. The United States has limited power to influence policies inside developing countries and directly affect the course of development. However, U.S. policy is extremely important in the international financial system and multilateral trading system. For many countries U.S. policy can at times be decisive.

U.S. economic policy toward Latin America may be divided into four overlapping elements: U.S. development assistance, multilateral finance, trade and investment policy, and the Caribbean Basin Initiative. The first element includes the administration's development assistance program. The second involves its policies toward the multilateral development banks and the International Monetary Fund. The third treats those aspects of commercial policy which affect Latin America's trade with the United States and U.S. investments in the hemisphere. The Caribbean Basin Initiative, a fourth component, is a special package of development assistance, trade, and investment incentives. This chapter deals with the first three aspects of U.S. economic policy toward Latin America (see chapter 14 for a discussion of the CBI); its first section describes the program, its second section evaluates it, and its concluding section suggests alternative policies.

The Administration's Program

The administration unveiled its program toward developing countries in a series of speeches and policy statements in the fall of 1981, prior to and during the Cancun Summit in October. The following three ideas are central to the program.

U.S. economic recovery. Growth in the world economy will be vastly aided by economic growth in the United States itself.

Security. World prosperity is contingent upon the security of the United States and all countries of the West.

Reliance on the private sector to promote economic development.

U.S. ECONOMIC RECOVERY

In his principal address on U.S. development policy on 15 October 1981 in Philadelphia, President Reagan stated that U.S. foreign policy proceeds from two important premises: "The need to revitalize the U.S. and world economy . . . and . . . adequate defenses to remain strong and safe." James Baker, Richard Allen, and Secretary of the Treasury Donald Regan all echoed this point on separate occasions in October. Secretary Regan put it this way: "The United States has been working on a plan of action to strengthen its own economy. And the most important contribution that we can make to greater growth and development abroad is sound economic policies at home."

The administration correctly recognizes the strong link between its domestic macroeconomic program and its development policy. Its macroeconomic policies often have more long-term impact on the world's poor than

195

do its development policies. An expanding U.S. economy creates demand for developing countries' exports. Growth and prosperity at home relieve pressures for protection against imports from developing countries. The lower interest rates that stem from a soundly managed U.S. economy can lead directly to lower interest rates abroad. This can help relieve the awesome debt servicing burden of most developing countries.

SECURITY

Few would deny the central role of security in the administration's program. The administration has labored hard to restructure the federal budget in favor of defense spending. In its first eight months in office, it focused on the Soviet Union almost to the exclusion of foreign policy unrelated to superpower relations. It seems clear that U.S.–Latin America and North-South relations are viewed most frequently through the lens of East-West competition and conflict. The administration has evaluated social turmoil in Latin America and elsewhere as the result of Soviet subversion that must be countered rather than as an opportunity for social reform to be facilitated.

RELIANCE ON THE PRIVATE SECTOR

A final pillar of the foreign economic policy is renewed emphasis on the role of the private sector working through free markets as instruments of growth. The administration's philosophy is encapsulated in the president's statement to the IMF and World Bank boards of directors in September 1981: "The societies which achieved the most spectacular, broad-based economic progress in the shortest period of time are [those that] believe in the magic of the marketplace."

Administrative policy, wherever possible, is to encourage and facilitate the growth of the private sector in developing countries. The administration has developed a five-point program, that accords a large role to private-sector-led growth. The program aims to:

> stimulate international trade;
> create regional development strategies (such as the Caribbean Basin Initiative);
> guide assistance into self-sustaining production capacities;
> improve the climate for private investment; and
> create a political atmosphere in which free-market solutions can move forward rather than "founder on a reef of misguided policies that interfere with the international marketplace."

Even the Caribbean Basin Initiative included a number of measures that relied on the private sector and markets.

The emphasis on the private sector can be seen in other actions as well. The administration created a new Bureau for Private Enterprise within the Agency for International Development to involve the U.S. private sector. The administration has also moved to expand the Overseas Private Investment Corporation, a program that stimulates direct investment overseas by insuring U.S. companies against exporpriation, damage during civil strife, and non-convertibility of local currency. In speeches before the IMF and World Bank, the administration repeatedly called for policies to strengthen markets, speed structural adjustment measures, and tie loans to reliance on the market.

The administration's approach to development assistance has three major elements: (1) tepid support for resource transfers, continuing the trend toward real decreases in foreign aid; (2) a reversal of recent U.S. policy favoring multilateral aid over bilateral programs; and (3) increased security-related assistance.

Over the past two decades, foreign economic assistance has been provided in four forms: multilateral assistance (about 14 percent), bilateral development assistance (33 percent), bilateral P.L. 480 "Food for Peace" (20 percent), and bilateral security-supporting assistance (now known as the Economic Support Fund), excluding military (33 percent). The Reagan administration has sought to rely more heavily on bilateral assistance on the grounds that it increases the U.S. political leverage. Early Office of Management of the Budget proposals for fiscal 1982 cut back greatly in concessional multilateral assistance (the International Development Association, the IDA) and cut back modestly in bilateral assistance and P.L. 480; security-supporting assistance was left intact. The eventual compromise with Congress for 1982 increased security assistance by approximately 6 percent (about $150 million), while development assistance for fiscal 1982 was cut by $300 million. The real value of outlays for development assistance was cut by about 10 percent between 1981 and 1982 (see table 13.1).[1]

For fiscal year 1983 the administration proposed to increase outlays from $6.6 billion to $7 billion, a net real decline of about 2 percent after subtracting the effects of inflation. The administration also proposed to increase bilateral balance of payments support through the Economic Support Fund and to offset by increase by decreasing multilateral development assistance, bilateral development assistance, and Food for Peace. By comparison, it proposed increase in military assistance (including guarantees) from $3.7 billion in 1981 to $5.8 billion in 1983 budget authority, a real increase of nearly 40 percent.

Latin America, which lately has received about 10 percent of all U.S. bilateral economic assistance, received a slight increase. About one-third of

[1]William R. Cline, "Foreign Economic Assistance," in *Setting 1981 National Priorities: The 1982 Budget*, ed. J. A. Pechman (Washington, D.C.: Brookings Institution, 1981), pp. 126–27.

Table 13.1
Federal Budget Outlays for Foreign Economic and Financial Assistance
Fiscal Years 1961–83
(billions of dollars unless otherwise specified)

Fiscal Year or Period[1]	Outlays		Percentage of Total Federal Budget Outlays	Percentage of Gross National Product
	Current Prices	Constant 1980 Dollars[2]		
1961–65	6.6	10.5	3.25	0.56
1966–70	3.9	9.9	2.34	0.38
1971–75	3.0	5.5	1.16	0.27
1976–78	4.0	5.3	0.97	0.26
1979	4.7	5.4	0.96	0.20
1980	5.6	5.6	0.97	0.21
1981	6.3	5.7	0.96	0.22
1982[3]	6.6	5.4	0.91	— —
1983[4]	7.0	— —	0.92	— —

SOURCES: *The Budget of the United States Government, Fiscal Year 1971* (Washington, D.C.: GPO, 1971), pp. 587–91; *The Budget of the United States Government, Fiscal Year 1975* (Washington, D.C.: GPO, 1975), pp. 324–28; *The Budget of the United States Government, Fiscal Year 1977* (Washington, D.C.: GPO, 1977), p. 360; *The Budget of the United States Government, Fiscal Year 1982* (Washington, D.C.: GPO, 1982), pp. 600–606; *Organization for Economic Cooperation and Development, Development Cooperation: Efforts and Policies of the Members of the Development Assistance Committee,* 1980 Review (Paris: OECD, 1980) and previous issues; *International Financial Statistics,* 29 (May 1976): 382–83; *Survey of Current Business,* 60 (December 1980); *Budget Revisions, Fiscal Year 1982* (Washington, D.C.: GPO, 1982), p. 37, as presented in William Cline, "Foreign Economic Assistance," in *Setting 1981 National Priorities: The 1982 Budget,* ed. J.A. Pechman (Washington, D.C.: Brookings Insitution, 1981); *The Budget of the United States Goverment, Fiscal Year 1983* (Washington, D.C.: GPO, 1983), pp. 5–23.

NOTE: This table is based on the OECD definition of official development assistance.
[1]The figures for the periods between 1961 and 1978 are annual averages.
[2]The OECD deflator is used for U.S. official development assistance between 1967 and 1977; the U.S. wholesale price index is used for other years.
[3]Estimated.
[4]Proposed.

this bilateral economic assistance was for El Salvador and Jamaica. This share increased with the 350-million-dollar fiscal 1982 authorization for the Caribbean Basin Initiative.

MULTILATERAL FINANCE

The move away from multilateral financing is particularly significant for Latin America. Because of its relatively high per capita income, Latin America receives less bilateral assistance than other regions and relies heavily on the World Bank and the Inter-American Developmental Bank (IDB). From the early 1970s until 1981, U.S. contributions to these institutions grew at a steady rate. From fiscal 1971 through 1980 U.S. contributions to the multilateral development banks totaled $12 billion. U.S. contributions to the

International Development Association, the "soft loan" facility of the World Bank which makes low-interest loans to the world's poorest countries, increased from a yearly rate of $320 million for fiscal years 1973 through 1976 to a high of $1.258 billion for 1979.

The Reagan administration initially viewed these transfers as international welfare programs, however, and sought to cut them. The private sector was encouraged to take up any slack. In February 1982 Treasury Undersecretary Berly Sprinkel announced that U.S. support for soft loans through the IDB and the World Bank would be cut by 26 percent, from $1.537 billion in fiscal 1983 to $1.139 billion in 1987. The cut would have amounted to slashes of 30 to 50 percent in real terms from the levels originally negotiated under previous administrations. The final agreement worked out with Congress was to spread out the commitments made in earlier years over a longer time horizon—from three to five years, or perhaps six years, depending on when Congress finally makes the appropriation. These cuts will have a contractionary multiplier effect, as many other industrialized countries peg their new contributions to the U.S. amount.

In addition to decreasing U.S. contributions to multilateral lending institutions, the administration has moved to tighten up eligibility for both hard and soft loans. For hard loans, the administration advocates a policy of "graduation" which would deny eligibility for countries whose annual per capita income exceeds approximately $2,160 (1980 dollars). Similarly, it advocates "maturation," or moving countries out of soft loan eligibility, when they attain a per capita annual income of about $750. A stringently applied graduation principle would immediately deny multilateral loans to (among Latin American countries) Argentina, which crossed the income threshold in the 1970s, and will soon effect Brazil, Chile, and Mexico, which will cross the threshold sometime in the 1980s. The Bahamas, Barbados, Costa Rica, and Panama may also cross the threshold in this decade. A maturation policy would adversely affect Bolivia, El Salvador, Guyana, Honduras, and Nicaragua, as these countries receive a blend of soft and hard loans.

The debt crisis of the most industrialized countries in Latin America and elsewhere heightens the importance of U.S. policy toward the International Monetary Fund, the international agency charged with helping all countries to overcome short-term balance of payments difficulties. The Reagan administration initially opposed any increases in the IMF's 67-billion-dollar capital. This reluctance grew out of the administration's monetarist philosophy, whose adherents opposed increasing international liquidity, as well as more general concerns with the size of the U.S. budget. But as several countries entered into economic crisis in 1982 and as the full domestic implications of possible default became clear, the administration reversed its position between June and November of 1982.

EVOLVING DIRECTIONS OF U.S. POLICY: TRADE AND INVESTMENT

Like financial policy, trade policy is made in the larger context of commercial relations with all countries, but it has enormous consequences for Latin America. The administration's trade policy appears to be a blend of strong support of an open international trading system against an increasingly protectionist Congress and more vigorous bilateral bargaining with major trading partners, especially Japan and advanced developing countries. The objective of the bilateral bargaining is to curb selected imports and gain greater access to foreign markets for U.S. products and investment.

The administration has taken action in three areas to appease domestic sentiments for increases in protection. In textiles and apparel, it renegotiated a more protectionist Miltifibre Agreement (MFA) in December of 1981.[2] In automobiles, the administration negotiated a "voluntary export restraint" (VER) in May of 1981 with Japan. Japan promised to limit export levels to the United States for two years and to consider a third year of restraint.[3] The steel industry also received increased protection. The administration succeeded in October of 1982 in getting the Europeans to agree to decrease their exports of certain products from 6.6 percent to 5.5 percent of the U.S. market.[4] The U.S. steel industry now seems likely to turn its attention to Brazil.

The administration has also moved to bargain more vigorously with trading partners, especially advanced developing countries, over the terms of access to their markets for both U.S. exports and investment. It has given verbal support to the concept of "reciprocity," meaning that markets in the foreign country should be as accessible to U.S. products and capital as markets in the United States are for that country's products. Several bills before

[2]The MFA, whose origins date back to 1961, is a quota system restricting the import of textiles. The administration dropped its goal of allowing developing countries' exports to rise by 6 percent per year. Instead, the new agreement allows the United States and other industrialized countries to set lower export growth levels in separate agreements with each supplier country. The major exporters, such as Hong Kong, Taiwan, and South Korea, will suffer most, while Latin America, Mexico, Brazil, and non–Caribbean Basin countries will also be denied important export earnings. Under the Caribbean Basin Initiative, quotas now allocated to the Far Eastern producers are slated to be transferred to the Caribbean Basin countries. Earlier the administration abandoned trade adjustment assistance to U.S. workers displaced by imports; this will certainly undercut U.S. labor support for freer trade in the future.

[3]First-year shipments were to be held to about 92 percent of their 1980 levels and those of the second year would rise only by 16.5 percent of the incremental increase in the market, a proportion equal to their U.S. market share. As the recession worsened and the fate of U.S. industry became more problematic, the industry has lobbied for more protectionist legislation.

[4]Several administrations had granted limited protection to the industry, first with VERs, then with the trigger price mechanism (which triggered countervailing duties if prices fell below a fixed price). The system, after several near-deaths, finally broke down in early 1982 under the weight of the recession and historically low rates of capacity utilization. The companies brought a series of countervailing duty suits against European producers before the International Trade Commission on the grounds that exports were subsidized. The U.S. trade representative sought to negotiate a way out of the crisis so as to avoid having to impose countervailing duties of large magnitudes, which risked triggering a retaliation in Europe.

Congress have sought to legislate reciprocity. While endorsing the concepts in general terms, the administration has eschewed support for specific legislation. Reciprocity legislation, together with the bilateral bargaining in steel and autos, is a significant step away from principles of nondiscrimination and multilateralism—principles that usually protect weaker members of the system against bilateral bargaining on unequal terms.

The administration sought to use the ministerial meeting of the General Agreement on Trade and Tariffs in November 1982 to push developing countries for more open markets for investments. The United States proposed a major initiative to have services covered in the `GATT. The initiative is designed to make restrictions on insurance, banking, and information subject to the same kinds of negotiations toward liberalization that now cover international trade. Developing countries opposed this initiative on the grounds that trade in services is not analogous to trade in products because regulation of the latter often involves matters of economic sovereignty. The meeting ended with an agreement only to study the matter.

A final major initiative involves the use of trade-related performance requirements. Many advanced developing countries such as Mexico, Brazil, and Argentina have required U.S. multinational companies (MNCs) to export a portion of their local production. This is a major quid pro quo that MNCs have been forced to accept in order to obtain access to third world markets. The United States has opposed these requirements as protectionist and distortions of trade that hurt its domestic industry. Its proposals in the GATT ministerial on performance requirements were not adopted.

The administration still has hopes for direct negotiations with the advanced developing countries. To coax them to the bargaining table, the administration may propose that Congress limit the trade preferences given to these countries when it seeks to renew the Generalized System of Preferences in the summer of 1983. These countries could then "buy back" the preferences through negotiating.

Program Appraisal

The broad outlines of U.S. economic policy are in place and merit a constructive appraisal. Ameliorating the current economic crisis and reducing poverty, unemployment, and social inequities in Latin America are in the national interests of the United States: security, economic self-interest (in growing overseas markets and resources), and humanitarian interests in alleviating misery. But the Reagan administration has emphasized security concerns, and long-term U.S. economic interests in growth have played a secondary role in the administration's policy. By late 1982, however, the prospect that many U.S. banks may go out of business if several large debtor countries default appeared to have raised the salience of economic interests within the administration. Traditional humanitarian concerns for the welfare of the poor have been relegated to a distant third position.

DEVELOPMENT EFFECTS OF U.S. MACROECONOMIC POLICY

The new emphasis on U.S. domestic economic recovery as a development program is being used to justify cutbacks in foreign assistance levels. For example, asked whether President Reagan was giving thought to more aid, Presidential Aide James Baker replied, "Before we can talk about increasing the percentage share of our gross national product which we give in aid . . . we first have to get our domestic house in order." This relationship between domestic austerity and development policy was restated by Secretary Regan and the president at Cancun.

Dollars transferred from development assistance to the domestic or military budget are not as likely to benefit developing countries as they would be if they were invested in development itself. Only if one dollar invested in the United States triggered a demand greater than one dollar for developing countries' exports could the administration correctly argue that cuts in foreign assistance in the name of U.S. recovery benefit developing countries. This is highly unlikely.

A second, perhaps more important, misgiving regarding the development impact of the domestic recovery program relates to the ill-advised combination of monetary and fiscal policy that has produced record high interest rates. Every percentage point of increase in the U.S. interest rate adds $500 million to the current account deficits of Mexico and Brazil and as much as $4 billion to the deficit of all developing countries. It sharply curtails the funds available to them through international capital markets. High interest rates have also produced an overvalued dollar, large U.S. trade deficits, and strong demands for protection against imports from developing countries. High interest rates have adversely affected economic growth in the United States and in developing countries. The 1983 budget proposals appear to continue with large deficits, although the third-quarter change in Federal Reserve policy has brought down short-term interest rates.

OVEREMPHASIZING SECURITY COULD DISTORT THE DEVELOPMENT EFFORT

Similarly, a heavy emphasis on perceived short-term U.S. security interests in our policy toward Latin America and developing countries has three adverse development effects.

First, the new emphasis on security almost certainly augurs a shift in foreign aid away from development assistance programs toward bilateral security assistance programs. This takes resources away from the effort to reduce poverty in two ways. First, since countries with a U.S. security interest are infrequently among the poorest, the policy shift has the effect of channeling more aid away from the poorest countries. In Latin America, Jamaica has become the largest recipient of U.S. aid, save for El Salvador, and is now among the largest recipients in the world on a per capita basis. Yet Jamaica's per capita income is among the top third of per capita incomes of countries in the region. Within recipient countries, the poor benefit far less from expenditures on arms than they do from development projects.

Second, the program's heavy emphasis on domestic defense spending will create minimal new demand within the United States for the products developing countries produce. When the United States invests in military hardware, the net purchases generated from developing countries are probably far less than if this country had invested in support programs for the U.S. poor, who buy less costly imported clothing and other basic goods. Furthermore, the U.S. military buildup will probably feed the fires of the arms race, reducing the amounts the industrialized countries as a group will have left to allocate to development assistance.

The security focus also affects our political relations with regimes in developing countries. Few knowledgeable observers of the development process would deny that social change and social reforms—in land tenure, in political structures, and in tax systems—are essential for more rapid, broadly shared economic growth in most countries. Yet the emphasis on security builds in a bias toward stability over social change, for supporting the status quo rather than reform. It may even extend to a bias toward sending arms when economic aid is needed. Consider Ambassador Jeane Kirkpatrick's recent statements suggesting that democratic Costa Rica, in the abyss of severe economic crisis, should create an army with U.S.-provided arms; or her statements on recent trips to Brazil and Argentina indicating a new U.S. tolerance for "friendly" authoritarian regimes.

THE PRIVATE SECTOR AND DEVELOPMENT

In the initial stages of the administration, it appeared that the private sector program was designed to justify cutbacks in foreign aid by emphasizing a diminished government role. The program also appealed to the interests of large multinational corporations by apparently offering more support for overseas business activities. Political realities undermined both these purposes. Former Secretary of State Alexander Haig argued vigorously against the early cutbacks on the grounds that foreign aid was an important instrument of U.S. foreign policy, and his view seems to have prevented large cuts. The international financial institutions, which came under close scrutiny in the initial stages of the administration as global welfare programs, by late 1982 came to be perceived as an essential underpinning of the international economic system. Finally, many U.S. businessmen reacted with indifference, even skepticism, to the administration's policies, primarily because the resources allocated to private-sector-related activities were few. (At the same time, the administration cut other programs of considerable importance to business, such as the Export-Import Bank.)

Within the Agency for International Development, the programmatic content has been limited thus far to the fairly small activities of the Private Enterprise Bureau, several internal policy papers, and a greater market orientation in advocating policies for developing countries. The actual resource shift in programs has been less than 2 percent away from existing programs and into private-sector-related programs. This may change as new bureaucratic constituencies gain power.

PRIVATE CAPITAL MARKETS AND MULTILATERAL LENDING

The private sector emphasis of the Reagan program implicitly places a heavy responsibility on the shoulders of large corporations and banks because it implicitly asks the private sector to lead the resource-transfer effort. Indeed, since World War II, private capital in the form of direct and indirect investment has poured out of the United States at dramatic rates. The stock of U.S. direct foreign investment has risen from $11.8 billion in 1950 to $213 billion in 1980. After two decades of being eclipsed by foreign direct investment, commercial bank capital transfers to the developing countries rose more rapidly in the 1970s. In 1980 private U.S. commercial banks lent $131.6 billion overseas.

Viewed from a development perspective, a major problem with private resource flows is that they go to the areas of highest profit and lowest risk—usually the wealthiest countries. About 70 percent of direct foreign investment goes to the industrialized countries; of the remaining 30 percent invested in developing countries, about two-thirds is concentrated in OPEC countries and the leading 10 (of 132) non-OPEC developing countries. Within Latin America, Mexico, Brazil, and Argentina account for about three-quarters of U.S. investment in manufacturing.

About one-half of private commercial bank capital goes to developing countries, but it too is concentrated in a select few. The leading debtor countries—Brazil, Mexico, Argentina, India, and Indonesia—are also among the wealthiest of developing countries. In late 1982 the foreign debt of Brazil and Mexico stood at an estimated $80 billion each.

But this long-term problem of developing finance is eclipsed by the near-term crisis facing much of Latin American and the developing world. Brazil, Mexico, Argentina, and Chile confront large balance of payments deficits. The current account deficits of the principal Caribbean Basin countries is projected to be more than $4 billion in 1982 and greater in 1983. The situation is dangerous not only for the countries involved. In 1982 nine of the largest U.S. banks had exposures in Mexico, Brazil, and Argentina equal to more than 100 percent of their equity.

The matter came to a head in August 1982 when Mexico announced it could no longer meet its external payment requirements and would suspend repayment of loan principal on its 70-billion-dollar debt, pending new negotiations with the banks. To avoid default, Mexico was forced into a massive devaluation and an internal compression of consumption. The United States arranged an "emergency" financial package in excess of $1 billion and Mexico announced later a three-year agreement with the IMF to provide $3.8 billion, conditioned upon slashing government expenditures and establishing a realistic exchange rate policy.

In November, Brazil also acknowledged that its foreign exchange reserves would be exhausted by the end of the year. With the private assurance that it would seek an IMF agreement after the 15 November Brazilian elections, U.S. banks authorized emergency loans of $600 million. During his November trip to Brazil, the president announced an even larger bilateral aid package.

The administration has slowly come to realize the severity of the crisis and begun to modify its position against additional financing of the multilateral financial institutions. The administration had steadfastly opposed increases in the country quotas on the grounds that increases would create excess world liquidity. In the summer 1982 meeting of the IMF in Toronto, the administration initially opposed European requests for a 50 percent increase, but during the course of the meeting softened its position to favor a moderate increase to begin by the end of 1985.

The August crisis in Mexico brought home the fact that more than two dozen developing countries are in positions fairly similar to that of Mexico. The prospect of a string of defaults on loans from U.S. and other foreign banks and the almost certain bailout that would be required by the Federal Reserve apparently convinced the administration to modify its position. In November, Under Secretary for Monetary Affairs Beryl Sprinkel reportedly offered a plan to increase IMF quotas at a meeting of Organization of Economic Cooperation and Development (OECD) partners. The United States also proposed injecting the funds as rapidly as possible (see *New York Times*, 17 November 1982.) A 40 to 50 percent increase is being discussed as well as a special 25-billion-dollar fund for assistance to precarious countries. If no increases of this magnitude occur, several developing countries may have no alternative but default, threatening the financial viability of several large banks in the industrialized countries and with them the entire international financing system.

NEEDED: A MORE VIGOROUS TRADE POLICY

At the very time when export earnings are desperately needed to cope with a severe debt crisis, new protectionist measures in the industrialized world may prevent the growth of Latin America's exports to the industrialized world. Increasing purchases of exports is a way the United States can facilitate new growth throughout the developing world.

The administration deserves credit for arguing persuasively in favor of open markets. Unfortunately, neither its macroeconomic policy nor its domestic labor market policy has aided its liberal trade policy. Macroeconomic policy has undercut the basis for renewed growth and with it the demand for exports from Latin America and elsewhere. To make matters worse, a cut in programs that help U.S. workers during recession, such as job retraining and food stamps, combined with regressive tax policies, worsened labor's plight and undoubtedly fed the fires of protectionism.

Nor has the administration tackled the difficult problem facing the General Agreement on Tariffs and Trade, the rules of the international trading game which protect the international order against protectionism. Instead of proposing a package of well-conceived measures that would strengthen GATT at the ministerial meeting in 1982, the administration sought to pry open markets of developing countries in services and curb trade-related performance requirements. The principal concession it offered was in reality a threat: the administration would fight against new protectionist measures in the United States.

To be sure, U.S. policy has been consistently more liberal than that of Europe, and European Economic Community intransigence on recommitting GATT members to principles of multilateralism and nondiscrimination proved a major stumbling block of GATT. Yet the United States is not totally virtuous: reciprocity, increased protectionism in textiles, apparel, and agriculture, and "voluntary" export restraints are measures that effectively move U.S. trade policy toward bilateralism and discrimination among trading partners. While it might fare better than other developing regions in bilateral bargaining, Latin America would undoubtedly do better in a multilateral context. To maintain its leadership in the multilateral system, the United States must present new wholistic initiatives that speak to the interests of Europe and the developing countries.

As in multilateral lending, graduation of developing countries to full membership in the international trading system is a central issue. The administration is right in proposing that as countries become wealthier and more industrialized they should become ineligible for privileges associated with "developing country" status and accept full responsibility for playing by the rules. On the other hand, they should not be victimized by restraints in products where they are most likely to gain a comparative advantage, for example, textiles, apparel, agriculture, and processed commodities, or even steel and autos. Thus, in negotiations on the terms for graduation in international trade, the United States should hold out real concessions in trade as an incentive to establish principles of graduation.

Of course, services and trade-related performance requirements are important investment issues. But as they are posed by the administration, these issues challenge the entire regulatory apparatus established in advanced developing countries. Many of these regulations were enacted to offset the much greater bargaining power of large multinational corporations. To draw developing countries into a discussion of these matters adequately, the administration must be willing to consider enforceable codes of conduct for MNCs to curb potential restrictive business practices and new policies toward the international treatment of patented technology. These matters are being considered in other international forums (e.g., United Nations Conference on Trade and Development and the World Intellectual Property Organization), but the administration has not been forthcoming in its negotiating position. A new policy will have to take a broader view of these issues and will have to be willing to negotiate a new and more comprehensive arrangement, perhaps in the spirit of the old International Trading Organization or perhaps a new, more comprehensive "GATT for Investment." Serious new initiatives are needed to deal with these interrelated problems.

Toward an Alternative Foreign Economic Policy

Most Latin American countries face several immediate economic problems: rising debt service payments, slow growth of exports, and stagnant or declining national income. In the optimistic scenario the mid- to long-term prospects are not bleak. *If* the industrialized countries fully recover and thereby create new demand for Latin American exports, *if* new trade barriers do not prevent expansion of exports, *if* commercial bank flows increase in real terms by 2 to 3 percent, and *if* official financial flows are sufficient to cover near-term resource gaps, the policy measures most countries have adopted will probably be sufficient to lay the foundation for future growth. The current liquidity crisis will not turn into a solvency crisis.

To these international "ifs" must be added a domestic uncertainty: What will be the internal political response to austerity measures? Serious political protests could undermine the stabilization programs and open major breeches between governments and the international economics system, the consequences of which are unforseeable. Obviously, the less responsive is one component of the optimistic scenario, the more the other components will have to shoulder the burden of adjustment. It is in the interests of the United States to see that the full measure of overcoming the current crisis does not fall solely on the domestic policy.

207

The policies of the administration weigh heavily on the international variables affecting Latin America's future. U.S. policies affect world growth, capital flows, and the openness of the trading system. The administration must reevaluate its economic recovery program, which has been foundering on the reefs of high deficits and, until recently, tight money. U.S. recovery is the single most important short-term palliative that the United States can offer the developing world.

Also, the administration must deal with the international financial and trade problems. Each set of problems is formidable in its own right, but coming together as they do the sets of problems magnify the effects of each other and pose an inestimable threat to the international economic system. If the economic system were to break down in a series of defaults and trade-contracting protectionist measures, the ensuing contraction would hurt all countries, especially the poorest, and within nearly all countries the poor would undoubtedly suffer the most.

Therefore, obvious short-term measures should be taken: the IMF must be expanded (perhaps with the authority to borrow on major capital markets), the World Bank and other multilateral development banks should be capitalized further, and official development assistance (especially multilateral) should be increased. On the trade front, the United States must search for ways to maintain its own openness while negotiating in multilateral forums to maintain the openness of the entire system. A first step would be a freeze on new protectionist measures. Another would be a serious manpower policy at home to ameliorate the plight of the unemployed, including those displaced by trade.

Finally, some effort should be made to coordinate financial and trade policies. The administration's policy toward the financial crisis has been to support adjustment programs in Latin America heavily oriented toward reducing imports and expanding exports. Indeed, increased trade surpluses are necessary in Latin America to service debt. But U.S. trade policy has been to seek increased "market access" for imports from the U.S. with the threat of reducing access of Latin American exports to the United States. This tension in U.S. international economic policy places some Latin American countries in an untenable, no-win situation.

These measures are unlikely to solve the long-term conflicts in finance, trade, and investment. The postwar system is not coping well with the huge expansion of largely unregulated international capital markets and resulting overlending and overborrowing. Nor has the postwar system fully drawn developing countries into an agreed upon set of trading rules that serves their interests. Given the increased connection between trade and investment and between publicly and privately created comparative advantage, it is doubtful that the commercial rules can survive the seismic changes brought on by dramatic increases in the volume of trade, abrupt and wide swings in competitiveness precipitated by floating exchange rates sensitive to financial flows, and changes in the international organization of business (e.g., proliferation of MNCs, state enterprise, and industrial policies affecting trade). Therefore the United States must begin to lay the analytical and political groundwork for a new international initiative designed to overcome these systemic flaws. The developing countries and the other developed countries, along with the United States, have an important interest in a viable, equitable international economic system. The United States should build on that mutual interest.

14. The Caribbean Basin Initiative: Bold Plan or Empty Promise?

Richard E. Feinberg and Richard Newfarmer

Introduction

The Caribbean Basin Initiative marks a radical departure in the international economic policy of the United States. In announcing the CBI, President Reagan swept aside the postwar tradition of globalism—the policy of nondiscrimination that has applied the same rules for trade and investment to all countries—and substituted preferential regionalism in the name of national security. The trade and investment incentives offered by the CBI will benefit the region exclusively, and then only the countries in the region that meet the administration's economic and political criteria. In its worst light, the program could be interpreted as a politicization of trade and investment that ultimately undermines U.S. interests in an expanding, nondiscriminatory trade and investment regime.

In other respects, the CBI is a recognizable mix of basic Reagan administration precepts. The initiative emphasizes anticommunism, bilateralism, private investment, and the free market.

Can the administration join these elements into a policy mix that will enhance political stability and economic growth in the Caribbean Basin, or will the CBI become, as the Alliance for Progress is now seen, just another empty promise? Will the gains to the region in renewed growth, and by inference to U.S. diplomacy, the sufficient to excuse the retreat from globalism?

The Economic Response to Political Problems

The concept of a "Caribbean Basin" is more geopolitical than economic. Central America differs from most of the Caribbean islands in culture, economic structure, and, most importantly, political institutions. In the Dominican Republic and much of the English-speaking Caribbean, relatively stable and democratic structures already exist. Since the negotiation of the new Panama Canal Treaties and the removal of this historic irritant in U.S.-Panamanian relations, Panama too has enjoyed stability and economic prosperity. The Caribbean Basin Initiative has a better chance of success on the Caribbean islands and Panama, where the requisite political stability exists.

In middle Central America, however, the political status quo has been challenged by powerful insurgencies, and violence and chaos are tearing at the very foundations of society. At bottom, the administration is more concerned about the political turmoil and economic decline in Central America than it is concerned about the Caribbean islands. This priority is reflected in the fact that $243 million of the $350 million of the proposed emergency supplemental assistance package is earmarked for Central America.

In Central America the administration's economic and political strategies have been working at cross purposes. The administration's economic plan aims to stimulate business, but a confrontationist diplomacy threatens to delay the restoration of investor confidence. Rather than seriously pursue negotiation among all the major parties to the conflict in El Salvador, the administration has hoped to exclude important sectors from the political process and to defeat them militarily. Rather than working to iron out major disagreements with Nicaragua, the administration has resorted to a policy of verbal threats and, according to media reports, perhaps even to covert paramilitary action. Rather than seeking to isolate Honduras from conflict, the administration proposes to increase military aid, lengthen air strips to handle large military cargo planes, and take actions that may plunge this fragile, imperfect democracy into war. By heightening political cocnflict the United States threatens to inflict deeper wounds on already badly mangled economies.

In response to the recent peace initiative of Mexican President José López Portillo, the administration has shown some renewed interest in negotiations. These efforts deserve commendation because the path of negotiated settlement offers the best hope of reinstating a political climate in which economic growth can occur. However, unless the administration fully commits itself to this new path with a willingness to compromise, negotiations are unlikely to bear fruit. In that case, the violence will escalate and the economies of Central America will continue to decline sharply.

Fearing that political strife will continue and even worsen, frightened Central American businessmen are stashing their savings in Florida's banks and condominium market. Because capital flight often occurs through illegal channels, it is not possible to measure its magnitude. One study sponsored by the Agency for International Development (AID) estimated capital flight during 1979 and 1980 to have surpassed $500 million. The investment climate in Central America has certainly deteriorated since then. Informed observers

211

believe that capital flight from El Salvador alone has reached $500 million annually.

The investment climate has been so bad in Central America that even U.S. government agencies have hesitated to commit their resources there. The Overseas Private Investment Corporation (OPIC) is virtually closed for business in El Salvador, Guatemala, and Nicaragua and has been considering only relatively small projects in Honduras and Costa Rica. The proposed changes contained in the CBI will allow for a greater OPIC involvement in the region, but its activities will still be constrained by its own risk criteria.

The Export-Import Bank (Eximbank) has also been unwilling to undertake major new exposures in Central America. It is noteworthy that the Eximbank, according to the language in the legislative package the administration sent to Congress, promises to expand its activity in the Caribbean Basin only "where its lending criteria allow."

The multilateral development banks, while increasing lending in unprecedented amounts to the Caribbean islands, have been unresponsive so far to the administration's appeals for sharply increased lending to Central America. Some member governments and staff in the World Bank and the Inter-American Development Bank doubt that investment projects can be safely and efficiently implemented amid political chaos. The World Bank has stopped approving loans for El Salvador.

In the absence of peaceful resolutions to political conflicts within and between nations, private capital will continue to flee Central America. Without investor confidence, two of the three prongs of the CBI—investment incentives and trade opportunities—will be irrelevant to Central America. The remaining prong—official aid—will in large measure be devoted to maintaining consumption levels and indirectly to purchasing weapons. Investment planning and implementation, whether by the public or the private sector, cannot proceed safely and efficiently in an environment of political turmoil.

An Absence of Multilateralism

The administration's diplomacy of confrontation has also prevented the realization of a truly multilateral Caribbean Basin Initiative. The administration has been consulting with Canada, Mexico, Venezuela, and Colombia. It has not, however, been willing to make the political compromises necessary to permit the elaboration of a cooperative and integrated approach to the region's economic problems. Each donor nation is pursuing its own development programs, largely as if the CBI had never been announced. As a result of its uncompromising diplomacy, the administration is actually working at cross purposes from other donors. Mexico, for example, has been concentrating substantial resources in Nicaragua. The United States has suspended some bilateral assistance programs and has been seeking to reduce Nicaragua's access to the multilateral development banks.

A genuinely multinational framework, based on a common political vision, would have several economic advantages. A multilateral mechanism would allow for a more efficient coordination of scarce resources. It would make other donors feel it in their interests to match the contributions made by others, thereby sharing the aid burden more widely. Moreover, multilateralism provides mechanisms for the transfer of aid resources without the political tensions and resentments that accompany bilateral programs. The Caribbean Group for Economic Cooperation and Development has, since 1977, provided such a multilateral vehicle for aid to the insular Caribbean. The administration's uncompromising bilateral and hardline diplomacy has impeded the formation of a similar group for Central America.

Administration officials have indicated that Cuba, Nicaragua, and Grenada may be excluded, not only from bilateral aid, but also from trade and investment incentives. Such an exclusionary policy would be counterproductive for four reasons. First, rather than adopting more moderate policies, excluded governments are likely to react with a defiant nationalism. Conversely, nations that participate actively in the U.S. economy are less likely to seek or maintain relations with countries hostile to the United States. Second, the heightened tensions between the United States and the excluded states will have negative repercussions on economies in other countries. For example, conflict between the United States and Nicaragua will adversely affect the economies of Costa Rica and Honduras. Third, by excluding Nicaragua and Grenada, the United States would seem to be attacking existing regional institutions. Yet the reverse policy, of seeking to strengthen the ties between Nicaragua and the Central American Common Market and between Grenada and the Caribbean Common Market, would be more likely to moderate those two governments. Finally, it has generally been U.S. policy throughout the postwar period to insulate international markets from politics. The United States objects when other countries use trade or finance for coercive purposes, but U.S. arguments lose force when the United States itself repeatedly violates these principles.

Therefore, the administration's confrontationist diplomacy and uncompromising bilateralism may well distort and even undermine the otherwise laudable Caribbean Basin Initiative.

Economic Consequences of the CBI

The separate components of the CBI package—trade, investment, and concessional aid—are intended to generate new resources in the form of foreign exchange as well as new employment and production. In the three sections that follow we present detailed estimates of the additional foreign exchange generated by each component of the CBI. This will allow us to match the anticipated benefits against the resource needs of the region.

The administration has not yet made such estimates. These calculations are admittedly difficult to make and require making some assumptions. But as with domestic forecasts of, say, the size of the budget deficit or rates of economic growth, one can make informed guesses about the direction and magnitude of change. Without such quantified estimates, policymakers are left to rely solely on impressions. The administration, with its superior access to information and staff time, should rightfully present this analysis with its own assumptions. We hope that our preliminary findings will trigger a more systematic response from the administration.

FREE TRADE AREA AND CHANGES IN QUOTAS

One of the most innovative components of the development package is the Free Trade Area (FTA). The one-way free trade area means that the United States will remove its tariffs on products originating in the Caribbean Basin. Textiles and sugar, however, are exempt from the FTA, and they are to be treated separately.

The Free Trade Area

The FTA has been heralded as the "centerpiece" of the CBI. Indeed, trade liberalization is potentially the most important development instrument at the disposal of the administration. Development economists have long contended that trade is a much more important stimulus to sustained growth in most poor countries than development assistance. Coming at a time of rising demands for protectionism, the FTA is a positive step—albeit small—in the direction of a more accessible U.S. market for developing countries.

The FTA is a violation of the principle of nondiscrimination in global trade long held by the United States and embodied in the General Agreement on Trade and Tariffs. It would certainly not be in the interests of the United States for the world to be carved up into trading blocs and for international trade and investment to become more politicized. However, the relative economic insignificance of the FTA-included states, the depth of the current economic crisis in the area, and the uniqueness of their geography taken in light of the limited duration of the FTA make an arguable case for this departure. In applying for the required waiver from GATT, the United States should make it clear that this departure from Most Favored Nation (MFN) treatment will not be extended to other countries or regions and that the exemption will last for only the twelve years requested.

The FTA, in reality, will affect only slightly more than 5 percent of the region's total exports to the United States (table 14.1). As the president

Table 14.1
Caribbean Basin Exports to the United States, 1980:
Percentage Affected by the Free Trade Area

Category	Value ($ millions)	Percentage
Total	10,205	100
Currently duty free	8,918	87
Oil and petroleum[1]	6,039	59
GSP	552	5
Other (coffee, tropical fruits, etc.)	2,327	23
Dutiable	1,282	13
Textiles	282	3
GSP exclusion, value added	182	2
GSP exclusion, competitive need	349	3
Products eligible for Free Trade Area[2]	469	5

SOURCE: U.S. Department of Commerce.

[1] Petroleum imports were admitted duty free for the first half of 1980 and later were made dutiable. The administration apparently does not intend to include petroleum in the Free Trade Area.
[2] Because of the lowering of the value-added criteria in GSP from 35 percent to 25 percent and the removal of the "competitive-need" test, some portion of these two categories will also be eligible.

mentioned in his formal announcement of the CBI before the Organization of American States, 87 percent of the region's exports into the United States already enter duty free. These exports include petroleum, products covered by the Generalized System of Preferences (GSP), and other goods, mainly agricultural products not produced in quantity in the United States.

Some categories of goods that are now "dutiable" will not be granted free entry under the CBI. These include textiles, products not eligible for GSP because their value-added criterion in the CBI country of origin is too low, and products not eligible for GSP because the country exports more than is allowed under the legislation (most of the category is sugar exports). The remaining 5 percent of the region's exports—$469 million in 1980—will be eligible for the Free Trade Area.

The exclusion of textiles from the program is particularly lamentable because this industry holds the greatest opportunity for expanding exports and creating jobs in the Caribbean. Some products now excluded from GSP because less than 35 percent of their value originates in the Caribbean may be made eligible for the FTA because the value-added criterion will be lowered to 25 percent. It is not possible to know how much of the $182 million of products excluded by the value-added criterion will be affected by this change. Also, about $49 million of $349 million of GSP exclusions due to competitive need will be eligible; the remaining $300 million is sugar, to be treated with quotas (discussed in the following).

The economic impact of the FTA upon the region will depend on two variables: (1) How much more consumers buy of the imported product because prices fall and goods are cheaper, and (2) how much more consumers buy of the imported product from the region favored with a price advantage and shift away from similar imported goods produced elsewhere. The total amount of new trade generated for the CBI countries therefore depends upon how high the original tariff was prior to cutting, the responsiveness of consumers to changes in prices, and the shift of consumer purchases into CBI imports at the expense of other imports.

Predicting these changes is always hazardous. Perhaps the largest unknown is the capacity of the CBI economies to expand their exports in response to new demand. Also, the effects of cutting tariffs have to be distinguished from other economic forces, such as upturns in growth of the U.S. or international economies. These other effects are not considered, since we wish to analyze the affects attributable purely to the CBI. Historical experience with other tariff cuts allows us to make some informed estimates of the general magnitude of the probable effects upon CBI exports, "holding constant" the impact of the international economy.

We analyzed the largest fifteen current export products eligible for the FTA. These accounted for $420 million, or 90 percent of the total (table 14.2). For each product, we estimated the effects of eliminating the U.S. tariff upon consumers' purchases of the product in response to the lower prices. The amount of new net U.S. demand created for the region's products is surprisingly small: $23 million, or about .2 percent of 1980 exports. The reason for this is that for many of these products tariff levels are not high and consumers are not particularly responsive to price changes.

The $23 million is only the new net U.S. demand created for imports. The region will also benefit from consumers shifting from already imported products to those imported from the region. This response will vary widely. For undifferentiated products where brand name are unimportant, such as beef, handbags, and scrap tobacco, the effect could be large, limited only by the capacity of the exporting countries to expand their production. For other products, such as differentiated brand names, certain consumer goods (e.g., cigars) and 806.3 and 807 products, the effects are likely to be somewhat smaller. Consumers with an attachment to branded products are less inclined to substitute products in response to a price change. In the case of 806.3 and 807 products, multinational firms may have to shut down a production unit in Mexico or the Far East and shift facilities into the basin in order to take advantage of the FTA. The effects on these firms will probably be minimal in the short run; they will be large in the long run only if the newly created price differentials more than offset the costs of shutting down operations abroad.

In the absence of experience on which to base estimates of consumer

Table 14.2
Estimated Trade Increases from CBI
(By Product, in 1980 U.S. $ millions)

Product	Current Duty[1] (%)	Imports 1980 ($ millions)	Estimated Trade Increases		
			New U.S. Imports ($ millions)	New CBI Exports Assumption[2]	
				A ($ millions)	B ($ millions)
Beef and veal	2	222	1.74	6.09	14.80
Electronic tubes[3]	5	59	1.41	4.21	9.83
Capacitors[3]	9	28	1.16	3.47	8.09
Cigars	9	25	2.35	4.42	8.55
Resistors[3]	5	18	.43	1.29	3.00
Benzenoid drugs[3]	12	14	2.48	3.98	6.98
Analgesics[3]	12	13	2.30	3.69	6.48
Leather handbags	10	9	3.27	4.09	5.73
Scrap tobacco	16	9	1.42	2.66	5.14
Pineapple	5	5	0.1	.33	.81
Iron and steel pipes	1	4	0.4	.08	.16
Wrapper tobacco	10	4	.42	.78	1.51
Luggage[3]	19	4	2.56	3.19	4.47
Footwear	8	3	.89	1.11	1.56
Tobacco, other	11	3	.34	.64	1.23
Total 15 products		420	20.88	40.02	78.32
Total all FTA[4]		469	23.20	44.47	87.02
CBI Trade as Percentage of 1980 trade			.2%	.4%	.9%

SOURCE: Calculated from U.S. Department of Commerce data, and from data in R. E. Baldwin, "U.S. Tariff Policy: Formation and Effects," U.S. Department of Labor Discussion Paper, June 1976. See Appendix for methodology.

[1] Ad Valorum Equivalent duty calculated on Caribbean Basin dutiable value.
[2] Assumption "A" assumes a cross-price elasticity of 1. Assumption "B" assumes a cross-price elasticity of 3.
[3] A large component of his product is imported under items 806.3 and 807 of the tariff code, contributing to some overstatement of the trade effects (Appendix A).
[4] Projected on the basis of the largest fifteen products.

shifts among import sources in response to price changes we present two different assumptions in table 14.2, one small and one large. Even relatively large consumer shifts to CBI country products, however, would generate additional exports of less than $100 million, about 1 percent of the region's 1980 exports.

In the first year, it is our judgment that the amount of new exports created by the Free Trade Area is unlikely to exceed about $40 million. Even if newly created demand were to exceed that amount, expansion in many product exports would be constrained by existing capacity limits. Any increases of as much as $100 million in the small base, however, would not come until the third and future years.

Changes in Quota Restrictions

The Free Trade Area is only one element in the administration's trade package. A potentially more important change in the short run is in the textile quotas and expansion of sugar quotas for some countries. In textiles, four countries—Haiti, the Dominican Republic, Costa Rica, and Jamaica—have restrictive bilateral agreements that currently cover exports to the United States. The administration has announced intentions of gradually allocating to the CBI countries a portion of the quota now held by the Far Eastern textile suppliers under the Multi-Fiber Arrangement. This process probably will be slow and wil be constrained to the volume increase normally contained in the quota.

The 1982 administration-supported farm bill raised nominal protection on sugar imports by 225 percent at the same time domestic price supports on sugar were raised. This depressed imports from countries not eligible for GSP privileges (i.e., those with more than the threshold level of exports, currently at $46 million). To mitigate the impact on the CBI sugar exports, the administration intends to give partial exemption from duties and import fees and establish quotas for the region's three principal suppliers, the Dominican Republic, Guatemala, and Panama. The new quotas will be roughly 10 percent higher than existing imports, amounting to 780,000 metric tons for the Dominican Republic, 210,000 metric tons for Guatemala, and 160,000 metric tons for Panama. Small producers in the region already have tariff-free access to the U.S. market under GSP. The increased share of the Dominican Republic, Guatemala, and Panama will almost certainly reduce the share held by other major producers in latin America such as Brazil and Peru.

Finally, two other trade effects are of minor consequence: (1) the easing of the GSP requirement to qualify for duty-free entry from 35 percent to 25 percent of the value of the product that must originate in the source country, and (2) some products of minor importance (other than sugar, not eligible for GSP because the countries supply more than 50 percent of U.S. impots (the "competitive need" test), will be permitted free access. These changes may produce another $32 million of new exports.

The total effects of the trade measures, including the Free Trade Area and the changes in textiles, sugar, and other categories are estimated in table 14.3. We have asumed that all the trade effects of the FTA will be felt in the first three years of the CBI. (New growth, of course, will continue to occur, but this will be because of the natural growth in the U.S. market that is not attributable to the tariff cuts.) The capacity of the CBI countries to respond to increases in demand may limit actual production increases to much lower levels.

These conclusions can be drawn from the table. First, the changes in the textile and sugar trade in the near term will account for about as much of the beneficial trade effects as the Free Trade Area. In future years the FTA should

Table 14.3
Estimated Projected Value of Export Increases
(By Trade Category, in 1980 U.S. $ millions)

	First Year	Second Year	Future Years
FTA[1]	40	70	100
Textiles[2]	15	30	30
Sugar[2]	40	80	80
Nonsugar GSP(CN)[3]	4	7	11
GSP(VA)[4]	9	15	21
Total trade increase	108	202	242
Percentage of 1980 total	1.0%	2%	2.4%

SOURCE: Estimated from U.S. Department of Commerce data.

NOTE: All increases are relative to the year prior to the initiation of the CBI.
[1] From table 14.2 and text; second and future years' effects are assumed greater due to lagged consumer shifts and shifts in 806.3/807 products, reaching a maximum in the third year.
[2] Five percent increases in both first and second year are due to changes in quotas.
[3] Base is $50 million (see text); this assumes the same rate of increase as other FTA products.
[4] Nineteen-eighty value equals $182 million; this assumes $100 million is eligible under new 25 percent value-added rule and is under the same rate of increase as other products in FTA.

account for a growing proportion. Second, the total effects of the trade package in the first year will probably not amount to much more than 1 percent of the region's 1980 total exports, though in future years effects should be greater. Even by the third year the increases will probably not amount to 3 percent of the region's 1980 exports.

Finally, these changes in trade regulations will probably have much less effect than would renewed U.S. domestic growth. An acceleration in the U.S. growth rate of from 0 to 3 percent annually would probably generate over $300 million in new export earnings for the region. Or consider the effects of lowered U.S. interest rates. Debt service not infrequently absorbs from 15 to 25 percent of export earnings of CBI countries. If interest rates were to fall by five percentage points on the debt of $5.4 billion owed to private creditors (as of 31 December 1980), interest payments would be reduced by more than $250 million. In the coming years, even if the CBI is tremendously successful, economic growth in the U.S. based upon a sound monetary and fiscal policy will probably have a far greater impact on the region's welfare than the CBI.

In summary, the Free Trade Area merits qualified support, even though its effects will probably be modest. It provides an opportunity for the region to increase in small measure its domestic employment, export earnings, and growth. However, its success hinges upon a significant administration turn toward the politics of negotiation and inclusion. Discrimination against

Nicaragua and other countries of the region because of their current politics heightens the tendency inherent in the program to politicize trade. Also, the administration should eventually move toward freer trade in textiles and sugar. Before doing so, however, it must reverse its stand on trade adjustment assistance, worker retraining, and addressing the legitimate trade concerns of domestic labor. A Department of Labor study estimates that an unlimited free trade area—unfettered by restrictions in textiles and other products—would cost about eighteen thousand U.S. jobs. Fifteen thousand jobs would be lost in textiles alone. The administration cannot hope to enlist the support of domestic labor for freer trade in the industry that would most benefit the region if it fails to aid American workers to make the painful adjustment to alternative employment.

INVESTMENT TAX CREDIT

A second major component in the CBI proposal is a five-year investment tax credit. A U.S. parent corporation may claim a credit against its total tax liabilities for an amount equal to 10 percent of new investment in plant and equipment in Caribbean Basin countries. The credit is only applicable to new equipment or used equipment not previously employed in the foreign country. Parents that are in joint venture with domestic partners may claim a credit proportionate to their share of the new investment. The credit is to be calculated as the lesser of two figures: (1) the increase in value of qualifying property, or (2) the increase in the parent's equity share devoted to increases in paid-in capital. This definition is slightly different from the domestic tax credit, which calculates the credit on the basis of actual investment expenditures, and will probably amount to slightly less, since qualifying domestic property is sometimes financed through debt.

These incentives are coupled with increased protection for foreign investment that is offered through the Overseas Private Investment Corporation. The U.S. private insurance sector is also being encouraged to become active in the Caribbean Basin to reduce the risk associated with investment.

The U.S. Treasury Department estimates that the cost of the investment tax credit in foregone tax revenues will be about $40 million in the first year. Its estimates represent 10 percent of the share of annual equity flows and reinvestment of retained earnings that were spent on new plant and equipment in 1980, about $400 million. The cost to the Treasury in uncollected taxes would presumably rise over the five-year period in direct relation to the amount of new investment in the region.

How much new investment would be generated by this $40 million? No one knows. New investment is highly sensitive to swings in the business cycle, changes in the perception of risk, and changes in overall levels of profitability. Econometric modeling techniques can only separate these various effects by building in debatable assumptions about financial and other relationships.

Studies of the U.S. experience with the domestic tax credit, however, offer reason for skepticism. Although this experience contains no "substitution" effect, i.e., the shifting among regions in response to changes in relative profitability, it does illustrate the uncertainty of this instrument. According to a recent study by the Office of Tax Analysis in the Department of Treasury of the 1973 investment tax credit on new domestic investment, every dollar of tax expenditure generated only seventy-six cents of new investment (Chirinko and Eisner, 1981).[1] Using the 76 percent figure, an investment tax credit in the CBI that costs the U.S. Treasury $40 million can be predicted to generate only $30 million of investment. This may be even less in the case of a foreign tax credit because of the increased risks associated with doing business abroad.

Although the estimates of the new investment generated vary depending on the assumptions, the relatively small payback for tax expenditures can be traced to a central weakness of this instrument. Much of the new investment would occur anyway because business activity is ongoing. Yet to get an *additional* investment, the Treasury has to include *all* investors in the tax credit. Thus, if U.S. investors in the region currently spend $400 million on new plant and equipment, and an investment tax credit creates an additional $30 million of investment, the total tax expenditures will be $43 million (10 percent of $400 and $30 million).

The administration hopes that credit, together with the trade incentives, will have a large impact. This is unlikely as long as business conditions in the region are precarious. Weak domestic economies, a weak international economy (particularly the U.S. economy), and, in some countries, high political risk have depressed expected profitability. Without growing markets, businessmen cannot justify new investments. In fact, capital flight now constitutes a serious drain to Caribbean Basin countries. For at least the foreseeable future, U.S. investors in many countries will probably invest only that amount which is absolutely necessary to maintain their ongoing plant and equipment. This investment would occur in any case, and the investment tax credit will be an unrequited loss to the Treasury. A second drawback of the tax credit is that not all of the additional investment will have a satisfactory development impact as measured by new employment or products relevant to the situation of the poor. A sizeable proportion of the credit will go into activities that are relatively capital-intensive and so fail to generate adequate employment. An investment in capital-intensive products, such as cosmetics or cigarettes, for example, arguably does not produce maximum development impact. Since the

---

[1]This conclusion is the mean increase in investment projected through the use of six different econometric models containing different assumptions. Only two of the models show increases in investment greater than losses to the Treasury in foregone taxes.

R. S. Chirinko and Robert Eisner, "The Effects of Tax Policies on Investment in Macroeconometric Model: Full Model Simulations," Office of Tax Analysis, Paper no. 46, (U.S. Department of Treasury, January 1981).

tax credit fails to disciminate among investments, these crucial development issues are ignored.

These considerations argue strongly against an investment tax credit. It is economically inefficient because it produces an uncertain amount of additional investment and provides a windfall gain for firms that would have invested even without the incentive. The 40-million-dollar cost to the Treasury could be better spent by channeling the funds directly into the economies without relying on intermediating companies.

The administration's objective of promoting private sector investment would be far better served if the funds were channeled through either the International Finance Corporation of the World Bank, which provides joint venture capital for developing countries, or the Private Enterprise Bureau of AID, which is strengthening its activities in private sector development financing. The funds could be targeted by either agency for particular countries in employment-generating private sector activities. Such an expenditure guarantees both new private sector investment in the targeted countries *and* investment with a direct development impact.

ECONOMIC ASSISTANCE

The administration has proposed $350 million in quick-disbursing funds to help the Caribbean Basin countries meet pressing balance of payments needs. Shortages of foreign exchange are a major cause of the profound economic crisis gripping the region. The cost of imported energy has risen, whereas the prices of such key commodities as sugar, coffee, bauxite, and nickel have declined. The drop in export prices in 1981 alone reduced the region's export earnings by over $485 million. In addition, high market interest rates have increased the burden of a swollen foreign debt.

The Caribbean Basin nations will need about $4 billion in net capital inflows in 1982. This sum will enable the region to cover its projected current account deficit (the difference between exports and imports and between the payments made to external investors and receipts from workers' remittances) (see table 14.4). The proposed emergency supplemental of $350 million will cover only about 9 percent of projected external financing needs.

Even if the region is able to borrow sufficiently to cover this estimated current account deficit, most countries will continue to suffer economic stagnation or decline. Indeed, it is likely that El Salvador, Costa Rica, Guatemala, Nicaragua, the Dominican Republic, Guyana, and Barbados will show little or negative growth this year, even assuming that they are able to finance their portions of the region's 4-billion-dollar deficit. Jamaica, Haiti, and Honduras may achieve very modest growth. Only Panama is expected to show a significant expansion in per capita gross domestic product.

The 350-million-dollar supplemental appropriation represents a sub-

Table 14.4
Current Account Balances in Principal Caribbean Countries

	1981 ($ million)	Growth Rate (%)	1982[1] ($ million)	1982 Projected Growth Rate (%)
Central America				
Guatemala	−570	1	−500	−2
El Salvador	−220	−10	−360	−5
Honduras	−270	0	−400	3
Nicaragua	−380	5	−460	0
Costa Rica	−390	1	−235	−3
Panama	−330	5	−400	5
Caribbean				
Jamaica	−450	1	−535	3
Dominican Republic	−440	4	−630	1
Eastern Caribbean	−245	−	−315	−
Haiti	−105	0	−60	3
Guyana	−190	−.5	−100	0
Total	−3,590		−3,995	

SOURCE: U.S. AID, multilateral development banks, U.N. Economic Commission on Latin America, and our own estimates.

[1] Estimate based on projected growth rate.

stantial increase over the $474 million provided in the fiscal year 1982 budget. In these times of budgetary stringency, it is a significant sum. Nevertheless, by itself the proposed supplement can only have a marginal impact on the region's economies. The supplement will not be enough to stimulate strong, positive growth through the basin.

The economic future of Central America is especially grim and will remain so if political solutions are not found to halt the fratricidal strife. El Salvador is to absorb $128 million, or a full 36 percent of the proposed supplement. This is in addition to the $105 million already earmarked for El Salvador in the 1982 budget. (The $164.9 million proposed in the fiscal year 1983 congressional presentation makes for a two-year authorization of $397.4 million, or $90 for every Salvadoran.) Given the poor climate for investment and planning in El Salvador, aid can, at best, serve to maintain living standards in government-controlled zones. A portion is likely to join the stream of capital fleeing to safer havens outside the country.

The administration has properly chosen to allocate substantial portions of the supplement to Jamaica, the Dominican Republic, Honduras, and Costa Rica. All are elected governments struggling seriously to overcome both underdevelopment and an adverse international economic climate. U.S. aid, however, should not be used as a lever with which to pressure Honduras and

Costa Rica into following confrontationist strategies with Nicaragua. The resulting political tensions would only destabilize the economies and possibly even the political systems of both democracies.

Nicaragua is excluded from the supplement and from the fiscal year 1983 AID congressional presentation. In fact, the administration seems prepared to marshal a wide range of instruments and resources for the express purpose of undermining the Nicaraguan economy. The actual effect, however, promises to be tragically counterproductive. A besieged Nicaragua is less likely to be democratic or to reduce its ties to Cuba. A frightened Nicaragua is more likely to seek Soviet protection.

Yet, economic aid could strengthen the private sector and political pluralism in Nicaragua as well as assist in meeting basic needs. Aid authorizations, if not overly burdened with restrictive and inflexible amendments, could be used as a carrot by the administration in a good-faith effort to reach an entente with Nicaragua.

For the whole region, the proposed aid supplement, even when taken together with the trade and investment incentives, will not be sufficient to cover resource needs. Even if the CBI package were to amount to as much as $500 million in the first year, it would not be enough to bridge the resource gap, projected to be $4 billion. Countries in the region will be forced to turn increasingly to the International Monetary Fund, the World Bank, and the Inter-American Development Bank for the large volume of resources they will most certainly need.

Yet, in its enthusiasm to gain bilateral leverage, the Reagan administration has tended to give reduced priority to these same multilateral financial institutions. It has opposed new quota increases for the IMF and has reduced U.S. commitments to the World Bank and the IDB. These measures are directly counterproductive to U.S. interests in the Caribbean Basin.

In sum, the emergency aid supplement is generous, given the constraints on the U.S. budget. It is modest, however, in comparison to the Caribbean Basin's economic problems, and should not be oversold. In the interests of creating a more stable business climate and preserving essential U.S. security interests, aid should be used to support a diplomacy of compromise and peace. The United States should increase its support of the multilateral institutions that are better able to cope with the region's economic adjustment.

Policy Recommendations

The Caribbean Basin Initiative is an imaginative and potentially important development initiative. It brings together several development instruments, including aid, trade, and investment policy, to the task of generating economic growth.

Yet the CBI is fundamentally flawed by its ties to an ill-conceived political strategy that relies too heavily on confrontationist policies. The CBI apparently incorporates the divisive bilateralism that has characterized the Reagan administration's hard-line diplomacy. Instead, the United States should pursue a diplomacy of compromise, true multilateralism, and inclusiveness as the better strategy to ensure American interests and to enhance the region's economic prospects. This requires seeking a negotiated solution to the civil war in El Salvador and de-escalating the confrontation with Nicaragua. Mexican Preident López Portillo has offered the administration the opportunity to alter directions gracefully not only toward these countries, but toward the entire Caribbean. Without such a change in policy direction, the CBI cannot successfully rekindle economic growth in the region.

In addition to their general policy change, five other changes would enhance the CBI's chances for effectiveness.

First, the CBI potentially is an important instrument to maintain and enhance the economic links of these economies to the West. The CBI should not exclude Nicaragua and Grenada or other countries. For obvious reasons, Cuba cannot be included at the outset of the program, but the CBI should be held out as yet another incentive for Cuba to reestablish trade relations with the United States.

Second, the Free Trade Area is an important measure, and, given a more complementary political strategy, it could eventually aid the region's recovery—even though its effects will probably be modest. Congress should support the FTA component of the bill, provided that (1) Nicaragua and Grenada are not excluded, and (2) that the United States commit itself to a program of limited duration and to no further discriminatory regional programs. With such commitments stated, the CBI is less politically discriminatory and represents less of a deviation from multilateral principles. It can better be seen in this light as a step toward freer trade rather than toward politicized trade. Consideration should be given to extending, eventually, its provision to textiles and sugar, where its impact would be greatest, although this should be contingent upon serious efforts to cope with the problems of the trade-induced dislocation in the U.S. domestic industry.

Third, the investment tax credit is economically tenuous. It is uncertain that the total cost to the U.S. Treasury of between $40 and 45 million will produce new investment approaching that amount. Furthermore, there is no guarantee that the new investment that does occur will have a strong developmental impact. Therefore the investment tax credit should not be enacted. Congress might more productively use the $40 million to enhance the private sector's growth directly by channeling the funds to the International Finance Corporation or by cofinancing programs of the Private Enterprise Bureau of AID.

Fourth, the economic aid is disproportionately directed at El Salvador.

225

Under current political conditions, over one-third of the 350-million-dollar supplement will be spent in this war-torn country, with no assurance that the funds will contribute to a reduction in hostilities. Aid can, however, be an important bargaining chip in the pursuit of a political solution. Therefore, we recommend that supplemental aid not be given to El Salvador unless the Salvadoran government undertakes a good-faith effort to seek a negotiated peace with the major opposition groups. Otherwise, economic aid should be channeled to the democratic regimes that are serious about development and the protection of human rights.

Fifth, the region's economic plight has been worsening at a rate far greater than the ability of the United States to ameliorate the situation unilaterally. A truly coordinated multilateral effort is needed to provide the large amounts of economic assistance that the Caribbean Basin countries require. We, therefore, recommend that the U.S. administration support significant expansion of the multilateral financial institutions. These institutions should take the lead in organizing the other multilateral and bilateral donors to increase both the quantity and effectiveness of external assistance.

The Caribbean Basin Initiative suggests that the United States possesses the talent to address creatively the difficult problems confronting a third world area in turmoil. But only an equally enlightened and courageous U.S. diplomacy coupled with more progressive trade and labor policies will allow the CBI to fulfill its potential.

Epilogue

As 1982 passed, the CBI came under attack from both liberals and conservatives in Congress, as well as special interest groups. Many liberals objected to the large amounts of aid earmarked for El Salvador. Many conservatives (and liberals) objected to the investment tax credit. Others attacked the measure for its token benefits, while organized labor attacked the benefits as too great, alleging that it would cost many U.S. jobs.

By the end of the 97th Congress in 1982, only the 350-million-dollar aid supplemental bill had been passed, and that with limitations on the amount of money to be spent in any one country. No single country could receive more than $75 million, which effectively cut the share destined for El Salvador.

The trade component was severely restricted. In the House of Representatives, two key items, leather products and footwear, were made ineligible for the Free Trade Area. By our calculations, these eliminations reduce the value of the CBI by 15 to 20 percent. The investment tax credit was eliminated because of the negative reaction within the House Ways and Means Committee. The amended measure passed Congress in the late summer of 1983.

Appendix: Methods Calculating Trade Effects

The value of the increase in U.S. demand for CBI imports for each product is given by the formula:

$$dM = M \cdot m \cdot dt/(1 + t),$$

where dM is the change in U.S. imports, M is the initial value of imports, m is the elasticity of demand for imports, dt is the change in tariff rate, and t is the tariff rate. This is the net trade creation effect of cutting import duties and is used to calculate the column labeled "New U.S. Imports" in table 14.2. But this does not give the gross trade creation for the CBI countries, since some of the already imported products would now be supplied from the CBI countries. This is given in the formula:

$$dE = E \cdot (m + n) \, dt/(1 + t),$$

where dE is the change in exports from the region, E is the initial exports from the region to the United States, and n is the cross-price elasticity of these exports with respect to a change in their price relative to the prices of exports of countries that do not receive the preferential treatment.

The import elasticities (m) were taken from R. E. Baldwin, "U.S. Tariff Policy: Formation and Effects," U.S. Department of Labor Discussion Paper, June 1976. The import and export levels for 1980 were kindly provided by the U.S. Department of Commerce. The cross-price elasticities in column "A" of table 14.2 are assumed to be 1, and in column "B" they are assumed to be 3.

The calculations for the "Total all FTA" row projects a total based upon the level of increase for the largest fifteen current export products.

Because of the inclusion of 806.3/807 commodities, the changes in export levels are somewhat overstated. This is because the ad valorem equivalents are based on value added for these products; this implies the tariff levels used in the calculations are somewhat overstated, magnifying the new demand created in response to the overstated cuts in tariffs.

15. Latin American Refugees: Problems of Mass Migration and Mass Asylum

Patricia Weiss Fagen

Introduction

The politically motivated flight of Salvadorans, Guatemalans, and Nicaraguans from their homelands to other countries of Central America and to Mexico and the United States has become a destabilizing force in the region. The refugee presence is now a major foreign policy consideration, affecting and being affected by every U.S. initiative from funding proposals for the Caribbean Basin Initiative to military aid to the Honduran government.

According to the United Nations High Commissioner on Refugees (UNHCR), in 1982 there were between 260 and 310 thousand refugees living precariously in Central America and Mexico. (The majority, 222 to 272 thousand, are from El Salvador; another 38 thousand are from Guatemala, Nicaragua, and Cuba.) Their presence has caused or added to existing political tensions and has placed a serious strain on the capacities of the area's fragile economies.

Costa Rica. Suffering the worst financial crisis of its history, Costa Rica has become a host country for some 10,000 Salvadorans, 2,700 Cubans, 2,000 Nicaraguans, and 300 Guatemalans, most of whom have entered in the past three years. Since Costa Rica cannot afford to provide assistance to them and is reluctant to grant them work permits, nearly all of the recent entrants are entirely dependent on international assistance.

Nicaragua. The majority of Nicaragua's own population was in exile or displaced until 1980, and its economy is far from recovered, but the country has managed to absorb some twenty-two thousand newly arrived Salvadorans. Nicaragua is sympathetic to the Salvadoran refugees and is supportive of the opposition to El Salvador's government. At the same time, however, Nicaragua and Honduras are involved in nearly open warfare that is fueled by armed incursions across the border involving elements of the Miskito Indians. The Miskitos have crossed the Nicaraguan border into Honduras in protest against the Sandinista government and are still located in a large camp close to the border.

Mexico. Like Costa Rica, Mexico is facing its worst financial crisis; the country has had to absorb some 120 thousand Salvadorans and, with even greater reluctance, over 60 thousand Guatemalans who have crossed Mexico's southern border. The Guatemalans are largely indigenous Maya-speaking peasants who have fled in the wake of their government's State of Siege, which reportedly has decimated many of the small villages in the northern part of the country. The Mexican government is willing to provide only temporary relief and assistance to the Guatemalans in flight. In the meantime, the Mexicans have only weakly protested Guatemalan pursuit of alleged guerrilla sympathizers across the border. The refugee presence not only creates new tensions between Guatemala and Mexico but, in the Mexican view, contributes to social unrest in one of that country's poorest regions.

Honduras. Honduras is the insecure refuge for over 17,000 Salvadorans and approximately 10,050 Miskitos and 500 Guatemalans. The Salvadoran refugee camps, which Honduran and Salvadoran military claim are havens of leftists, have been invaded by the armed forces and police of both countries. Refugees and relief workers have accused the Hondurans of collaborating in military operations with the Salvadoran army on both sides of the border.

THE UNITED STATES

For the United States, the problem of Central American refugees is now a domestic concern as well as a foreign policy issue. The United States itself, however unwillingly, has become a country of first asylum for Central Americans as well as for Cubans and Haitians. Their entry has added a new and dramatic dimension to the complex and longstanding debates over illegal immigration and the rights of aliens. There is virtually unanimous consensus that the United States has proved itself ill prepared, both institutionally and politically, to manage the recent massive entries of, that is, to serve as a country of first asylum for, Cubans, Haitians, Salvadorans, and others who originate overwhelmingly in the Caribbean Basin area. It is also generally agreed that entries from neighboring and contiguous countries are likely to reoccur.

With respect to politically motivated exiles, U.S. foreign policy has contributed to the very flows that are now so difficult to stem. The Reagan administration continues to support governments that violate human rights, fail to provide for the basic needs of their citizens, and repeatedly unleash security-force violence against their civilian populations. Such governments, in effect, drive people who otherwise would remain in their countries into exile.

229

Were the human rights situations to improve in the current refugee-producing countries of Latin America, most people would return to their homelands. This would generally ease tensions and resource drains, especially in Central America and Mexico. It would also meaningfully reduce the flow of illegal immigration into the United States. We have already seen this occur with respect to Nicaragua. During the Somoza dictatorship, as many as one million Nicaraguans left the country, one hundred thousand of whom fled during the 1978–79 civil war. The overwhelming majority of these people have been repatriated since the overthrow of the Somoza government. While Nicaraguans continue to leave the country because of the present Sandinista government, the number seeking political asylum is a fraction of former numbers. Brazil is another case in which nearly the entire exile population voluntarily returned once the government began to open the political system and passed an amnesty law that permitted exiles to participate fully in the nation's political and economic life. It is likely that political exiles from other Latin American countries would return if they were given similar opportunities. And, if peace can be negotiated in El Salvador, the majority of the more than three hundred thousand Salvadorans who have fled violence and civil war will return, as well.

Latin Americans and U.S. Refugee and Asylum Law

Southeast Asians, who comprise the vast majority of the recent U.S. refugee influx, are processed and admitted from third countries, and their entries are coordinated and controlled. Latin Americans, who claim to be refugees as well, are likely to arrive as illegal entrants, uninvited and having undergone no prior selection process. Moreover, they are apt to request political asylum only upon apprehension at the border or in this country.

Appeals for political asylum from people who are already in the United States or who are crossing into the United States have increased from approximately thirty-eight hundred in 1978 to about forty thousand in 1981. Over 140 thousand applications were pending as of September 1982. These applicants are not only people who have entered illegally; an even greater number of persons come to the United States on nonimmigrant visas and apply for asylum when these visas have expired and they face deportation. Latin Americans comprise a major portion of these requests as well.

Whether a person requests refugee status in the United States from a third country or asks for political asylum once in this country, the person must meet the definition of a refugee as stated in the 1980 Refugee Act. As a signatory in 1968 to the United Nations Protocol Relating to the Status of Refugees, the United States was prohibited from forcibly returning anyone meeting the UN refugee definition to his or her country of origin, but prior to 1980 the refugee definition for resettlement was limited to persons fleeing communist regimes or coming from the Middle East, thereby excluding Latin Americans outside of Cuba. Congressional passage of the 1980 Refugee Act was a substantial step toward providing a legal framework for accepting and resettling refugees. The act removed ideological and geographical distinctions from the refugee definition, thereby bringing the United States into closer compliance with its international obligations as a party to the protocol. The act also mandated federal support for refugee resettlement.

U.S. practice in the refugee area, however, continues to be criticized for lacking coherent decision-making procedures, retaining politically motivated biases, fostering individual abuses, and placing unfair burdens on certain U.S. communities. The Carter administration and, to an even greater extent, the Reagan administration have been accused of discriminating against Latin American refugees through the procedures and regional allocations in the 1980 Refugee Act. They have also been cited for ideologically based discriminatory treatment of non-Cuban Latin American asylum seekers through harsher detention policies and more stringent requirements of proof to establish asylum claims.

Each year the president designates refugee allocations overall and by region, and these designations indicate both a general U.S. reluctance to accept refugees and the persistence of ideological and geographical distinctions among those recommended for admission. The total fiscal year 1980 peak admission figure was 231 thousand. The overall ceiling was lowered both in 1981 and in 1982, and for fiscal year 1983 the president proposes a ceiling of only ninety thousand. The regional proportions within this ceiling have not been greatly altered, and are as follows: sixty-four thousand for East Asia; fifteen thousand for the Soviet Union and East Europe; six thousand for the Near East and South Asia; three thousand for Africa; and two thousand for Latin America.

The low Latin American allocation is incongruous in view of the continuing massive displacement of persons throughout the hemisphere due to political persecution, official violence, and war. Administration officials claim that other Latin American nations will settle refugees because of the region's tradition of granting asylum. However, the Latin American asylum tradition was designed for individuals, not for mass entries; the few countries that might accept refugees have already absorbed more of them than their governments feel they can reasonably absorb, and representatives of the inter-American system through the Organization of American States have repeatedly acknowledged their inability to assure adequate protection or sustained relief to refugee populations. In fact, the low U.S. admission level for Latin Americans reflects U.S. political preferences and ignores hemispheric needs. Even facilities and consular personnel trained to work with refugee claims are concentrated, as they were prior to the 1980 Refugee Act, in

Southeast Asia, Europe, and the Middle East. Latin Americans face far more complicated and discouraging bureaucratic procedures when they apply for refugee status than do persons from other regions.

Because Latin Americans in flight for political motives attempt to enter the United States for asylum far more often than as refugees, they are more affected by U.S. asylum procedures than by refugee allocations and facilities. These procedures are the subject of the three case studies that follow. In the United States, the arrival of large numbers of refugees from Latin America as well as from Asia has created problems for the communities in which they have concentrated. This is particularly so in southern Florida, which has a heavy inflow of Cubans and Haitians and smaller numbers of Nicaraguans, Argentines, and other Latin Americans. The U.S. government has refused to grant full refugee status to the majority of these people and has supplied less in the way of federal funds or resources than local officials have requested for resettlement and other services.

The massive inflow of Latin American immigrants has strained U.S. resources and raised concerns about the capacity of this country to control its borders. The Carter administration appointed a Select Commission on Immigration and Refugee Policy, the Reagan administration named an Inter-Agency Task Force on Immigration and Refugee policy, and the 97th Congress has debated an immigration reform and control bill at length during two sessions. These efforts reflect the official recognition that the United States must deal more effectively with longstanding patterns of illegal immigration and at the same time develop an adequate and coherent policy on the admission of large groups of people fleeing injustice and persecution in their home countries. In theory there are two separate issues. First, immigration policies must establish the admission criteria and limits of persons who for economic, social, or personal reasons, or political preferences, wish to emigrate to the United States and must also formulate appropriate sanctions for those who enter the country illegally. Second, refugee and asylum policies must develop mechanisms for judging claims of fear of political persecution and adopt measures designed to protect and assist the resettlement of those who are accepted as refugees and those who are seeking asylum. In practice the two issues have been inadequately separated. This is due both to the fact that the political and economic causes for flight frequently overlap (e.g., loss of land or ability to work due to political decisions and official acts or because of civil strife) and to the U.S. presumption that migrants from most Latin American countries are economically motivated and hence are to be handled as illegal entrants.

The Reagan administration has adopted policies of deterrence and detention to turn away entrants and to discourage migrants. Much of the ongoing debate concerning U.S. immigration practices and structures is outside the scope of this chapter. What is essential here, however, is to recognize that the effect of present policies is to treat economically and politically motivated migrants alike—as illegal entrants—and to deny even a temporary haven for many persons who have legitimate claims of political persecution, persons the United States is bound by law and treaty to protect.

The Reagan administration, seeking to reduce refugee admissions generally, appears for the first time to be making entry more difficult for applicants from many leftist-ruled as well as rightist-ruled countries, including Ethiopians, Afghans, and even Eastern Europeans. There is no longer a blanket presumption that all Cambodians and Vietnamese are political refugees. Since political presumptions based on ideological preferences run counter to the spirit of the 1980 Refugee Act and international refugee conventions, their diminution is welcome. However, the intent of present policies seems to be to exclude people whenever possible, no matter how compelling their need for, or claim to, U.S. protection, rather than to improve existing procedures or create new ones that operate in a more efficient and consistent manner.

SALVADORANS

The U.S. government's refusal to grant political asylum to Salvadorans fleeing civil war strife after 1980 has led to considerable protest from international organizations and domestic groups concerned with refugees. In late 1981 the United Nations High Commissioner for Refugees asserted that because of its Salvadoran deportation policies, the United States was in apparent violation of its responsibilities as a signatory to the UN Convention and Protocol Relating to the Status of Refugees. In an act of civil disobedience to protest U.S. treatment of Salvadoran asylum seekers, a coalition of U.S. church groups established a network that provides sanctuary and assistance to Salvadorans who are in danger of deportation.

At the end of 1981 only two Salvadorans had been granted political asylum; 6,043 applications were still pending. Responding to pressures from the State Department's own Human Rights and Humanitarian Affairs Bureau, among others, the Immigration and Naturalization Service (INS) approved six more applications in February 1982. In fiscal year 1982 a total of 74 applications had been granted, 1,067 had been denied, and 22,326 were pending. The Central American Refugee Center maintained in congressional testimony in December 1981 that the INS was sending back between two hundred and three hundred Salvadorans daily. The level of combined deportations and voluntary departures remained at about the same level until May 1982. Well over one hundred thousand Salvadorans are estimated to have arrived illegally in the United States since 1980; the INS estimates that it apprehends about one in four of them.

Since 1 May 1982 the UNHCR has considered all Salvadorans to be eligible for protection as refugees because, regardless of the motives for which they left the country, they may face danger if they are forced to return. The UNHCR also maintains that a large portion of individual Salvadorans would qualify for asylum in the United States if they were afforded proper and unbiased hearings. In a report following an October 1981 mission to U.S. detention facilities, the High Commissioner for Refugees confirmed many of the allegations made by lawyers of Salvadorans seeking asylum, and by refugees themselves, concerning the negligence and abuse of due process rights. Later, on 1 May 1982, following a major lawsuit filed in the federal district court of Los Angeles, Federal District Judge David Kenyon issued an injunction against the INS, charging it with having engaged in verbal and physical abuse to induce Salvadorans to sign voluntary departure forms. The judge ordered the implementation of strict procedures to assure the rights of asylum applicants. As a result of this decision, deportations rose in proportion to voluntary departures, but the overall number of Salvadorans sent home declined.

Until a May 1982 court decision ruled against the INS, over 90 percent of Salvadorans apprehended were deported after having signed voluntary departure forms. Although INS practices improved after the decision, voluntary departures remain high, usually over one hundred monthly. Even persons who claim their lives are in danger or whose friends and families have been killed sign these voluntary departure forms, either unwittingly or because of strong psychological pressure. Signatures have often been obtained as a result of an absence of due process rights and the intentional efforts of INS officials to misrepresent the contents of what the Salvadorans are asked to sign. Young people between the ages of 12 and 18 years have been the most frequent victims of such pressures. Lawyers, particularly in the Southwest, have reported attempts by INS officials in the detention centers to interfere with their contact with clients in order to induce them to sign voluntary departure forms. They have also cited cases of clients who were deported while in the process of revoking their signatures on these forms in order to initiate asylum pleas.

Salvadorans are still held for long periods in detention facilities with disproportionately high bonds. Those who are able to post bond are rarely granted work permits, although by law persons with nonfrivolous asylum claims may be permitted work authorizations upon release.

Despite widespread criticisms of human rights violations in El Salvador, both the Carter and the Reagan administrations have generally supported the Salvadoran government. Both administrations have contended that the overwhelming majority of entrants are economically rather than politically motivated and hence are not entitled to asylum status. Neither administration has been willing to extend to the entrants a collective parole (extended voluntary departure status) based on the danger faced by the group as a whole if it returned to its violence-ridden land. The U.S. position has probably been based on two considerations. First, the U.S. government has defended El Salvador's overall human rights record, even while admitting abuses. Large-scale political asylum granted by the United States would constitute an admission that the Salvadoran government is both unable to defeat the guerrilla insurgents and unable to control its own security forces. Second, a sympathetic U.S. reception for fleeing Salvadorans would encourage an even larger Salvador entry, which would involve a U.S. obligation to grant some legal status and benefits to the entrants.

Because of the persistent violence in that country, many human rights groups and members of Congress have been urging the U.S. government to grant extended voluntary departure protection for Salvadorans in this country. This status has been routinely granted in the past to Ethiopians, Lebanese, Ugandans, Iranians, and Nicaraguans who, like the Salvadorans, were fleeing civil war situations in which individual claims of political persecution were difficult to document but in which the collective danger was apparent. Official reply to a formal request from Senator Edward Kennedy (D-Mass.) to the State Department and INS for a grant of extended voluntary departure to Salvadorans was that conditions in El Salvador were neither sufficiently dangerous nor sufficiently disruptive to warrant this measure. At least one person who was returned from the United States to El Salvador is known to have been killed. Santana Chirino Amaya was apparently not a political activist, and he probably could not have won political asylum, but his life would have been spared had the extended voluntary departure option existed.

HAITIANS

Haitians have been entering the United States for more than a decade for a mixture of economic and political motives. According the INS forty to fifty thousand Haitians were legally admitted as immigrants between 1972 and 1979. They constituted a small portion of total net immigration to the United States during this period, but their presence has been strongly felt in southern Florida, where most recent arrivals have landed. The number of arrivals increased sharply after 1978, when the Bahamian government began deporting Haitians.

In September 1981 President Reagan proclaimed that, due to the "continuing illegal migration by sea of large numbers of undocumented aliens into the Southeastern United States," he was ordering the interdiction of vessels carrying such aliens (Haitians). He instructed the U.S. Coast Guard to board suspicious boats, to search for persons attempting illegal entry, and to return boats and passengers to Haiti. This action has been widely criticized in terms of international law despite the fact that the Haitian government has concurred with it. It has also been condemned because it singles out black Haitians for interdiction. It is also difficult to enforce.

Government sources claim that because of the highly publicized interdiction practice, the number of Haitian arrivals has declined. This may well be the case, but there is no way to ascertain how many of those now presumably discouraged from attempting to reach the United States have valid political reasons for fleeing Haiti.

There is considerably less protection of the rights of those who do decide to flee. The interdiction orders require qualified individuals to examine claims for political asylum on the Coast Guard vessels, but persons fleeing for fear of political persecution are unlikely to speak fully and truthfully before uniformed U.S. officers. In addition, it is arguable whether U.S. government officials are the most appropriate advocates for Haitian claimants, or whether they are competent to make proper determination. There is no information as to whether asylum applications have been requested, but no political asylum request has been processed, much less granted, to any Haitian on an interdicted boat.

Haitian emigration has long been debated in Congress, in the press, and in the courts. Haitians are willing to risk death by traveling nearly eight hundred miles through difficult seas in unseaworthy boats. Yet the Reagan administration, like the Carter administration, asserts that the overwhelming majority of Haitians flee because of economic desperation, not political persecution. The UNHCR agrees that a relatively small percentage of them probably qualify for political asylum under U.S. and international law. Nevertheless, human rights groups and scholars have documented continuing political repression in Haiti. At least some Haitians are likely to be attempting to escape that repression by fleeing to the United States. Haitians contend that those who return to the country after having left it are subject to persecution and arrest.

In June 1980 Federal Judge James L. King ruled on a class action suit on behalf of over four thousand Haitians requesting political asylum. He found that the Carter administration was violating "the Constitution, the immigration statutes, international agreements, INS regulations and INS operative procedures" by its mass deportations of Haitians. Judge King's decision protected from deportation all Haitians who where facing exclusion hearings prior to the end of 1979.

In spring 1980 a massive exodus of Cubans to the United States began. When the Cubans first arrived, several groups, including the Congressional Black Caucus, complained the the INS operated on a double standard with regard to Cubans and Haitians. Although both groups claimed political motives for flight, only the Haitians were obliged to prove, individually, why they should not be deported as economic migrants. Soon after the boatlift was underway, President Carter announced that Haitians and Cubans would be treated equally, and the administration finally admitted members of both groups—120 thousand Cubans and 50 thousand Haitians—as "entrants." The entrant status initially was a six-month parole, but subsequently it was extended indefinitely for Haitians and Cubans who were known to INS officials prior to mid-October 1980.

Haitians arriving after 1980 were not protected from detention and deportation. In May 1981 the Reagan administration adopted a policy of obligatory detention without bond for Haitians attempting to enter, and in September it initated the interdiction of Haitian boats. Haitians were subsequently detained at seventeen different facilities, most of which were located in isolated areas where it was difficult to obtain legal counsel and where the climate was exceptionally unpleasant, e.g. Fort Allen, Puerto Rico, and Ottisville, New York. In the past, Haitians making asylum applications normally had not been kept in detention, were routinely released to relatives and sponsors, and were allowed to work.

Lawyers representing Haitians brought a class action suit to U.S. District Court in Miami contending that the detention policy was illegal and discriminatory. On 29 June 1982 Judge Eugene Spellman ruled against that policy and ordered the release of the detained Haitians. The ruling was based on the failure of U.S. authorities to give notice of changed procedures; the judge did not find the policy per se to be discriminatory, although a subsequent appeals court in 1983 did. Having given adequate notice, the government may again detain incoming Haitians. The nineteen hundred released Haitians still face hearings at which they will have to present their asylum pleas.

It is likely that most of the Haitian pleas will be denied. Of the more than five thousand Haitian applications filed in 1981, only five were approved. In fiscal year 1982, 8 applications were approved, 125 were denied, and 6,036 were still pending. U.S. immigration courts continue to be unsympathetic to, and unconvinced by, Haitian claims of fear of political persecution.

CUBANS

Trends in present immigration and refugee policies are possibily best illustrated by the treatment of recent Cuban exiles. The Cuban boatlift experience also demonstrated how badly prepared the United States is to cope with a large-scale entry, even of people toward whom the U.S. government is sympathetic.

Over one hundred and twenty-five thousand Cubans arrived in the United States between spring and fall of 1980. They expected, but did not find, the same warm welcome that had been extended to the nearly seven hundred thousand Cubans who had been accepted and generously provided for during the 1960s.

The massive Cuban exodus that became known as the Mariel Boatlift did not occur without warning. Since the end of the U.S. Cuban airlift in the early 1970s few Cuban exiles had come to the United States, but there were continuing pressures in both countries for family reunification. The absence of normalized relations has prevented either legal immigration or comprehensive negotiations on immigration problems and family reunification concerns between the two countries.

During 1980, attracted by the success of family members in the United States and encountering both persistent economic difficulties and tighter political controls at home, Cubans increasingly hijacked small boats bound for the United States. This had not occurred to any extent for several years. The Cuban government complained to the United States on two grounds: first, that the U.S. government was not returning the hijacked boats as stipulated in the treaty signed by both governments in 1973; and second, that the United States was slow to process the entry permissions for several political prisoners who had been released by the Cuban government and who wanted to and expected to leave for the United States. In other words, the U.S. government appeared to be encouraging illegal entries while placing obstacles in the way of legal channels of migration.

Following an occupation of the Peruvian embassy in Havana by over ten thousand Cubans (a conflict that in large part was resolved through the collaboration of the United States, the Andean Pact nations, and the UNHCR), Fidel Castro announced that Cuban exiles in the United States could come to the Port of Mariel and pick up relatives and others who wished to emigrate. The Cuban community responded at once. The resulting boatlift was at first encouraged by U.S. officials, then discouraged, and finally formally—but not effectively—prohibited. Ultimately the boatlift was declared to have been illegal, but the Cubans were permitted to remain.

About twenty thousand of the one hundred and twenty-five thousand Cubans were detained upon arrival, some for long periods, in federal camps. There were serious problems, especially with the 950 Cubans interned at Fort Chaffee, Arkansas, who rioted and tried to escape. About thirteen hundred Cubans remain in an Atlanta prison. The government claims they are not exiles, but felons and physically or mentally handicapped persons. Some of the jailed Cubans claim their previous crimes were political in nature. They have not been accused of or tried for crimes in this country.

The United States reacted angrily to what appeared to be a Cuban attempt to rid the island of misfits and criminals by placing them on Miami-bound boats. A few of the *Marielitos* who were not detained upon arrival or who were released shortly thereafter became involved in criminal activity in the United States and these activities have received considerable publicity. The newcomers have often found adjustment difficult. The established Cuban community and many residents of southern Florida feel that the U.S. government shares some of the blame for the disorder. Had the United States better provided for the needs of the new arrivals and organized sponsorship for the *Marielitos* more efficiently, they contend, much of the social disruption would have been avoided. Instead, this country dealt with the massive emergency caused by the Cuban entry by expanding detention facilities and then rushing to empty them, often by placing Cubans with sponsors who were not well prepared—or willing—to care for them adequately. Southern Florida officials complain that their social service organizations and policy have inherited the problems caused by the federal government's organizational disarray.

Funding is a major issue. The Cubans were not given political asylum, but were designated as "entrants" along with a specified group of Haitians as described earlier. By declaring the Cubans to be entrants the government avoided what would have been its responsibility under the Refugee Act of 1980 to bear the full costs of refugee resettlement. It also avoided what would have been the embarrassment of granting political asylum to one hundred and twenty-five thousand Cubans, when the total number of refugees foreseen in the act was a mere fifty thousand.

The Reagan administration maintains that the Cuban boatlift presented a "question of illegal immigration under cover of applications for asylum."[1] At the same time government officials speak of the Cubans' "flight to freedom." Whatever administration officials attitudes toward the Cubans' political cause, this country clearly does not wish Cubans to migrate to the United States. In January 1982, for the first time in twenty-three years, the U.S. government deported a Cuban who arrived as a stowaway. It did so on the grounds that the individual was not able to prove a fear of persecution.

General Policy Recommendations

The United States is bound by its national and international obligations not to return forcibly persons who have a well-founded fear of persecution. Neither the United States nor any other country is obliged to resettle all those who seek asylum. It is in the U.S. national interests to work for greater international cooperation on refugee questions and to explore feasible alternatives, including programs to help settle refugees in other countries, pressing governments that have expelled large numbers of their citizens (or forced them to leave) to allow them to return with guarantees for safety, offering financial assistance and other forms of aid to governments burdened with large refugee populations and to private and intergovernmental organizations involved in refugee resettlement.

U.S. refugee policy should be an integral part of U.S. foreign policy, consistent with U.S. stated concerns for human rights and humanitarian objectives. It is in the national interests of this country and in the interest of international stability to relieve the political and economic pressures caused by

---

[1]Attorney General William French Smith, Senate Committee on the Judiciary, 22 September 1981.

239

massive refugee flows. The United States is in a position to take a leadership role in this task, not only by providing a safe haven for refugees, but also by addressing the root causes of refugee flows: wide-scale human rights violations and economic misery. U.S. human rights policies can be used effectively to reduce the flow of refugees. Economic aid and trade policies that promote economic justice will also diminish the likelihood that large numbers of people will flee their homelands for a mixture of economic and political motives.

Taking the national groups separately: The thousands of *Salvadorans* seeking refuge throughout Central American and Mexico are a burden on the scarce resources of these countries and have been another destabilizing influence in the already volatile region. In the United States Salvadorans have been unwelcome and badly treated. Increasingly, they are a source of contention between community and religious groups and the INS. The massive exodus from Salvador is a direct consequence of the current civil strife and wide-scale repression and the resulting economic collapse. For certain groups, especially young peasants, it is simply unsafe to remain in the country. A negotiated settlement to the present fighting would enable people to return, and the majority would do so. If there were meaningful land reform and other economic improvements, the number of Salvadorans seeking economic exile would probably also decline in the long run. The first step toward a resolution of the Salvadoran refugee problem, clearly, is for the United States to cooperate with Mexico, Venezuela, and other countries in the region to negotiate an end to the fighting and subsequently to support the efforts of Salvadorans promoting greater social justice and reform.

A government less corrupt than the present Haitian regime, one that respected human rights and held its security forces accountable for their criminal acts, would be able to stem the massive flight of *Haitians* to other countries. The United States is in a position to put pressures on the Haitian government for considerable improvement in human rights practices and financial accountability for aid. As one of the poorest countries in the hemisphere, Haiti cannot support its population. For the foreseeable future, Haitians will continue to leave for survival. Aid alone will not improve the economic situation. But it is essential that aid be effectively channeled to basic needs and economic development, which is not the case at present.

Much of the chaos of the *Cuban* Mariel Boatlift might have been avoided had the U.S. and Cuban governments negotiated differences to the mutual satisfaction of both countries, e.g., the hijacking agreement, the fishing rights agreement, and the establishment of Interest Sections. The Cuban government has said it might discuss the return of some Cubans as part of more general talks. The Mexicans have offered their good offices for U.S.-Cuban discussions. The implacable hostility of the Reagan administration toward

Cuba appears entirely counterproductive to the purposes of resolving the refugee question and others.

In *Nicaragua*, as in Cuba, the U.S. posture has been one of untempered hostility. A U.S. policy that combined support for human rights with efforts to ease tensions would make it easier for the Nicaraguan government to tolerate opposition activities and might facilitate the development of a more pluralist society there. Under such conditions Nicaragua would be less likely to produce refugees seeking to settle in this country.

As hundreds of thousands of *Guatemala's* peasants flee their northern villages with stories of the Guatemalan army's scorched earth policies, of massacres, and of repression, the Reagan administration continues to advocate military and other aid for Guatemala. Administration spokesmen have also concurred with claims by the Guatemalan government that many of those who have fled across the border to Mexico are guerrilla sympathizers or guerrillas themselves, but this allegation has been denied across the board by reputable human rights organizations, the Mexican government, and, needless to say, the Guatemalan refugees. These refugees have been driven from their villages by violence, most of which is of government origin. The United States should oppose the government to save the lives and prevent the desperate flight of huge numbers of peaceful Guatemalan peasants.

Conclusions

The Latin American mass entries into the United States described in these pages were of fundamental importance in leading first the president and later Congress to consider major revisions in the U.S. Immigration and Nationality Act. The changes initially proposed by President Reagan appeared, by and large, to be attempts to address a humanitarian crisis by diminishing due process rights and imposing stronger police and military controls, made possible by emergency executive powers. The president's bill, as presented to Congress, also violated the spirit of the 1980 Refugee Act by reasserting ideological biases and singling out specific groups for reprisals. Congressional deliberations on the immigration reform and control act of 1982—the Simpson-Mazolli bill—many result in a more creative and balanced approach than the president's with respect to immigration and asylum issues.

The 97th Congress did not complete action on the Simpson-Mazolli bill. It remains to be seen what the 98th Congress will do with regard to asylum questions; it does appear that the United States will provide training for asylum officers who judge applications made by persons who claim well-founded fear of persecution, a step long advocated by public interest law and humanitarian groups. On the other hand, humanitarian groups are concerned by proposed measures in the bill that appear to curtail due process rights by permitting the summary exclusion without hearings of illegal entrants, severely limiting the possible appeals on asylum determinations, and making it easier for immigration officials to implement deportation.

In a period of high unemployment and general economic difficulty, it is logical that public opinion should turn against large-scale influxes of immigrants, and especially against those who arrive illegally. Nevertheless, it is clear that neither U.S. nor humanitarian interests are served by policies designed to exclude indiscriminately. There are many steps the United States can take, not only to reduce the flow of politically motivated exiles through a more enlightened foreign policy, but also to more efficiently and humanely manage asylum emergencies that do occur.

The federal government should recognize that it has primary responsibility for bearing the cost of refugee resettlement and should work with community groups to reduce tensions within the communities among the refugees themselves. Voluntary agencies (rather than the government) are better equipped to carry out resettlement tasks efficiently in almost all cases. A more knowledgeable and better trained corps of officials who hear asylum cases and determine refugee status is desirable and is apparently to be legislated. It would also enhance the consistency and fairness of refugee and asylum determinations if the United States was to create a genuinely impartial review board to hear appeals. Such a board would include immigration law judges, as presently proposed, and would also provide formal roles for U.S. public interest and humanitarian groups and for the UNHCR.

State Department evaluations of country conditions should be taken into account in deciding if a refugee or asylum applicant has a legitimate claim, but these evaluations should not be as decisive as they are now.

A greater role for the UNHCR is especially important, since that organization has the longest experience and the greatest expertise in refugee and asylum matters. A number of countries have invited the UNHCR to participate directly in making decisions on refugee cases, but the United States has rarely requested its services, and then only for very limited purposes. Perhaps it is unrealistic to expect U.S. authorities to invite direct international participation in domestic administrative procedures, but UNHCR advisory opinions ought to be more systematically sought and accorded greater weight.

The Reagan administration's desire to expedite asylum procedures is justifiable, since long delays cause anguish to legitimate claimants. Delays also encourage people who have only frivolous asylum claims to file applications simply to gain time. Expedited procedures should be approached with the idea of improving existing structures and shortening unnecessary bureaucratic processes, for example. Many decisions presently made on a case-by-case basis would be more appropriately handled as group determinations. Expedited procedures should not, however, be implemented solely as a means to exclude and discourage migrants, as the intent of current policies appears to be.

Finally, in cases of massive but temporary flights due to warlike conditions, the United States should routinely provide extended voluntary departure for those affected, as it has in the past. It should be provided now for the Salvadorans, and possibly for Guatemalans as well.

Selected Bibliography

Chapter 1. The New Realism in U.S.–Latin America Relations: Principles for a New U.S. Foreign Policy

Collier, David, ed. *The New Authoritarianism in Latin America*. Princeton: Princeton University Press, 1979.

Comblin, José. *The Church and the National Security State*. Maryknoll, New York: Orbis Books, 1979.

Farer, Tom J. "Searching for Defeat." *Foreign Policy* (Fall 1980):155–74.

Feinberg, Richard E. *The Intemporate Zone: The Third World Challenge to U.S. Foreign Policy*. New York: W. W. Norton & Co., 1983.

Gaddis, John Lewis. *Strategies of Containment: A Critical Appraisal of Postwar American National Security Policy*. New York: Oxford University Press, 1982.

LaFeber, Walter. *America, Russia, and the Cold War, 1945–1980*. 4th ed. New York: Wiley, 1980.

Chapter 2. From Monroe to Reagan: An Overview of U.S.–Latin American Relations

Cable, James. *Gunboat Diplomacy*. New York: St. Martin's Press, 1981.

Gellman, Irwin F. *Good Neighbor Diplomacy*. Baltimore: Johns Hopkins University Press, 1979.

Gil, Federico Guillermo. *Latin American–United States Relations*. New York: Harcourt Brace Jovanovich, 1971.

Grunwald, Joseph. *The Alliance for Progress*. Washington, D.C.: Brookings Institution, 1965.

Levinson, Jerome. *The Alliance That Lost Its Way*. Chicago: Quadrangle Books, 1970.

May, Ernest R. *The Making of the Monroe Doctrine*. Cambridge, Mass.: Belknap Press of Harvard University Press, 1975.

Nearing, Scott. *Dollar Diplomacy*. New York: Monthly Review Press, 1966.

Perkins, Dexter. *A History of the Monroe Doctrine*. Boston: Little, Brown, 1955.

Rogers, William D. *The Twilight Struggle: The Alliance for Progress and the Politics of Development in Latin America*. New York: Random House, 1967.

Steel, Ronald. *Pax Americana*. New York: Penguin Books, 1970.

Williams, William Appleman. *The Shaping of American Diplomacy*. Vol. 1, Vol. 2. Chicago: Rand McNally & Company, 1956.

———. *The Tragedy of American Diplomacy*. Cleveland: World Publishing Company, 1959.

Chapter 3. Mexico: The Continuing Quest for a Policy

McBride, Robert H., ed. *Mexico and the United States*. Englewood Cliffs: Prentice-Hall, 1981.
Montgomery, Tommie Sue, ed. *Mexico Today*. Philadelphia: Institute for the Study of Human Issues, 1982.
Purcell, Susan Kaufman, ed. *Mexico–United States Relations*. New York: Academy of Political Science, 1981.
Reyna, José Luis, and Richard S. Weinert, eds. *Authoritarianism in Mexico*. Philadelphia: Institute for the Study of Human Issues, 1977.
Smith, Peter H. *Labyrinths of Power: Political Recruitment in Twentieth-Century Mexico*. Princeton: Princeton University Press, 1979.
———. *Mexico: The Quest for a U.S. Policy*. New York: Foreign Policy Association, 1980.

Chapter 4. Guatemala: The Long-Term Costs of Short-Term Stability

Aguilera Peralta, Gabriel, et al. *Dialéctica del terror en Guatemala*. San José, Costa Rica: Editorial Universitaria Centroamericana, 1981.
Davis, Shelton H., and Julie Hodson. *Witnesses to Political Violence in Guatemala: The Suppression of a Rural Development Movement*. Boston: OXFAM-America, 1982.
Fried, Jonathan L., et al., eds. *Guatemala in Rebellion: Unfinished History*. New York: Grove Press, 1983.
Immerman, Richard H. *The CIA in Guatemala: The Foreign Policy of Intervention*. Austin: University of Texas Press, 1982.
Rarihokwats, ed. *Guatemala!: The Horror and the Hope*. York, Pennsylvania: Four Arrows, 1982.
Schlesinger, Stephen, and Stephen Kinzer. *Bitter Fruit: The Untold Story of the American Coup in Guatemala*. Garden City, New York: Doubleday and Company, 1982.

Chapter 5. El Salvador: The Policy That Failed

Armstrong, Robert, and Janet Shenk. *El Salvador: The Face of Revolution*. Boston: South End Press, 1982.
Baloyra, Enrique. *El Salvador in Transition*. Chapel Hill: University of North Carolina Press, 1982.
Montgomery, Tommie Sue. *Revolution in El Salvador: Origins and Evolution*. Boulder, Colorado: Westview Press, 1982.
U.S. Congress. House. Inter-American Affairs Subcommittee of the Committee on Foreign Affairs. Various hearings on certification of El Salvador.
———. Senate. Committee on Foreign Relations. Various hearings on certification of El Salvador.
White, Alistair. *El Salvador*. Boulder, Colorado: Westview Press, 1973.

Chapter 6. Honduras: An Emerging Dilemma

Gleijeses, Piero. "La Política del President Reagan en Centro América." In *CentroAmerica: Más Allá de la Crisis,* edited by Donald Castillo. Mexico: Ediciones Siap, 1983.
Meza, Víctor. *Honduras: La Evolución de la Crisis*. Tegucigalpa: Editorial Universitaria, 1982.
Millet, Richard. "Central American Paralysis." *Foreign Policy* (Summer 1980).

Rosenberg, Mark. "Honduran Scorecard: Democrats and Military in Central America." *Caribbean Review* (Winter 1983).

———, and Phil Shepherd. "Two Approaches to the Understanding of U.S.–Honduran Relations." Dialogue Series, Latin American Caribbean Center. Florida International University (April 1983).

Selser, Gregorio. *Honduras: República Alquilada*. Mexico City: Mex-Sur Editorial, 1983.

Chapter 7. Costa Rica: The End of the Fiesta

Ameringer, Charles D. *Democracy in Costa Rica*. New York: Praeger, 1982.

Carvajal, Manuel. *Report on Income Distribution and Poverty in Costa Rica*. Washington, D.C.: Agency for International Development, 1979.

Goodman, Chester Zelaya. ¿ *Democracia en Costa Rica?* San José, Costa Rica: Universidad Estatal a Distancia.

Montealegre, Flora. "Costa Rica at the Crossroads." *Development and Change* 14, no. 2 (April 1983).

Seligson, Mitchell A. *Peasants of Costa Rica and the Development of Agrarian Capitalism*. Madison: University of Wisconsin Press, 1980.

Chapter 8. Nicaragua: The United States Confronts a Revolution

Black, George. *Triumph of the People: The Sandinista Revolution in Nicaragua*. London: Zed Press, 1981.

Collins, Joseph. *What Difference Could a Revolution Make? Farming and Food in the New Nicaragua*. San Francisco: Institute for Food and Development Policy, 1982.

EPICA Task Force. *Nicaragua: A People's Revolution*. Washington, D.C.: EPICA, 1980.

Fagen, Richard R. *The Nicaraguan Revolution: A Personal Report*. Washington, D.C.: Institute for Policy Studies, 1981.

Gelly,· Adolfo. *La nueva Nicaragua: antiimperialismo y lucha de clases*. Mexico: Editorial Nueva Imagen, 1980.

Ramirez, Sergio, ed. *El pensamiento vivo de Sandino*. 5th ed. San José, Costa Rica: EDUCA, 1980.

Sunol, Julio. *Insurreccion en Nicaragua: la historial no contada*. San José, Costa Rica: Editorial Costa Rica, 1981.

Walker, Thomas W., ed. *Nicaragua in Revolution*. New York: Praeger, 1982.

Weber, Henri. *Nicaragua: The Sandinista Revolution*. London: Verso Editions, 1981.

Chapter 9. Cuba: Going to the Source

Bender, Lynn Darrell. *Cuba vs. the United States: The Politics of Hostility*. San Juan, Puerto Rico: Inter-American University Press, 1981.

Blaiser, Cole, and Carmelo Mesa-Lago, eds. *Cuba in the World*. Pittsburgh: University of Pittsburgh Press, 1979.

Domínguez, Jorge I., ed. *Cuba: Internal and International Affairs*. Beverly Hills, California: Sage Publications, 1982.

———. "Cuban Foreign Policy." *Foreign Affairs* 57 (Fall 1978):83–108.

Gonzalez, Edward. *A Strategy for Dealing with Cuba in the 1980s*. Santa Monica, California: RAND Corp., 1982.

———. "Complexities of Cuban Foreign Policy." *Problems of Communism* 26 (November-December 1977):1–15.

LeoGrande, William M. *Cuba's Policy in Africa, 1959–1980*. Berkeley, California: Institute of International Studies, University of California, 1980.

Mesa-Lago, Carmelo, and June Belkin, eds. *Cuba in Africa*. Pittsburgh: Center for Latin American Studies, University of Pittsburgh, 1982.

Robbins, Carla Anne. *The Cuban Threat*. New York: McGraw-Hill, 1983.

Smith, Wayne S. "Dateline Havana: Myopic Diplomacy." *Foreign Policy*, no. 48 (Fall 1982):157–74.

Valenta, Jiri. "The USSR, Cuba, and the Crisis in Central America." *Orbis* 25 (Fall 1981):715–46.

Weinstein, Martin, ed. *Revolutionary Cuba in the World Arena*. Philadelphia: ISHI, 1979.

Chapter 10. Brazil: The Case of the Missing Relationship

Bacha, Edmar. "The IMF and the Prospects for Adjustment in Brazil." In *Prospects for Adjustment in Argentina, Brazil and Mexico: Responding to the Debt Crisis*, edited by J. Williamson. Washington, D.C.: IIE, 1983.

Baer, Wener. *The Brazilian Economy*. New York: Praeger, 1983.

Evans, Peter. *Dependent Development: The Alliance of Multinational, State, and Local Capital in Brazil*. Princeton: Princeton University Press, 1978.

Roett, Riordan. "The Brazilian Debt Crisis: Social and Political Consequences." Testimony before the Subcommittee on International Economic Policy of the Foreign Relations Committee of the U.S. Senate, September 28, 1983.

———. "Brazil's International Relations in Perspective." *Orbis* 26, no. 1 (Spring 1982).

Wiarda, H., and J. Perfit, eds. *Changing Dynamics of the Brazilian Economy*. AEI Occasional Paper, no. 5. Washington, D.C.: American Enterprise Institute, 1983.

———. *Trade, Aid, and U.S. Economic Policy in Latin America*. AEI Occasional Paper, no. 6. Washington, D.C.: American Enterprise Institute, 1983.

Chapter 11. Argentina: Rebuilding the Relationship

del Carril, Bonifacio. *El futuro de las Malvinas*. Buenos Aires: EMECE, 1983.

Ferrer, Aldo. *Puede Argentina pagar su deuda externa?* Buenos Aires: El Cid Editor, 1982.

Freedman, Lawrence. "The War of the Falkland Islands, 1982." *Foreign Affairs* 61, no. 1 (Fall 1982):196–210.

Maechling, Charles. "The Argentine Pariah." *Foreign Policy*, no. 45 (Winter 1981–82):69–83.

Purcell, Susan Kaufman. "War and Debt in South America." *America and the World 1982*. New York: Council on Foreign Relations, 1982.

Turner, Frederick. "The Aftermath of Defeat in Argentina." *Current History* (February 1983):58–62, 85–87.

Wynia, Gary. *Argentina in the Postwar Era*. Albuquerque: University of New Mexico Press, 1978.

Chapter 12. Chile: From Democracy to Authoritarianism

Handelman, Howard, and Thomas G. Sanders, eds. *Military Government and the Movement toward Democracy in South America*. Bloomington: Indiana University Press, 1981.

Ricardo Lagos, Frederico G. Gil, and Henry A. Landsberger, eds. *Chile at the Turning Point: Lessons of the Socialist Years, 1970–73*. Philadelphia: Institute for the Study of Human Issues, 1979.

Orrego Vicuña, Francisco. *Chile: The Balanced View*. Santiago: Institute of International Studies, University of Chile, 1975.

Sigmund, Paul E. *The Overthrow of Allende and the Politics of Chile, 1964–76*. Pittsburgh: University of Pittsburgh Press, 1977.

Stallings, Barbara. *Class Conflict and Economic Development in Chile, 1958–1973*. Stanford: Stanford University Press, 1978.

Valenzuela, Arturo. *The Breakdown of Democratic Regimes: Chile*. Baltimore: Johns Hopkins University Press, 1978.

Valenzuela, Arturo, and J. Samuel Valenzuela, eds. *Military Rule in Chile*. Baltimore: Johns Hopkins University Press, 1984.

Chapter 13. U.S. Economic Policy toward Latin America: The Deepening Problem

Cline, William. *Trade Policy in the 1980s*. Washington, D.C.: Institute for International Economics, 1982.

Helleiner, G. K. *Protectionism: Threat to International Order*. London: Commonwealth Secretariat, 1982.

Hufbauer, G. C., ed. *U.S. International Economic Policy 1981: A Draft Report*. Washington, D.C.: Georgetown University Law Center, 1982.

Newfarmer, R. S., ed. *Policies for Industrial Growth in a Competitive World*. Report prepared for the Joint Economic Committee, U.S. Congress. Washington, D.C.: U.S. Government Printing Office, 1983.

————. "The Reagan Revolution in Development Policy." *Challenge Magazine* (September-October 1983).

U.S. Congress. House. Hearings before the Subcommittee on Latin American Affairs of the House Foreign Affairs Committee. "U.S.–Latin American Economic Policy." Washington, D.C.: Government Printing Office, June 1983.

————. House. Hearings before the Subcommittees on International Economic Policy and Trade and Western Hemisphere Affairs of the Foreign Affairs Committee. "Latin America in the World Economy." Washington, D.C.: Government Printing Office, June 1983.

————. House. Hearings on U.S. Economic Policy toward Latin America before the Inter-American Affairs Subcommittee of the Committee on Foreign Affairs. June 9, 1983. Washington, D.C.: Government Printing Office, 1983.

————. House. Joint Economic Committee. *U.S. International Economic Policy: Selected Essays*. Washington, D.C.: Government Printing Office, February 11, 1982.

Williamson, John. *IMF Conditionality*. Washington, D.C.: Institute for International Economics, 1983.

————, ed. *Prospects for Adjustment in Argentina, Brazil and Mexico: Responding to the Debt Crisis*. Washington, D.C.: IIE, 1983.

Chapter 14. The Caribbean Basin Initiative: Bold Plan or Empty Promise?

Feinberg, R. E., and R. S. Newfarmer. "The Battle Over the Caribbean Basin Initiative: The Debate in Washington." *Caribbean Review* (Winter 1983).

Forum on the Caribbean Basin Initiative. *Foreign Policy,* no. 47 (Summer 1982).

Johnson, Kyle, and Donald Russlang. "Tariff Duties as a Measure of the Effect of Tariff Elimination in the Caribbean Basin." Report prepared for the U.S. Department of Labor. Bureau of International Labor Affairs, April 27, 1982.

Pelzman, Joseph, and Donald Russlang. "Effects on U.S. Trade and Employment of Tariff Elimination among the Countries of North America and the Caribbean Basin." Report prepared for the U.S. Department of Labor. Bureau of International Labor Affairs, January 1982.

U.S. Congress. House. Hearings and Mark-up before the Committee on Foreign Affairs, March 25, 30; April 1, 27, 29, 1982. "Caribbean Basin Initiative." Washington, D.C.: U.S. Government Printing Office.

————. House. Hearings before the Subcommittee on Inter-American Affairs of the Committee on Foreign Affairs, July 14, 21, 28, 1981. "Caribbean Basin Policy." Washington, D.C.: U.S. Government Printing Office.

Chapter 15. Latin American Refugees: Problems of Mass Migration and Mass Asylum

Hanson, Christopher T. "Behind the Paper Curtain: Asylum Policy versus Asylum Practice." *New York University Review of Law and Social Change* (Winter 1978).

Mac Eoin, Gary, and Nevita Riley. *No Promised Land: American Refugee Policies and the Rule of Law.* Boston: Oxfam, America, 1982.

Refugee Policy Group (Washington, D.C.). "Political Asylum: A Background Paper on Concepts, Procedures and Problems." Prepared by Ronald Copeland and Patricia Weiss Fagen. December, 1982.

————. "United States Refugee Policy and Latin America." Prepared by Dennis Gallagher. February, 1983.

Scanlan, John, and Gilburt D. Loescher. "Mass Asylum and Human Rights in American Foreign Policy." *Political Science Quarterly* (Spring 1982).

Teitelbaum, Michael S. "Right versus Right: Immigration and Refugee Policy in the United States." *Foreign Affairs* (Fall 1980).

Contributors

MORRIS J. BLACHMAN is an associate professor of political science at the University of South Carolina. He has lectured on development in the third world at the Foreign Service Institute (1978) and has consulted on numerous projects with both nongovernment and government agencies. His publications include "Mexico and Multinational Corporations: An Exploration of State Action," coauthored in *Latin America and World Economy: A Changing International Order; Terms of Conflict: Ideology in Inter-American Politics,* coedited with R. G. Hellman; and *Eve in Adamocracy: The Politics of Women in Brazil.*

PATRICIA WEISS FAGEN is staff associate of the Refugee Policy Group in Washington, D.C., and is on leave from the History Department at San José State University in California. She is the author of *Exiles and Citizens: Spanish Republicans in Mexico* and has written a number of articles on Latin America, human rights, U.S. foreign policies, and political asylum. In addition to her academic work, she serves on the board of directors and coordinates the refugee work of Amnesty International, USA. She has also been a consultant on protection and assistance of Latin American refugees for the Inter-American Commission on Human Rights of the Organization of American States.

RICHARD E. FEINBERG is vice president of the Overseas Development Council and an adjunct professor to the Landegger Program of International Business Diplomacy at Georgetown University. He has worked as an international economist at the Treasury Department and the House Banking Committee and was a member of the Policy Planning Staff of the State Department from 1977 to 1980. He has published articles in such journals as *Foreign Affairs, Foreign*

251

Policy, and the *Washington Quarterly.* He is the author of *The Intemperate Zone: The Third World Challenge to U.S. Foreign Policy* and *Subsidizing Success: The Export-Import Bank in the U.S. Economy.* He is the editor of *Central America: International Dimensions of the Crisis.*

ALBERT FISHLOW is professor of economics at the University of California, Berkeley. He was a member of the economics faculty and director of the Concilium on International and Area Studies at Yale University from 1978 to 1983. He was deputy assistant secretary for Inter-American Affairs in 1975–76. He has been a consultant to the World Bank, Inter-American Development Bank, and several foundations, and serves on the editorial boards of *Foreign Policy, International Organization,* and *Latin American Research Review,* as well as on the council of the Overseas Development Council. Among his recent monographic publications are *The Mature Neighbor Policy: A New United States Economic Policy for Latin America, Rich and Poor Nations in the World Economy* (co-author), *Latin America's Emergence: Toward a U.S. Response* (co-author), and *Trade in Manufactured Products with Developing Countries: Reinforcing North-South Partnership* (principal author).

ROBERT KAUFMAN is a professor of political science at Rutgers University. He has been a member of the Institute for Advanced Studies at Princeton University and an associate at the Center for International Affairs at Harvard University. His publications include "Industrial Change and Authoritarian Rule in Latin America," in *The New Authoritarianism in Latin America; Transitions to Stable Authoritarian Cooperative Regimes: The Chilean Case?;* and *The Politics of Chilean Land Reform, 1950–1970.*

JAMES R. KURTH is a professor of political science at Swarthmore College. From 1967 to 1973 he taught in the Department of Government at Harvard University, where he was also editor of the journal *Public Policy* and a research associate in the Center for International Affairs and in the Center for European Studies. Since 1973 he has taught in the Department of Political Science at Swarthmore College. He has been a visiting member of the Institute for Advanced Studies and a visiting professor at the U.S. Naval War College. He has published on American foreign and defense policies and on European and Latin American politics. His recent publications on Latin America include "Industrial Change and Political Change: A European Perspective," in *The New Authoritarianism in Latin America,* and "The United States in Central America: Hegemony in Historical and Comparative Perspective," in *Central America: The International Dimensions of the Crisis.*

252

Contributors

WILLIAM M. LEOGRANDE is director of political science in the School of Government and Public Administration at the American University in Washington, D.C. He has been published widely in the field of Latin American politics and U.S.–Latin American relations; his publications include *Cuba's Policy in Africa, 1959–1980*; "The Revolution in Nicaragua," in *Foreign Affairs;* and "Drawing the Line in El Salvador," in *International Security*.

RICHARD MCCALL is deputy staff director and foreign policy specialist for the Senate Democratic Policy Committee.

RICHARD L. MILLETT is a professor of history at Southern Illinois University, Edwardsville. His publications include *Guardians of the Dynasty; The Restless Caribbean;* and "Central American Paralysis," in *Foreign Policy*.

RICHARD NEWFARMER is an economist in the Latin America and the Caribbean Region at the World Bank. He was a senior fellow at the Overseas Development Council from 1981 to 1983 when this book was written. He was formerly on the economics faculty at the University of Notre Dame. He has served as a consultant to the US Agency for International Development, the Democratic Policy Committee of the U.S. Senate, and the Subcommittee on Multinational Corporations of the Senate Foreign Relations Committee. He is editor of *Profits, Progress and Poverty*. He is author of *Transnational Conglomerates and the Economics of Dependent Development; Multinational Corporations in Brazil and Mexico* (with Willard F. Mueller); and *The International Electrical Association: A Continuing Cartel* (with Barbara Epstein). He has published various articles on economic and foreign policy in journals such as *Foreign Policy, Challenge Magazine, World Development, Journal of Development Economics, Journal of Development Studies,* and *Cambridge Journal of Economics*.

LARS SCHOULTZ is a professor of political science specializing in the study of U.S.–Latin American relations at the University of North Carolina. He is the author of *Human Rights and United States Policy toward Latin America* and coeditor of *Latin America, the United States and the Inter-American System*. His articles have appeared in a variety of journals, including the *American Political Science Review*, the *American Journal of Political Science, Comparative Politics*, the *Journal of Politics, International Organizations*, the *Latin American Research Review*, and *Political Science Quarterly*.

KENNETH SHARPE is an associate professor of political science at Swarthmore College. He has had over five years of field work experience in Mexico, Central America, and the Caribbean. He is the author of *Peasant Politics:*

Struggle in a Dominican Village and co-author (with Douglas Bennett) of *Transnational Corporations and the Mexican State: The Political Economy of the Mexican Automobile Industry*. His articles have appeared in a variety of journals and newspapers including *World Politics, Comparative Politics, International Organizations*, the *New York Times*, the *Christian Science Monitor*, the *Miami Herald*, the *Philadelphia Inquirer*, and the *St. Louis Post-Dispatch*. He is a co-chairman (with Morris Blachman and William LeoGrande) of the policy research group preparing a book on U.S. foreign policy and its effect on Central America.

PETER H. SMITH has concentrated his research on Argentina and Mexico. His most recent publications include *Labyrinths of Power: Political Recruitment in Twentieth-Century Mexico* and *Mexico: The Quest for a U.S. Policy*. A past president of the Latin American Studies Association, he is a professor of history and political science at the Massachusetts Institute of Technology.

ROBERT H. TRUDEAU is an associate professor of political science and director of the Latin American Studies program at Providence College. He is also a member of the Latin American Studies Association Task Force on Human Rights and Academic Freedom and was a Fulbright Fellow in political science in Guatemala for the 1980 academic year. His papers include ''The Effects of Malnutrition and Repressions on Political Participation in Guatemala''; ''Politics and Terror: The Case of Guatemala''; and ''Democracy in Guatemala: Current Status and Future Prospects.

ARTURO VALENZUELA is a professor of political science at Duke University. In 1981–82 he was a fellow with the Woodrow Wilson International Center for Scholars. He was a visiting fellow in 1977–78 at the Institute of Development Studies, University of Sussex, England, and has been a visiting professor at the Catholic University in Santiago, Chile, and visiting researcher at the University of Chile. He is the author of *Political Brokers in Chile* and *The Breakdown of Democratic Regimes: Chile*, and coauthor and coeditor of *Chile: Politics and Society*. His articles have appeared in *Comparative Politics, Proceedings of the Academy of Political Science, Rivista Italiana di Scienza Politica, Latin American Research Review, Revista Mexicana de Sociologia*, and other journals and edited volumes.

GARY W. WYNIA is a professor of political science at the University of Minnesota. His publications include *Politics and Planners: Economic Development Policy in Central America; The Politics of Latin American Development; Argentina in the Postwar Era: Politics and Economic Policy-Making in a Divided Society*.

The Johns Hopkins University Press

From Gunboats to Diplomacy

*This book was composed in Times Roman text
and Antique Olive display type by Brushwood Graphics, Ltd.
from a design by Cynthia W. Hotvedt.
It was printed on S.D. Warren's 50-lb. Sebago Eggshell paper
and bound in Kivar 5 by Port City Press, Inc.*

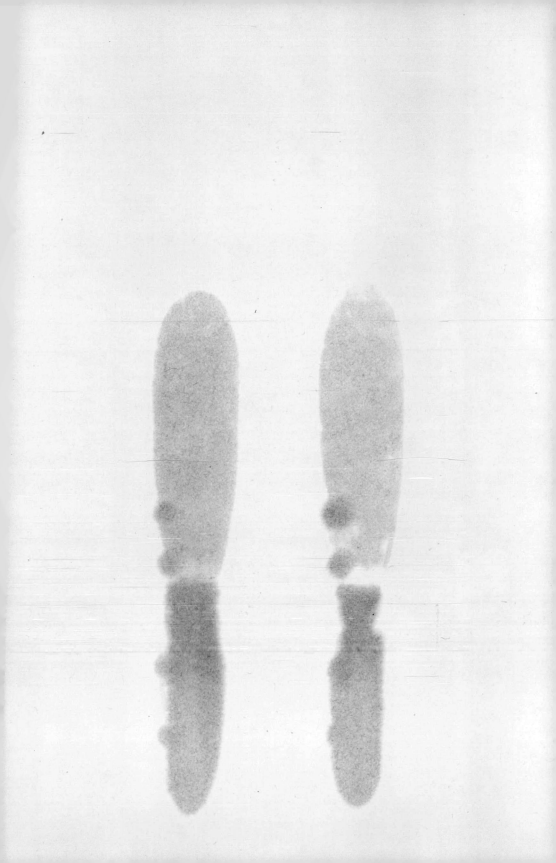

96436

F
1418
.F9
1984

FROM GUNBOATS TO DIPLOMACY.

DATE DUE

GAYLORD   PRINTED IN U.S.A.